MASTERS AND SERVANTS IN ENGLISH
RENAISSANCE DRAMA AND CULTURE

EARLY MODERN LITERATURE IN HISTORY

General Editor: Cedric C. Brown
Professor of English and Head of Department, University of Reading

Within the period 1520–1740 this series discusses many kinds of
writing, both within and outside the established canon. The
volumes may employ different theoretical perspectives, but they
share an historical awareness and an interest in seeing their texts
in lively negotiation with their own and successive cultures.

Published titles

Anna R. Beer
SIR WALTER RALEGH AND HIS READERS IN THE
SEVENTEENTH CENTURY: Speaking to the People

Cedric C. Brown and Arthur F. Marotti (*editors*)
TEXTS AND CULTURAL CHANGE IN EARLY MODERN
ENGLAND

James Loxley
ROYALISM AND POETRY IN THE ENGLISH CIVIL WARS:
The Drawn Sword

Mark Thornton Burnett
MASTERS AND SERVANTS IN ENGLISH RENAISSANCE
DRAMA AND CULTURE: Authority and Obedience

The series Early Modern Literature in History is published
in association with the Renaissance Texts Research Centre
at the University of Reading.

Masters and Servants in English Renaissance Drama and Culture

Authority and Obedience

Mark Thornton Burnett

© Mark Thornton Burnett 1997

Published by
PALGRAVE
Houndmills, Basingstoke, Hampshire RG21 6XS and
175 Fifth Avenue, New York, N.Y. 10010
Companies and representatives throughout the world

PALGRAVE is the new global academic imprint of
St. Martin's Press LLC Scholarly and Reference Division and
Palgrave Publishers Ltd (formerly Macmillan Press Ltd).

ISBN 0–333–69457–0

This book is printed on paper suitable for recycling and made from fully managed and sustained forest sources.

A catalogue record for this book is available from the British Library.

Transferred to digital printing 2001

Printed and bound in Great Britain by
Antony Rowe Ltd, Chippenham, Wiltshire

To my parents

Contents

Acknowledgements

I would like to thank Emrys Jones who guided my interests in the Renaissance in their early stages and who was always ready to offer criticism and encouragement. I equally appreciate the assistance of Keith Thomas, both for his comments on my work and for the intellectual stimulus he provided. Julia Briggs and Martin Butler kindly read the first draft of the manuscript and offered numerous useful suggestions for improvements. Rick Waswo has been generous in his support of my researches. I am particularly thankful to those friends and colleagues who took time to read draft chapters. For responses to sections of the book, I would like to thank Ian Archer, Christina Britzolakis, Brian Caraher, Fran Dolan, François Laroque, Ted Leinwand, Chris Marsh, Jyotsna Singh and Peter Stoneley. Ramona Wray offered advice and invaluable comment on how the manuscript might be improved: without her the book could not have been written. My parents have offered love and support, and to them this book is gratefully dedicated. The infelicities and errors that remain are my responsibility alone.

Part of chapter 1, 'Apprentice Literature and the "Crisis" of the 1590s', first appeared in *The Yearbook of English Studies*, 21 (1991), pp. 27–38, and I am grateful to the editors and publishers for permission to use versions of this earlier material.

For kind permission to consult, refer to or quote from documents or manuscripts in their possession I thank the following estates, individuals, libraries and offices: the Marquess of Bath (Dudley Papers at Longleat House), Bethlem Royal Hospital, the Bodleian Library, Bristol Record Office, the British Library, Buckinghamshire Record Office, Cambridge University Library (Ely Diocesan Records), Chatsworth House (Devonshire manuscripts), the Clothworkers' Company, Clwyd Record Office, Corporation of London Records Office, the Right Honourable the Viscount Daventry, Essex Record Office, the Trustees of the Estate of the Late Earl Fitzwilliam, Gloucestershire County Library, the Worshipful Company of Goldsmiths, Greater London Record Office (crown copyright material is reproduced by permission of the

Controller of Her Majesty's Stationery Office), the Trustees of Grimsthorpe and Drummond Castle Trust, the Guildhall Library, Hampshire Record Office, Hertfordshire Record Office, the Huntington Library, San Marino, California, Kent Archives Office, Lambeth Palace Library, Lancashire Record Office, Mrs C. McLaren-Throckmorton, Major More-Molyneux, His Grace the Duke of Norfolk, Norfolk Record Office, North Yorkshire County Record Office, Public Record Office (crown copyright), Lord Salisbury, Sheffield City Library, Somerset Record Office, Staffordshire Record Office, Suffolk Record Office, Bury St Edmund's Branch, the Marquess of Tavistock and the Trustees of the Bedford Estates, Tyne and Wear Joint Archives Service, Newcastle (by permission of the Chief Archivist), Warwickshire County Record Office, West Sussex Record Office, West Yorkshire Archive Service, Leeds, and Wiltshire Record Office.

I am indebted to the Queen's University of Belfast for a period of sabbatical leave and financial support; Wolfson College, Oxford, for electing me to a Visiting Scholarship; the Huntington Library, San Marino, for appointing me to a Fletcher Jones Fellowship; and the British Academy for research grants.

Abbreviations and Conventions

A.C.	Arundel Castle
A.O.	Archives Office
Bodl. Lib.	Bodleian Library
B.L.	British Library
B.R.H., B.C.B.	Bethlem Royal Hospital, Bridewell Court Books
C.L.R.O.	Corporation of London Records Office
Co.	Company
C.U.L.	Cambridge University Library
G.C.L.	Gloucestershire County Library
G.L.	Guildhall Library
G.L.R.O.	Greater London Record Office
H.H.	Hatfield House
H.L.	Huntington Library, California
H.M.C.	*Historical Manuscripts Commission*
L.H.	Longleat House
L.P.L.	Lambeth Palace Library
P.R.O.	Public Record Office
R.O.	Record(s) Office
S.C.L., B.F.M.	Sheffield City Library, Bacon Frank Muniments
S.C.L., W.W.M.	Sheffield City Library, Wentworth Woodhouse Muniments
S.T.C.	A.W. Pollard and G.R. Redgrave, eds, *A Short-Title Catalogue of Books Printed in England, Scotland, and Ireland, and of English Books Printed Abroad 1475–1640*, 2nd edn, 3 vols, London, 1976–91. Vols. I (1986), II (1976) and III (1991) ed. by Pollard and Redgrave, revised and enlarged by W.A. Jackson, F.S. Ferguson, Katharine F. Pantzer and Philip R. Rider.

W.A.   Woburn Abbey
Wing   Donald Wing, ed.,
            *Short-Title Catalogue of Books Printed in
            England, Scotland, Ireland, Wales, and British
            America and of Books Printed in other Countries*,
            2nd edn, 3 vols, New York, 1982–94.
            Vol. I (1994) ed. by Wing.
            Vol. II (1982) ed. by Wing, rev. and ed. by
            Timothy J. Crist with Janice M. Hansel,
            Phebe A. Kirkham and Jeri S. Smith.
            Vol. III (1988) ed. by Wing, rev. and ed. by
            John J. Morrison, Carolyn W. Nelson,
            Matthew Seccombe,
            Mark E. English and Harold E. Selesky.
W.Y.A.S.   West Yorkshire Archive Service

In quotations from manuscript sources and original texts, I have
not modernized, although I have made slight changes in cases
of manifest error. First editions of S.T.C. and Wing material have
been used, except where later editions offer striking expansions
or developments of earlier material. Dates are given in Old Style,
but the year is taken to begin on 1 January. References to Shakespeare are taken from the Arden editions. Modern editions have
generally been used for citations from other plays of the period.
Quotations from Deloney are taken from *The Novels of Thomas
Deloney*, ed. Merritt E. Lawlis (Bloomington, IN, 1961). A full
reference to a play is given in the notes with the first citation;
thereafter references appear within the body of the text. For the
dates of composition of plays, I have initially consulted *A Survey and Bibliography of Recent Studies in English Renaissance Drama*,
edited in four volumes by Terence P. Logan and Denzell S. Smith
(Lincoln, 1973–8), supplemented in almost every case, however,
by more recent estimations in editions, books and articles.

Introduction

In that barrage of explosive exclamations which marks Iago in the first scene of *Othello* (1601–2), one complaint looms above the rest. The confusion that colours his speech emphasizes his outraged response to diminished prospects of promotion:

> Why, there's no remedy, 'tis the curse of service:
> Preferment goes by letter and affection
> And not by old gradation, where each second
> Stood heir to th' first. Now sir, be judge yourself
> Whether I in any just term am affined
> To love the Moor.[1]

It is striking that Iago, an 'ancient' (ensign) and intimate of Othello, should conceive of his relationship according to a master and servant paradigm. As the play goes on to demonstrate, Iago's function hardly conforms to the role of the domestic servant; nevertheless, the analogy highlighted in the passage offers a potent impression of the institution's central importance.

Among the many differences which divide present-day English society from the organization described by Iago, arguably the greatest is the virtual disappearance of the servant. Servants are still in existence but they are rarely in evidence, generally live independently of their employers, and are permanently recruited only by a fraction of the population. Such a state of affairs would have been inconceivable in early modern England where service played a vital part in the economy and constituted one of the main sources of employment. Usually between 10 and 30 years of age and unmarried, servants were to be found in 29 per cent of all households during the period, and a substantial proportion of young people of both sexes could expect to be servants at some stage in their lives.[2] From apprentices learning a trade to the officials of the great noble households, servants were perhaps the most distinctive socio-economic feature of sixteenth- and seventeenth-century society.

DEFINITIONS AND FEATURES

What exactly defined a servant in early modern England was far from universally agreed or established, and the multiplicity of definitions is eloquent testimony to the institution's pervasive influence. Many writers argued that 'servant' was a term with a wide application, and that among those who could be classed as such were players, monks, grooms, gentlemen, lords or courtiers, and even kings.[3] Other definitions were more capacious still, and maintained that any individual bound by a contract was a 'servant'.[4] Most often, however, such broadly-based statements were offset by precise attempts to place servants in relation to other forms of employment. In a reduction of available descriptions, for instance, Thomas Morrice averred in 1619 that chaplains and schoolmasters should not be thought of as servants as they were educated and exercised professional duties.[5] By contrast, Simon Daines endeavoured to solve the difficulty in 1640 by ranking all the possibilities:

> as there are differences and diverse degrees of Masters, so ought there severall respects to be had to servants, according to their place, and manner of service. For it were absurd to think, that Gentlemen in those places that may befit their rank and fortune, though subject to their masters call, should be tied to the obsequious termes of every pedantique Groome. As first, he that waits voluntary, and at his own expence; then Secretaries in their severall ranks; then such as serve in the places of Gentlemen, as Ushers, and the like. Then Clarks to men eminent, and of quality; and Clarks appertaining to Offices, Factors, and Apprentices (especially about *London*) men perhaps (as is usuall in that kind) better derived than their Masters.[6]

Even by the end of the seventeenth century, definitions were still circulating and colliding, for in 1700 Timothy Nourse could offer yet another interpretation and assert that there were only ever domestic servants, those working in husbandry and 'Mungrel-Labourers'.[7]

If definitions of service in the period were conflicting and diffuse, there were some areas of agreement and points of contact. The receipt of a wage came to be one of the chief characteristics of a period of service, as the Statute of Artificers, introduced in 1563 to establish 'an unyforme ordre ... concernynge the wages ... for ... seruauntes', exemplifies.[8] In 1615 the Protestant writer, Edward Elton, formulated the situation explicitly in such terms, commenting, 'seruants of any sort whatsoeuer, [are] such ... who serue for wages', and he was joined in 1690 by John Locke, who wrote, 'a free man makes himself a servant to another by selling him for a certain time the service he undertakes to do in exchange for wages he is to receive'.[9] Taking the example provided by Locke as their basis, and endeavouring to narrow these definitions, some historians in the 1960s and 1970s suggested the important distinction that labourers 'lived out' and were hired in a casual fashion, whereas servants 'lived in' as part of the master's household and served by the year.[10]

With some qualifications and additions, these contemporary and modern descriptions afford a useful working definition. Historians of the early modern period, however, have been hesitant to recognize that a wage did not always involve a cash payment, and that in the term 'wage-earner' other kinds of recompense, such as 'board', may be implied.[11] In this respect, apprentices are a case in point. Although training took the place of wages, apprentices were nevertheless regarded as servants. They were placed in a position of subordination, served for a fixed term, were instructed to conduct themselves with diligence, and were expected to show reverence to the master, who ideally combined the roles of commercial employer and caring *paterfamilias*.[12] The wage element, in addition, does not apply to and even limits the diversity of servants that marked the period as a whole. With such older servants as ladies-in-waiting, gentlemen ushers and stewards, for instance, who belonged to upper gentle and aristocratic households, there may not have been an annual contract; rewards may have been granted in the form of land or political privileges; and accommodation may have been located at some distance from the employer's residence.[13]

Wage-earners occupied a particular niche in the social hierarchy, and a second area of agreement about servants is apparent in contemporary comment on the subordinate positions with which they were inevitably associated. In political theory, the social order was imagined in terms of strictly gradated divisions: men and women were placed according to their 'estate', mobility was discouraged and the virtue of obedience was repeatedly praised and underlined.[14] 'An Exhortacion concernyng Good Ordre and Obedience to Rulers and Magistrates', the 1547 homily, advises: 'Every degre of people . . . hath appoynted to them their duetie and ordre . . . masters and servauntes . . . have nede of other'.[15] For Sir Thomas Smith, writing in 1562–5, servants occupied a rung below that of yeomen, and were therefore consigned, with day labourers, poor husbandmen and other artificers, to the 'fourth sort'. 'These', Smith states, 'have no voice nor authoritie in our common wealth, and no account is made of them but onelie to be ruled.'[16]

But the very existence of such comment provides fertile soil for speculation about the more complex and unpredictable ways in which authority and obedience in the social order may, in practice, have operated. Following recent developments in Cultural Materialism and the New Historicism, such constructions of early modern society have been increasingly scrutinized and contextualized. As Jonathan Dollimore states, didacticism can often be seen as reflecting not 'the occasional articulation of the collective mind but . . . an anxious reaction to social change'.[17] Sir Thomas Smith's division of England into four 'sorts' may suggest an ideological response to anxieties in the period about new emerging forces which seemed to threaten cherished ideals, while the attention given to the 'wage' in sixteenth- and seventeenth-century writing illuminates the expansion of the commercial and professional sectors, and the concomitant difficulty of maintaining hard-and-fast definitions of status and rank. The language of 'estates' and 'orders', moreover, was gradually being whittled away, and by the beginning of the eighteenth century a vocabulary of class was taking its place.

One of the energies animating Iago's corrosive expostulations is the conviction that justice has not been done, that his experience has been overlooked and that promotion has come to depend upon the master's whimsical selectivity exercises. The charges he levels follow the contours of views voiced by a number of popular writers, who held that the institution of service was at a critical stage in its development. Walter Darell's *A short discourse of the life of seruing-men* (1578), I. M.'s *A health to the gentlemanly profession of seruing-men* (1598) and William Basse's *Sword and Buckler* (1602) all lament the fact that liberality has decayed, that the nobility are dissolving their households and that servants are now treated with indifference. In agreement on the material manifestations of social transformations, the writers differ, however, in their analyses of the causes. Darell states that servants are disdained because of their 'lewd gouernment', riotousness and prodigality; I. M. locates the problem in the compounding of the pure metal of the institution with 'vntryed dregges and drosse of lesse esteeme'; while Basse blames the 'dunghill clowne' and 'Drone', who vilify servants 'In Dunsicall reproch, and blockish phrase'.[18] Although these writers, who claim to have had some personal experience of service, are principally concerned with the upper ranks of society, the issues they raise provide a provocative starting-point for a discussion of servants at other social levels and in literary texts of different genres.

It is the argument of this book that the ways in which servants are represented in English Renaissance drama and culture articulate some of the period's deepest sensitivities and aspirations, point to attempts to understand and control the changes that were challenging the contemporary order, and disclose fears of political instability, disorder and social frustration and unrest. In a wide range of literary materials – from plays and ballads to satirical verses – servants are given prominence, and their presence throws considerable light on mixed attitudes towards patterns of labour, a developing class consciousness, court and country relations and growing opportunities for social aggrandizement.[19] In a wider context, by returning to the claims of Basse, Darell, I. M. and other commentators, I intend to open up some fresh approaches to the current historical orientation in literary and cultural studies.

POWER AND RESISTANCE

Since the early 1980s, critics, known collectively if sometimes misleadingly as Cultural Materialists and New Historicists, have challenged the idea of literature as an aesthetic category which transcends historical contingencies.[20] There is now a greater recognition of the socially embedded nature of literary texts and of their relationship to other discursive practices. Exemplary of New Historicist work is Stephen Greenblatt's *Shakespearean Negotiations* (1988) in which Shakespearean texts, travel narratives, anti-Catholic propaganda, court depositions and accounts of exploration and imperialism all circulate as charged indicators of the 'energies' and 'transactions' of English Renaissance culture.[21]

Opponents of the New Historicism in particular, however, have held that this interlacing of diverse cultural products is misleading, rhetorical sleight of hand, and that it elides precise matters of evidence, place and date. Frequently heard is the criticism that the New Historicism has failed to clarify its own theoretical assumptions and methodological principles. The vocabulary favoured by New Historicists – of wonder or exchange – has been dismissed for its vagueness, while a more urgent but contradictory accusation sees in New Historicist work a nostalgic harking back to liberal values of freedom and autonomy, and even an essentialist undertow which goes against the claims for the historicity of all written utterances.[22]

While alive to such critical pitfalls, the present study grows out of the New Historicism and, perhaps more directly, Cultural Materialism in several ways. As a sample I have selected not only from the drama of the period but also from the popular culture as part of a dislodgement of canonical texts and aristocratic cultural modes. My readings are therefore stimulated by the ephemeral literature of the English Renaissance, by the productions of the breed of university-educated professional writers who swelled the marketplace with their recreational wares. In a related respect, this book endeavours to extend the contextual approaches which are characteristic of Cultural Materialism and the New Historicism, since I construct relations between texts and their material circumstances through substantially archival work. In order to pinpoint the anxieties which shaped and were shaped by representations of servants, I draw upon wills, court records, household accounts, correspondence, diaries and state papers, many of which are still in manuscript.

Of course, such contextual work carries its own questions and difficulties. Correspondence mostly records the worries and concerns of the employers rather than their servants, and diaries were often written out of a sense of moral obligation or religious commitment. Depositions in which servants protest against injustices may have been the exception rather than the rule (stable relations are more difficult to trace), while court minutes embrace an 'official' version of criminal activities. Any recovery of 'history' must always be provisional, since the 'evidence' available is fragmentary and selective, and conceals as well as exposes a culture's material 'realities'.

Despite the difficulties of recovering 'history from below', as

Jonathan Dollimore terms it, this book takes its form from an urge to prioritize not so much the master's voice as the servant's, to concentrate on the margins of literary discourse rather than the centre, and to be alive less to the exercise of power than to expressions of resistance.[23] With these aims in mind, theories of power relations assume a particular relevance. In his chapter on lordship and bondage in *Phenomenology of Spirit*, Hegel expounds a theory of the binarisms of 'self-consciousness', which he defines as existing 'in and for itself when, and by the fact that, it so exists for another; that is, it exists only in being acknowledged'.[24] Various commentators have suggested that this account indicates the reciprocal nature of power relations, which involve 'autonomy and dependence' pulling '"in both directions"' at one and the same time.[25] The master's existence is predicated upon maintaining his status as employer and upon the slave's subservience, without which neither of them is able to survive. Ultimately, then, the most authentic mastery can be said to reside with the slave whose work transforms the world and himself. 'And thus in the long run,' writes Alexandre Kojève, a commentator on Hegel, 'all slavish work realizes not the Master's will, but the will – at first unconscious – of the Slave, who – finally – succeeds where the Master – necessarily – fails.'[26]

In the work of Hegel's philosophical successor, Michel Foucault, is found a more pointed elaboration of the ways in which subordinated social groups can agitate to gain representation or privilege. Power in the Foucauldian sense is never static; it is always shifting and turbulent. As Foucault writes: 'power relationships' depend 'upon a multiplicity of points of resistance: these play the role of adversary, target, support, or handle in power relations. These points of resistance are present everywhere in the power network.'[27] What is important is that power originates in competing sections of the hierarchical structure, and that servants as well as masters are an integral part of the perpetuation of forms of social control. Pluralized rather than unitary, power is not owned by a particular group but is distributed over wide areas; the balance can be modified in a contradictory process whereby those who appear to exercise authority may also become its most unlikely casualties.

While Hegel and Foucault recognize the potential for resistance, they generally neglect to offer concrete descriptions of how it might be realized. Useful in this connection, therefore, is sociologist James C. Scott's book, *Domination and the Arts of Resistance* (1990), which details the strategies utilized by subordinate groups, such as rumours, trickster folktales, songs, gestures, dissimulation, flight, petitions, carnival, the cultivation of scatalogical languages and organized confrontations at the marketplace.[28] The value of Scott's study, however, mainly lies in its inventory of examples, and the particularities of the English Renaissance do not enter its discussions. It is by attending to the reception and appropriation of literary texts, and to the ideological work which they perform, that the potential for resistance in the period can be most forcibly apprehended.

In exploring anxieties at a number of social levels, and in addressing a range of textual materials, I argue that, partly through their participation in popular culture and their access to developing cultural networks, subordinated groups could be empowered and even contest existing hierarchical arrangements. Chiefly in the popular theatres, apprentices, servants and journeymen – often referred to as 'youth' in contemporary documents of control – were a recurrent presence, at least to judge from the anxious statements issued by moralists and the city authorities.[29] Escalating literacy levels contributed to an expansion of opportunities for the servant classes, and an expression and a product of these developments was an increase in the availability of printed works.[30] Although literacy standards differed according to the educational knowledge of particular servant groups, and were unequally distributed among the men and women who belonged to those groups, the general trend in the period seems to have been towards the dramatic rise of reading and writing abilities.[31]

As part of this process, texts began to be specifically targeted at servant interests. Occasional statements in prefaces which identify servants as readers survive from the earlier sixteenth century; in the seventeenth century, however, can be found the majority of apposite instances.[32] *A brothers gift* (1623), Humphrey Everinden's compendium of moral exempla, includes a series of complicated instructions to be absorbed and acted upon by the intended servant consumer, and *Cupids schoole*, a 1632 book of compliments, prints a group of epistles from Roger, the servingman, to Susan, the chambermaid, informing the aspiring servant how to write a love-letter.[33] Godly admonitions, such as Thomas Sorocold's *Supplications of saints* (1612) and Michael Sparke's *The crums of comfort with godly prayers* (1628), featured prayers designed for men and women servants in which questions about social company, status, sexuality and economic foresight receive detailed consideration.[34] In constructing servants as consumers, the authors of such texts played a key part in creating a servant culture, and spaces within which particular preoccupations and projects could be highlighted.

But it was in the range of literary representations of servants, as opposed to moral works in which they were addressed, that a greater scope for resistance resided. As I argue in chapter 1, possibilities for resistance are broached in representations in plays and pamphlets of apprentices who declare a dissatisfaction with the exercise of power through murmurs, violence or open revolt. Chapter 2 looks at the role of servants in crafts and trades in popular entertainments, while chapter 3 attends to inversions of the social order brought about by male domestic servants. Although these representations show attempts to control servants' infractions, the move to closure is deceptive. For, as Alan Sinfield remarks, 'a text that aspires to contain a subordinate position must first bring it into visibility . . . once that has happened, there can be no guarantee that the subordinate will stay safely in its prescribed place.'[35] In fact, these two chapters maintain that the theatre made manifest both the servant's dangerous mobility and the concerns of the employing class. Questions about the distribution and ownership of privileges take on a gendered dimension in chapter 4, where discussion concentrates on the ways in which patriarchal norms are upset by representations of women servants who share in the prerogatives that should be their employers' province. In the noble household, these questions acquire a particular urgency. The final chapter accordingly traces the intersections between mainly dramatic representations of negligent gentlemen ushers and stewards, and aristocratic anxieties about a loss of prestige and influence.

It is the very multiplicity of points of resistance that this book explores. In moving through various servant categories (apprentices, journeymen, male domestic servants, women in service and the 'chief officers' of the noble household), I employ a convenient arrangement which enables key concerns to be addressed, different anxieties to be confronted and a variety of literary genres to be examined. While keeping mainly within the limits of the English Renaissance, I also occasionally move outside its borders:

this permits changes and continuities in the representation of the early modern servant to be described, and makes possible a reassessment of Iago's view that service is not so much a blessing as a curse.

NOTES

1. *Othello*, ed. E. A. J. Honigmann (London and New York, 1997), I.i.34–9.
2. Barry Coward, *Social Change and Continuity in Early Modern England 1550–1750* (London and New York, 1988), p. 19; Paul Griffiths, 'Masterless Young People in Norwich, 1560–1645', in Paul Griffiths, Adam Fox and Steve Hindle, eds, *The Experience of Authority in Early Modern England* (Basingstoke and London, 1996), p. 150; John Hajnal, 'Two Kinds of Preindustrial Household Formation System', *Population and Development Review*, 8 (1982), p. 473. It is less easy to ascertain how servants entered employment, but correspondence and letter-books suggest that, at least among the upper levels of society, a personal recommendation was highly influential. See Angel Day, *The English secretorie* (London, 1586; S.T.C. 6401), pp. 191–2; Kent A. O., U269 098/1; L.P.L., MS. 3199, fo. 221ʳ.
3. E. K. Chambers, ed., *The Elizabethan Stage*, 4 vols (Oxford, 1923), vol. II, p. 208, vol. IV, pp. 263–4, 296, 334; Abraham Cowley, *Several Discourses by way of Essays, in Verse and Prose* (published 1668), in *The English Writings*, ed. A. R. Waller, 2 vols (Cambridge, 1905–6), vol. II, p. 381; John Davies, *Wits Bedlam* (London, 1617; S.T.C. 6343), sig. G4ᵛ; Owen Felltham, *Resolves, Divine, Moral, Political* (c. 1620) (Oxford, 1840), p. 14; Stefano Guazzo, *The ciuile conuersation*, tr. B. Young (London, 1586; S.T.C. 12423), fos 166ʳ, 167ʳ; Paul Whitfield White, *Theatre and Reformation: Protestantism, Patronage, and Playing in Tudor England* (Cambridge, 1993), p. 43.
4. William Gouge, *Of domesticall duties* (London, 1622; S.T.C. 12119), p. 160; Nicholas Ling, *Politeuphuia wits common wealth* (London, 1597; S.T.C. 15685), p. 139.
5. Thomas Morrice, *An apology for schoole-masters* (London, 1619; S.T.C. 18170), sigs B2ᵛ, B4ʳ, C1ʳ, C2ʳ.
6. Simon Daines, *Orthoepia Anglicana: or, the first principall part of the English grammar* (London, 1640; S.T.C. 6190), p. 86.
7. Timothy Nourse, *Campania foelix* (London, 1700; Wing N1416), pp. 202–3, 213.
8. R. H. Tawney and Eileen Power, eds, *Tudor Economic Documents*, 3 vols (London, 1924), vol. I, p. 338.
9. Edward Elton, *An exposition of the epistle to the Colossians* (London,

1615; S.T.C. 7612), p. 1145; John Locke, *Two Treatises of Government*, ed. W. S. Carpenter (London, 1990), pp. 157–8.

10. Peter Laslett, 'Market Society and Political Theory', *Historical Journal*, 7 (1964), pp. 150–4; C. B. Macpherson, *Democratic Theory: Essays in Retrieval* (Oxford, 1973), pp. 207–23; C.B. Macpherson, *The Political Theory of Possessive Individualism: Hobbes to Locke* (Oxford, 1962), pp. 107–11, 282–6; Keith Thomas, 'The Levellers and the Franchise', in G. E. Aylmer, ed., *The Interregnum: The Quest for Settlement 1646–1660* (London and Basingstoke, 1972), pp. 71–2. See also Ann Kussmaul, *Servants in Husbandry in Early Modern England* (Cambridge, 1981), p. 135.

11. See J. A. Sharpe, *Early Modern England: A Social History 1550–1760* (London, 1987), p. 211; J. A. Simpson and E. S. C. Weiner, eds, *The Oxford English Dictionary*, 20 vols (Oxford, 1989), vol. XIX, pp. 803–4.

12. Sir William Blackstone, *Commentaries on the Laws of England*, 4th edn, 4 vols (Dublin, 1771), vol. I, pp. 422–31; Elton, *An exposition*, p. 1145. On master–servant duties more generally, see Mark Thornton Burnett, 'Masters and Servants in Moral and Religious Treatises, *c.* 1580–*c.* 1642', in Arthur Marwick, ed., *The Arts, Literature, and Society* (London and New York, 1990), pp. 48–75; Mark Thornton Burnett, 'The "Trusty Servant": A Sixteenth-Century English Emblem', *Emblematica*, 6 (1992), pp. 237–53. The portrait of the 'Trusty Servant' is reproduced on the cover of this book.

13. I address these exceptions in chapters 4 and 5.

14. Keith Wrightson, 'Estates, Degrees and Sorts: Changing Perceptions of Society in Tudor and Stuart England', in Penelope J. Corfield, ed., *Language, History and Class* (Oxford, 1991), pp. 30–52; and '"Sorts of people" in Tudor and Stuart England', in Jonathan Barry and Christopher Brooks, eds, *The Middling Sort of People: Culture, Society and Politics in England, 1550–1800* (Basingstoke and London, 1994), pp. 28–51.

15. Ronald B. Bond, ed., *'Certain Sermons or Homilies' (1547) and 'A Homily against Disobedience and Wilful Rebellion' (1570): A Critical Edition* (Toronto, Buffalo and London, 1987), p. 161.

16. Sir Thomas Smith, *De Republica Anglorum*, ed. Mary Dewar (Cambridge, 1982), p. 76. In his account first published in 1577, William Harrison arrived at similar conclusions. See his *The Description of England*, ed. Georges Edelen (Ithaca, NY, 1968), p. 119.

17. Jonathan Dollimore, review of *James I and the Politics of Literature: Jonson, Shakespeare, Donne and Their Contemporaries* by Jonathan Goldberg (Baltimore and London, 1983), *Criticism*, 26 (1984), p. 84.

18. Walter Darell, *A short discourse of the life of seruing-men* (London, 1578; S.T.C. 6274), sig. Aiii^v; I. M., *A health to the gentlemanly profession of seruing-men* (London, 1598; S.T.C. 17140), sig. C3^r; William Basse, *Sword and Buckler* (1602), in *The Poetical Works*, ed. R. Warwick Bond (London, 1893), p. 14.

19. In addition to my own studies, there have been several recent specialized discussions of servants and service in the early modern period, which include: Linda Anderson, 'Shakespeare's Servants',

The Shakespeare Yearbook, 2, Spring (1991), pp. 149–61; Mario DiGangi, 'Asses and Wits: The Homoerotics of Mastery in Satiric Comedy', *English Literary Renaissance*, 25 (1995), pp. 179–208; Frances E. Dolan, *Dangerous Familiars: Representations of Domestic Crime in England, 1550–1700* (Ithaca, NY and London, 1994); David Evett, '"Surprising Confrontations": Ideologies of Service in Shakespeare's England', *Renaissance Papers 1990*, pp. 67–78; Thomas Moisan, '"Knock me here soundly": Comic Misprision and Class Consciousness in Shakespeare', *Shakespeare Quarterly*, 42 (1991), pp. 276–90; Judith Weil, '"Household stuff": Maestrie and Service in *The Taming of the Shrew*', in A. L. Magnusson and C. E. McGee, eds, *The Elizabethan Theatre, XIV* (Port Credit, 1994), pp. 71–82.

20. For representative studies, see Richard Wilson and Richard Dutton, eds, *New Historicism and Renaissance Drama* (London and New York, 1992).

21. Stephen Greenblatt, *Shakespearean Negotiations: The Circulation of Social Energy in Renaissance England* (Oxford, 1988), pp. 1–20.

22. See Alan Liu, 'The Power of Formalism: The New Historicism', *English Literary History*, 56 (1989), pp. 721–71; Carolyn Porter, 'Are We Being Historical Yet?', *South Atlantic Quarterly*, 87 (1988), pp. 743–86.

23. Jonathan Dollimore, 'Introduction: Shakespeare, Cultural Materialism and the New Historicism', in Jonathan Dollimore and Alan Sinfield, eds, *Political Shakespeare: New Essays in Cultural Materialism* (Manchester, 1985), p. 15.

24. G. W. F. Hegel, *Phenomenology of Spirit*, tr. A. V. Miller (Oxford, 1977), p. 111.

25. Anthony Giddens, *Central Problems in Social Theory: Action, Structure and Contradiction in Social Analysis* (London and Basingstoke, 1979), p. 149.

26. Alexandre Kojève, *Introduction to the Reading of Hegel*, ed. Allan Bloom, tr. James H. Nichols (New York and London, 1969), p. 30.

27. Michel Foucault, *The History of Sexuality: An Introduction*, tr. Robert Hurley (Harmondsworth, 1990), p. 95.

28. James C. Scott, *Domination and the Arts of Resistance: Hidden Transcripts* (New Haven, CT and London, 1990).

29. Chambers, ed., *Elizabethan*, vol. IV, pp. 187, 197, 207, 209, 239, 244, 247, 287, 288, 307, 317, 322.

30. Servants did not generally write or commit themselves to print, the exception being Thomas Whythorne's autobiography, composed in 1576; see *The Autobiography*, ed. James M. Osborn (London, New York and Toronto, 1962).

31. David Cressy, *Literacy and the Social Order: Reading and Writing in Tudor and Stuart England* (Cambridge, 1980), pp. 4, 41, 128–9. It also needs to be recognized that reading constituted only one route to knowledge. Visual and aural literacy may have been as important as scribal: black-letter broadsides were pasted up as wallpaper, and ballads, if they were not performed by the minstrel as part of the selling process, could be dramatized or displayed in taverns, nurseries and private houses. See Tessa Watt, *Cheap Print and Popular*

Piety 1550–1640 (Cambridge, 1991), pp. 6, 7, 12, 14, 16, 148, 167, 220, 328; Natascha Würzbach, *The Rise of the English Street Ballad, 1550–1650*, tr. Gayna Walls (Cambridge, 1990), pp. 13–14, 22.

32. Thomas Blundeville, *A new book containing the arte of ryding* (London, 1561?; S.T.C. 3158), sig. Ai[r]; *von Braunschweig* Hieronymus, *The noble experyence of the vertuous handywarke of surgeri* (London, 1525; S.T.C. 13434), sig. Aii[r].

33. Humphrey Everinden, *A brothers gift: containing an hundred precepts, instructing to a godly life* (London, 1623; S.T.C. 10601), sigs B3[r]–4[r]; *Cupids schoole: wherein, yongmen and maids may learne divers sorts of complements* (London, 1632; S.T.C. 6123), sigs C2[v]–4[r].

34. Thomas Sorocold, *Supplications of saints* (London, 1612; S.T.C. 22932), pp. 333, 336, 341, 344; Michael Sparke, *The crums of comfort with godly prayers* (London, 1628; S.T.C. 23016), sig. B5[v].

35. Alan Sinfield, *Faultlines: Cultural Materialism and the Politics of Dissident Reading* (Oxford, 1992), p. 48.

1
Apprenticeship and Society

Apprenticeships were usually arranged between a boy's father and a prospective master, and once contracted the apprentice left the parental home to learn a particular craft or trade.[1] The apprentice undertook to work hard, to conduct himself soberly, to keep his master's secrets and not to marry until his terms had been completed; in return, the master offered accommodation, maintenance and technical training. Instruction in skills was accompanied by moral lessons, since masters, guardians *in loco parentis*, were obliged to ensure that their apprentices observed saints' days and attended divine service.[2] This was, then, an essentially familial mode of organization through which the apprentice would ideally be elevated to the positions of established citizen, freeman of the livery company and respected adult member of society.

In this chapter, I argue that representations of apprentices in ballads, didactic literature and drama were dialectically related to contemporary social and political dislocations and developments. To appreciate these representations fully, it is to an apprentice culture that we first need to turn. Throughout the period, apprentices entertained a corporate identity, which is revealed in their consumption of popular literary materials as well as their political activities. Literacy was a general prerequisite for the would-be apprentice. From the 1520s to the 1540s, 72 per cent of the apprentices in the Ironmongers' Company managed to write out a long oath, and the Barber-Surgeons in 1556 were disallowed from taking on any apprentice who could not understand Latin or read and write.[3] Such abilities were crucial factors in the production of texts which addressed specifically apprentice interests. Thomas Heywood was not alone in writing his *The Four Prentices of London* (*c.* 1594) for 'the honest and hie-spirited Prentises The Readers', and later accounts testify to the popularity of romances with a literate apprentice audience.[4]

In the popular theatres, apprentices responded enthusiastically to a familiar repertory, and were represented gorging on custard and cream and even precipitating violence.[5] On Shrove Tuesday, the religious festival traditionally associated with the licensed indulgence of excessive behaviour prior to a period of Lenten abstinence, apprentices placed exacting commercial pressures on the playhouses, and on several occasions would begin to dismantle the building if their demands for the staging of their favourite plays were not met.[6] The bloodiest Shrove Tuesday occurred in 1617, when apprentices destroyed the new theatre in Drury Lane, responding to the action of the theatre manager, Christopher Beeston, who had removed the popular repertory of the Red Bull to the more expensive Cockpit, thereby infuriating his citizen audiences.[7] On this day of the year, apprentices acted against institutions which they otherwise seem to have patronized, reflecting a powerful system of communication, a set of common cultural imperatives and a shared political agenda.

James C. Scott has suggested that carnival provided a 'time and . . . place to settle, verbally at least, personal and social scores', and his formulation is pertinent to the ways in which apprentices perennially gathered to oust traditional enemies and favourites.[8] A carnival dimension, similarly, may be seen in apprentice uprisings in London in the 1590s, some of which were directed at the metropolitan authorities. It is with a discussion of the shifting literary manifestations of the apprentice's social attitudes and economic horizons in this period of acute distress that the chapter begins. The repressive nature of his contract, I go on to argue, can help to account for the evolution of early seventeenth-century plays and pamphlets, which deliberated the relationship's potential for breakdown and asked questions about the legitimacy of male sexual inclinations. I link a later critical conception of the institution, in turn, to the popularity of new theatrical tastes and to changes within the livery companies themselves. Throughout these three main sections, I examine writings as discourses of control and in relation to the regulatory procedures of the livery companies, in order to arrive at a denser understanding of the means whereby master and apprentice relations were inscribed within an expanding and predominantly urban culture. The theatre, moral treatises and popular literature, in different ways and at different times, fulfilled several ideological purposes simultaneously, underscoring prevailing establishment views, qualifying the ideals of particular literary conventions, and creating a culture within which dissident apprentice energies might be articulated.

THE CRISIS OF THE 1590s

In many texts of the 1590s and even the early Jacobean period, the apprentice's virtues of hard work and obedience are singled out in ways which evoke and engage with the economic difficulties and social uncertainties of the contemporary metropolis. These productions gave shape to apprentices' opportunities for betterment, corporate sense of themselves, vexed relations with groups opposed to national security, and military ambitions, ideas and material practices which are most succinctly communicated in the play, *Sir Thomas More*.

Publications of the moral exemplum genre depicted godly and sanctimonious apprentices, such as Sir William Sevenoak, a former mayor of London, who remembers in a pamphlet of 1592:

> To please the honest care my master tooke,
> I did refuse no toyle nor drudging payne,
> My handes no labor euer yet forsooke
> Whereby I might encrease my masters gayne:
> Thus *Seuenoake* liud (for so they cald my name,)
> Till Heauen did place mee in a better frame.[9]

Perhaps 60 per cent of apprentices in this period of rising poverty failed to work for a full term, and the response of didactic writers was to seek to persuade them that training, successfully completed, was a moral necessity. Sevenoak underscores the importance of social stability and contentment.[10] A parallel point is made via Piers, the titular apprentice hero of *Piers Plainness: Seven Years' Prenticeship* (1595) by Henry Chettle, who had himself served as an apprentice to a stationer. After having helped in putting down a rebellion and served various corrupt masters, Piers has the opportunity to live at court but decides, instead, to become a shepherd's servant: 'for my plaine condition I found them too curious: therefore hetherward I bent my course, intending to live Menalcas man if he accept it, or keepe my owne Heard, when I can get it'.[11] Piers's course lies in happily accepting the manacles of serving Menalcas, in amassing sheep rather than money and in anticipating a position that will not affect his essential humility.

The broad outline of such fictions espouses community values and affirms the inviolability of the political structure. In popular advice to apprentices, in contrast, it is implied that serving an apprenticeship will lead to material gain and public honours. Dick Whittington, the quasi-legendary apprentice who rose to be Lord Mayor of London, was celebrated in ballads from at least the sixteenth century onwards; the following construction of his story is from a 1613 version of an earlier set of verses:

> Brave *London* 'Prentices, come listen to my Song,
> 'Tis for your glory all, and to you doth belong;
> And you, poor Country Lads, though born of low degree,
> See by God's providence what you in time may bee.[12]

Steve Rappaport has remarked that Dick Whittington 'legends became popular because they reflected not only immigrants' aspirations but also the existence of opportunities for social mobility . . . which attracted so many young people to the capital'.[13] The ballad bears out the appositeness of the statement, since it promotes an ideal of a divinely ordained rise to greatness, which is essentially divorced from the material pressures of economic exigency.

But the insistence on the apprentice's pleasurable acceptance of discomfort and implicit approval of the hierarchical order masked an unstable social environment. The common concerns registered in these texts, and the idealized cast which they assume, are thrown into relief by the more politically subversive nature of apprentices' periodic demonstrations. Beyond the tales of riches and advantages advanced by popular writers lay the spectre of dearth and critical shortages. Moderation, abstemiousness and discipline conveniently mediated the problems which plagued an overburdened economy; the perceived inadequacies of Elizabethan distribution systems were countered by promises of civic reward and achievement. Famine was a pervasive fear in the mid-1590s, and the apprentices took it upon themselves to attempt to implement their own solutions to the economic crisis in ways which pointed to a dissatisfaction with the economic policies of contemporary officials. At Billingsgate in June 1595, in two separate incidents, they stole butter and fish in order to sell them at reduced prices.[14] In October 1595, riotous apprentices in Cheapside made off with a cart-load of starch, the property of the Queen's patentee of an unpopular monopoly.[15] Even in 1596, libels which probably complained about the conditions of dearth were still circulating in the city.[16]

James C. Scott states that there were established 'horizontal links among subordinates' and opportunities to join 'public gatherings', which were commonly regarded 'as an implicit threat to domination', and his comment works both as a useful summation of the articulation of apprentice anxieties and as a reminder of an extended history of political involvement.[17] On May Day in 1517, 2000 apprentices had demonstrated anti-alien feelings, sacked the houses of French and Flemish merchants, assaulted the Spanish ambassador and opened the gaols. Twelve apprentices were executed after the troubles had subsided.[18] In 1549, there had been an unsuccessful attempt to persuade the apprentices to join the Norfolk rebels.[19] When writers voiced the complicating view that apprentice activity could exacerbate rather than resolve social conflicts, therefore, contemporaries may not have received the possibility as a fanciful extravagance.

For the apprentice who failed to submit himself 'vnder the yoake', to adopt the words of a contemporary pamphlet, there was little doubt of his conduct's dangerous social implications.[20] Wrote Samuel Rowlands, another pamphleteer, in 1602:

> There are a certaine band of Raggamuffin Prentises about the towne, that will abuse anie vpon the smallest occasion . . . such men . . . dare neuer meete a man in the face to auouch their rogarie, but forsooth they must haue the help of some other their complices. Of this base sort you shall commonly find them at Playhouses on holy dayes . . . or at some rout, as the pulling downe of Baudie houses, or at some good exploit or other, so that if you . . . thinke your selfe not able to make your part good with anie that you owe a grudge to, no more but repaire to one of these, and for a canne of Ale they will do as much as another for a crowne.[21]

Rowlands offers a dispassionate reading of the actions of apprentices, for here they represent a floating crowd, a pressure group that can be exploited. More disconcerting still is Thomas

Rogers's *Leicester's Ghost* (1602–4) in which Robert Dudley, the Earl of Leicester, recalls his manipulation of metropolitan interests:

> The Prentises did likewise take my part,
> As I in private quarrels often tryde,
> Soe that I had the very head and hart,
> The *Court* and *Citty* leaning one my side,
> With flattery some, others with guifts I plide,
>   And some with threats, stearne looks, and angry words,
>   I woone to my defence with clubbs and swords.[22]

The lines are ambiguous, since Dudley either bribes or threatens his supporters, but the overriding point is that the unscrupulous services of apprentices are readily available. That this assembly of open voters, and flotsam of the social order, can be so easily persuaded lends Rogers's verse a sinister edge and elaborates a more cynical assessment of an institution's corporate identity and aspirations.

Judging from outbreaks of apprentice disorder in which 'class' tensions were played out, it is entirely appropriate that these representations should countenance the possibility of conjunctions among and oppositions between diverse social 'sorts' and constituencies. In practice, apprentices seem to have come into conflict with their social superiors, as a 1576 proclamation, protesting against the violence offered by apprentices towards the pages and lackeys of noblemen, suggests.[23] A 1581 incident, when some apprentices in Smithfield assaulted the servants of Sir Thomas Stanhope, caused similar concern.[24] In 1584 the apprentices made 'mutines and assembles' after one of their fellows, sleeping on the grass outside the theatre, the Curtain, had been kicked in the stomach and called a rogue and scum by a passing gentleman.[25] The frustrations culminated in 1590: vagrants and apprentices assembled, attacked the gentlemen of Lincoln's Inn and broke into their chambers.[26] Though the insurrection was put down, it was still necessary to introduce in 1591 stringent measures against unlawful gatherings to prevent further outbreaks of violence.[27]

It is with such contexts in mind that we need to read the preoccupation with social conflict in a number of dramas, which address with a greater sensitivity the stability of ascribed roles and the permanence of allegiances, and interrogate the lines that might keep an 'apprentice' and a 'gentleman' distinct. A disagreement erupts between two prosecutors of vice, and some dandies in *Every Woman in Her Humour* (1599–1603), possibly by Lewis Machin, and the hostess of the tavern appeals to the apprentices to separate the fighting parties.[28] On a later occasion in the play, in a parodic reading of an indenture, she drills the apprentices: 'you must bee eyed like a Serieant, an eare like a Belfounder, your conscience a Schoolemaister, a knee like a Courtier' (IV.i.14–16). When two gallants insult George, the journeyman, in Dekker and Middleton's *The Honest Whore, Part I* (1604), he rouses the apprentices to rise to correct the hierarchical balance: 'Sfoot clubs, clubs, prentices, downe with em, ah you roagues, strike a Cittizen in's shop.'[29] Once again a moral dimension is stressed in these passages, as the apprentices, in their role as part of a local militia, confront the affectations of an aspiring bourgeoisie and assume the characteristics of a figure of justice. That dandies and gallants are realized as targets of opprobrium and threats to the privileges of civic institutions is not coincidental. As Ian W. Archer states, conflicts involving apprentices, servants and students 'reflected the status uncertainties of apprentices, which derived from gentry snobbery about the demeaning effects of trade. Such attitudes had a sharper cutting edge in London because many apprentices were recruited from the younger sons of the gentry or from the ranks of the yeomanry, the same groups as provided so many servingmen in gentry households.'[30] Between these groups in London, there were long-established and particularized social tensions.

In the 1590s, therefore, the apprentice's diligence was put to a variety of metaphorical uses, which both reduced and magnified interrelated economic and social imperatives. The contrasting roles played by the apprentices illuminate the sometimes irreconcilable causes which they supported, while the guises assumed by authority are debated in all their manifestations. If attacks on the satellites of the court were legitimized in dramatic representations, however, attacks by apprentices on their employers presented a particularly intractable difficulty. 'O! where is loyalty?', asks Henry in *King Henry VI, Part II* (1590–91), lamenting the treachery that afflicts his kingdom, adding, 'When such strings jar, what hope of harmony?'[31] The scenes between Peter, an armourer's apprentice, and his master, Horner, take up these questions, and explore the ways in which literate petitioners might defend common rights and protest against injustice, even at the highest levels. From Peter's evidence, Horner has proclaimed the Duke of York as the 'rightful heir to the crown' (I.iii.26), which represents a treasonable offence. As Peter accordingly prepares to fight his master, he is comforted by his fellows:

> 2 *Prentice.* Be merry, Peter, and fear not thy master: fight for credit of the prentices.
> *Peter.* I thank you all: drink, and pray for me . . .
> Here, Robin, and if I die, I give thee my apron; and, Will, thou shalt have my hammer: and here, Tom, take all the money that I have. (II.iii.68–70, 72–4)

Even though Peter dispatches his master in the duel, he is given royal approval, for thanks to Horner's deathbed confession of guilt ('I confess, I confess treason' [II.iii.91]) the apprentice is distinguished from his master, who thinks only of his own interests and of justifying his accusations.[32]

In its realization of a community defending its values through fraternal spirit, *King Henry VI, Part II* prompts a testing debate. Peter is a comic figure who mistakes a 'usurer' (I.iii.30) for a usurper: he is also a threatening force whose act of 'petty treason' (the murder of a master by a servant) is left neatly unresolved. As an armourer's apprentice, Peter has a tangential role to play in the war effort, which places in an ironic light the angry discussion about the loss of Anjou and Maine at the start of the play. At the same time, the apprentice's victory foreshadows the insurrection of Jack Cade, a more dangerous species of rebel, an opponent of literacy and a self-styled aristocrat. Most worrying, perhaps, is that Peter's action points to flaws inherent in the family and the state, and to divisions and discrepancies within those structures, and in so doing touches upon a complex of contemporary associations. For the play's representation of the camaraderie shared by apprentices anticipates a series of tumults in the 1590s in which they acted in concert to support their members.

When a feltmaker's apprentice was imprisoned in the Marshalsea for debt in 1592, his fellows met at a play to plan his rescue. In the attempt, innocent bystanders in Southwark were jostled and hurt, leading to a strengthening of the watch soon afterwards.[33] On 6 June 1595, a silkweaver, who faced punishment for having

criticized the Lord Mayor, was rescued by a crowd of apprentices.[34] The attempt later in the month to imprison in the Counter (a prison attached to the city court) some servants who had
fallen foul of the magistrates gave rise to further apprentice rescue
efforts.[35] The discontent came to a climax at the end of the month:
encouraged by vagrant soldiers and in revenge for the way in
which their fellows had been treated after the butter and fish
dispute, 1800 apprentices pulled down the pillories in Cheapside
and Leadenhall on 27 June, and s et up gallows against the door
of the Lord Mayor, Sir John Spenser.[36] Coming home from the
Spanish wars, without obvious means of support and often waiting
for long overdue wages, demobilized soldiers nurtured specific
frustrations, and some of them may even have had experience
of apprenticeships themselves.[37] A gathering of apprentices outside the Tower on 29 June, the stated intention of which was to
rob the wealthy inhabitants and to take the sword of authority
from the governors, resulted in the enforcement of a state of
martial law, a search for the culprits, proclamations, a spate of
libels, the arrest of the leaders, their conviction for treason and
on 24 July their subsequent execution.[38]

While *King Henry VI, Part II* does not prefigure these disturbances precisely, it still represents a point of intervention in a
discursive field marked by questions about political loyalty, the
practices of constituted authorities and the circumstances within
which treasonable offences could be identified and exorcized.
Given the extent and longevity of disorders in the 1590s, the
legitimization of apprentice antagonisms in dramatic representations, it might also be argued, constituted a strategic interpretation of practices that were unpredictable in their social effects,
despite apparently common ideological assumptions. A play which
traces the contours of the 1590s more explicitly, and which expands
the range of targets selected for apprentice attack, is Heywood's
Edward IV, Part I, in existence in an early version in 1594 but
not printed until 1599. As his drama was associated with the
popular amphitheatres, such as the Red Bull, moreover, it may
have been in a particularly strong position to air the interests of
apprentice spectators. The play contains scenes in which apprentices band together to repel, not their employers, but an invading rebel army from the city gates. What is at stake is not so
much the city as the ideal of freedom which it represents: the
second apprentice cries, 'And, *London* prentices, be rul'd by me;

/ Die ere ye lose fair *Londons* liberty', and he denounces the rebels as 'those desperate, idle, swaggering mates, / That haunt the suburbes in the time of peace', reflecting a diagrammatic conception of the city as a site of moral values and the suburbs as a haven for sedition and vagabondage.[39] The first apprentice's speech culminates in a celebration of civic sentiments:

> The Chronicles of *England* can report
> What memorable actions we haue done,
> To which this daies achieuement shall be knit,
> To make the volume larger than it is. (p. 18)

Edward IV, Part I develops and separates the examples set by *King Henry VI, Part II*, distinguishing the apprentices from the rebels rather than, as in the case of Jack Cade, suggesting points of contact between apprentice petitioning and popular protest. By discovering apprentices who act to write themselves into the text of London's posterity, the play also papers over the differences that apprentices experienced with the city's oligarchical authorities. However, as Kathleen E. McLuskie states, the allegiance between the city, the apprentices and the crown 'works symbolically in the theatrical psychomachia of the alarums and excursions but the overdetermined insistence of the speeches' suggests 'tensions in the political understanding which are far from completely resolved'.[40] Like Shakespeare, Heywood elaborates dramatic mechanisms for situating disorder, only to expose its uncertain status and and internal contradictions.

Rebels outside the city gates may have been the stuff of fantasy, but foreigners within the city itself posed a threat of greater material urgency to trading and commercial interests. War and rapid population growth exacerbated already well-established grievances. Dutch and French refugees, in particular, were charged with causing unemployment, a decline in trade and a rise in prices. Hostilities surfaced in a libel of 1567 and a plot of 1586 hatched by the plasterers' apprentices against the foreign artisans.[41] Again in 1593 a litter of apprentice libels menacing the strangers swept the capital.[42] Although riot was only threatened, not executed, the anxieties aroused by foreigners continued and revealed themselves in a variety of prosaic, dramatic and poetic forms. Jest-books, such as *Wits fittes and fancies* (1595), worked to diffuse the frustrations attendant upon popular xenophobia.

A London printer asks his apprentice to fetch him some French mustard, telling him ironically that it is only to be found in France; the servant rushes to Billingsgate, boards a ship bound for France and returns home after a year's absence, triumphantly bearing the hard-won condiment:

> The said Prentise entring by and by into his maisters Printing-house, and finding a Dutch-man there working at the Presse, straight stept vnto him, and snatching the balles out of his hands, gaue him a good cuffe on the eare, & sayd: Why how now (Butter-boxe?) Cannot a man so soon turne his back to fetch his maister a messe of Mustard, but you to step straight into his place?[43]

The butt of the joke is the apprentice, a parody of the 'good servant' who will go to any lengths to obey orders. But such a parody has a specific relevance in the light of fears about evaporating sources of employment: the apprentice is afraid that English practices are being usurped by the consuming Dutchman ('Butter-boxe'), and as he fills his master's mustard-pot, so is he worried by the possibility of his own place being filled by a foreign worker.

Diffusing anxieties, however, was only one part of a more complex literary engagement with the hostile feelings excited by a foreign population. Not content with attacking local forms of aberration, apprentices in some texts steal abroad to fight traditional enemies and to express their nationalistic inclinations, recalling, perhaps, the precedent set by those apprentices who enlisted or were impressed to fight in foreign wars, such as in the Low Countries.[44] In Heywood's *The Four Prentices of London* (*c.* 1594), the sound of a drum lures the apprentices to leave their trades and join the Holy Wars in Jerusalem: *en route*, they liberate Boulogne and other besieged cities from the Spanish forces, and during the course of their campaigns indulge in invective against demagogic tyrants, foreigners and 'proud *Italians*' (l. 1012). Adventure and romance in Heywood's play assuage anxieties about the possible erosion of the trading liberties of London: Heywood's heroic apprentices are presented for approbation as they deliver Syon and Jerusalem from the domination of a foreign power, restoring to them their cultural and religious importance. Of a similar cast is Henry Roberts's 1595 celebration of Captain

James Lancaster's sea adventures against the Spanish, which specifically addresses apprentices:

> And gallant Brutes which yet are bound,
>   your masters to obay:
> When time shall make you free againe,
>   think then what I now say.
> Learne by this man of woorth to guyde,
>   your selues in euerie place:
> By land or sea to gaine renowne,
>   and enemies to disgrace,
> your Countrey then your honor shall,
>   for Prince doe seruice good:
> and men that see your woorthynes,
>   for you will spend their blood.[45]

Although the figure of the foreigner is only dimly present, the economically inflected recommendation for apprentices to save themselves belongs with the poem's polemical point that a sound England is built upon its citizens' faithful service and allegiance. Adventure genres served to direct aggression into realms of heroic fantasy: dramatists and pamphleteers, with one eye on the censors and the other on apprentices who clamoured for new publications, negotiated contemporary questions by relocating them to an exotic environment.

The majority of these concerns are crystallized in *Sir Thomas More*, a play which is usually dated 1593–4 and which was severely censored because deemed to be subversively topical: it never received a theatrical performance. Although apprentices do not feature prominently, there are numerous complaints about consuming strangers, the theft of foodstuffs and the loss of property, considerations of particular relevance to an apprentice audience.[46] It may have been that the inflammatory power of *Sir Thomas More* prohibited particularity; it is certainly the case that more general terms, such as 'artisans' and 'others', are employed when the text suggests apprentice involvement. Of the specific allusions, they work towards underwriting the apprentices' fragile economic circumstances – Lincoln, a broker, claims that the strangers 'bring in strange roots, which is merely to the undoing of poor prentices' (II.iii.10–11) – and the importance of keeping servants under the master's control: the Sheriff orders that 'every householder, on pain of death' should 'Keep in his prentices' (II.iv.23–4) during the troubles.

Apprentice concerns in the play, therefore, are covertly ventilated, and often through the central character. More functions as a synecdochal comment upon the ideals apprentices were encouraged to emulate, and his harmonious household reflects an image of the smoothly operating unit in which they theoretically served. Scenes involving his servants neutralize the threat of ambitious and restless behaviour: after he has impersonated his master by dressing in his clothes, Randall is made newly humble, while Falkner, the long-haired servant, is normalized when his locks are forcibly cut. More himself is a hard-working commoner who has risen in the hierarchy. He is ennobled by his restrained response to unrest and by his sensitive dispensation of justice, and loyalty and stoicism eventually define the gentility he is awarded in the final scenes. *Sir Thomas More* resists, however, too neat an interpretation, as the relationship between More and central authority is ambiguous; he espouses a doctrine of the body politic which he does not strictly obey; and it is unclear if he is a servant of the court or a master of the people.

James C. Scott observes that 'subordinates have a fairly extensive social existence outside the immediate control of the dominant. It is in such sequestered settings', he adds, 'where, in principle, a shared critique of domination may develop.'[47] Two of the uprisings in the 1590s started in or near theatres, which represent 'sequestered settings', and plays themselves could be viewed as incitements to riot. It is hardly surprising, in the circumstances, that the intervention of the Master of the Revels precipitated the endless revisions to which *Sir Thomas More* was subjected. Furthermore, references in the play to the imprisonment of rebellious artisans (I.i.40–4), to petitions (I.i.88–90), to the unpopularity of the mayor (I.iii.74–5), to the breaking open of the prisons (II.ii.11), to the fixing of food prices (II.iii.1–4), to the execution of the rebels (II.iv.1–4) and to clashes with servants (III.i.85–7) recall an earlier stage of the crisis and reach beyond the immediate context of 1593–4 to anticipate developments characteristic of a later moment of the 1590s.

In this section, I have argued that a broad range of literary representations of apprentices dwelled upon and looked forward to a late Elizabethan crisis. Conventional recommendations as to behaviour were given specific applications; social satire revealed economic injustices; and narratives of apprentice group activity manifested a critique of and a disillusionment with municipal authority. As discursive forms, representations contributed to and reacted against the political mechanisms deployed in the period, in combinations which, with varying degrees of invention, passed comment on contemporary events. Even if the disturbances would seem to have been quelled following the executions of 1595, fictions of apprentice solidarity and discontent persisted, which might account, in part, for the reflective tone adopted by a number of early Jacobean writers. The Oxfordshire rebels in 1596 planned to join with the apprentices when they marched on London, and more libels were distributed.[48] There were libels discovered in 1597 which claimed that the mayor was 'engaged in a *pacte de famine*', and a further apprentice libel vowing revenge against magisterial injustice was reported in 1598.[49] As late as 1601, there were rumours that the apprentices would rise to free the Earl of Essex after his ill-fated rebellion, and a scrivener's apprentice suspected of writing libels was brought before the London Bridewell governors.[50]

The separate circumstances of these later threatened disorders encourage speculation about the ways in which apprentices' political involvement was initiated. Although aldermen may have recognized that some apprentice grievances were justified, and may even have sympathized with the urge to rid the capital of alien artisans, nothing specifically indicates that they filled an organizational role. Only on one occasion did a key figure emerge, which suggests that the majority of the uprisings were spontaneous or accidental: the riot at Tower Hill on 29 June, 1595 was led by 'Captain Grant', presumably a demobilized soldier, and 'other euill disposed persons'. Those 'Prentises' who valued 'faithfulnes', however, to quote a contemporary account, 'reuealed their offence', which implies that, in contrast to some literary perceptions of political uniformity, apprentices were not always identical in their alignments and that there were competing agendas among their ranks.[51] Traces of these differences colour related representations of apprentice rebellions and the conflicting meanings which they provoke. For apprentices in a variety of texts assume punitive functions although they themselves may be the rioters, and strive for ideals of order in the same moment as they contribute to the perpetuation of social strife. Even literary strategies of displacement, whereby apprentice aggression was diluted through humour or shifts in geographical location, could underline frustrations rather than dispel them completely. In the 1590s, constructions of the crisis articulated anxieties in an effort to consign them to silence, but suppressed them in such a way as to grant them a forceful voice, a process which took its features from the mixed fortunes of civil protest and the unstable social status of apprentices themselves.

ENDANGERED IDEALS

Explosions of popular violence in the 1590s were indicative of domestic conflicts, and instabilities inherent in the household had wider political ramifications. In the earlier seventeenth century, writers began to focus increasingly on the domestic aspects of the master and apprentice contract in representations which circulated most powerfully in the theatre. Images of the troublesome apprentice reflect the possibility that the servant can enjoy isolated moments of domestic power, and have an oblique relation to the policies of the guilds, which paradoxically aimed to control the energies of their youthful charges through granting them a measure of autonomy.[52] In this way, dramatists were able to meet the expectations of a number of possible audiences while also leaving open opportunities for expressions of apprentice resistance.

The submission of apprentices to the master's dictates encouraged antithetical feelings towards a system that forestalled the enjoyment of adult privileges. The gerontological bias of the period tended to place power in the hands of its older members, as the 1556 act passed by the Common Council, which ruled that no apprentice was allowed to take up the freedom of his company until he had reached at least 24 years, demonstrates.[53] Within and against these structures, the theatre assumed a vital role, appealing as a forum which entertained alternative distributions of power and permitted release of engrained frustrations. Drama staged in different theatres acknowledged the apprentice's predicament. In Lyly's *Campaspe* (1583), Psyllus, an apprentice to a painter, complains:

> It is always my master's fashion, when any fair gentlewoman is to be drawn within, to make me to stay without; but if he should paint Jupiter like a bull, like a swan, like an eagle,

then must Psyllus with one hand grind colours and with the other hold the candle.[54]

A Blackfriars play, *Campaspe* may have found favour with spectators primed to laugh at bourgeois ambitions, but it also touches upon concerns which, at this stage, lay beyond the immediate experience of a more courtly audience. It confronts the nature of the apprentice's domestic role, the marginal status he occupied and the disciplinary mechanisms that kept his adolescence in check. Psyllus suffers from social, creative and sexual impoverishment, and whereas his master, through his art, is able to enjoy enviable advantages, the apprentice is bound to a dull grind of existence outside the place of magical transformations.

Questions asked of prevailing authority structures could have dangerous implications, and a number of plays pushes further an interrogative treatment of the possible effects of companies' attempts to inculcate apprentice obedience. A variation on Psyllus, who is kept out, is Eustace, the grocer's apprentice in Heywood's *The Four Prentices of London* (*c.* 1594), who is kept in and prevented from attending entertainments and leisure activities:

> Mee thinkes I could endure it for seven yeares,
> Did not my Maister keepe me in too much.
> I cannot goe to breake-fast in a morning
> With my kinde mates and fellow-Prentises,
> But he cries *Eustace*, one bid *Eustace* come:
> And my name *Eustace* is in every roome. (ll. 107–12)

With apprentice spectators, Eustace's complaint would surely have struck a chord, since some companies required their apprentices not to be out after nine o' clock at night, to avoid football and to refrain from dancing, mumming or making music in the streets.[55] Given that apprentices entered trade in their late teens, faced a period of service which could range from seven to ten and even twelve years, and may have eventually advanced no further than the rank of a journeyman, moreover, this play can only have sharpened a sense of limited prospects and onerous domestic circumstances.[56] While Heywood quickly shunts Eustace and his brothers away from their constricted London environment, this does little to lessen the registration of the household as a form of imprisonment, which draws a heightened attention to pressure points in the apprentice's contract and speaks loudly to the grievances of a servant populace.

From complaints about household regulations, it was a small step to active resistance. In 1597, Thomas Awdley, an 'vnrulye' London fishmonger's apprentice, was presented before the company's court, accused of being 'a great swearer & blasphemer of god [who] ... will not be reformed by reasonable meanes'. He was 'impudent and shamles', 'lewde & vnreverend', and his master despaired of his 'foule faultes'.[57] Although the minutes do not clarify if Awdley was reformed, or even if his master was a provocative agent, the case offers a powerful impression of an adolescent temperament in conflict with civic corporations, and its broad features reappear in the records of numerous similar disputes.[58] Awdley's case equally permits a fresh appreciation of the work of sixteenth- and seventeenth-century balladeers and moralists, who often drew the apprentice in terms of a lust for gaming, bad language and libertinage, and of a number of recurring situations in the drama.[59] Quicksilver, the apprentice in Chapman, Jonson and Marston's *Eastward Ho* (1605), is a hardened prodigal who mocks at his 'betters', swears, is given to abuse – 'I will piss at thy shop posts and throw rotten eggs at thy sign' – steals, gets drunk and runs away.[60] Finally caught, he is reprimanded by a fellow-apprentice, Golding, disguised as an alderman:

> thou hast prodigally consumed much of thy master's estate: and being by him gently admonished at several times, hast returned thyself haughty and rebellious, in thine answers, thundering out uncivil comparisons, requiting all his kindness with a coarse and harsh behaviour, never returning thanks for any one benefit, but receiving all, as if they had been debts to thee, and no courtesies.
>
> (IV.iii.237–43)

Golding's economic terms underwrite a catastrophe of profit loss (the speech is structured around a series of disastrous commercial exchanges), while the social specifications suggest a weakening of the principles of authority and obedience and the fragile condition of the household's traditional symbolic functions.

In 1606, Walter Howell, a 'malaperte' goldsmith's apprentice, appeared in court, charged with having 'often hurled good sustenance about the howse fitte for goodmens tables' and called his master's 'daughter being a modest yonge woman priestes bable'.[61] At issue in Howell's case is the possibility that the master's status as a bourgeois provider will be jeopardized, and that divisions between servants and children, both of whom occupied comparable but different subordinate positions, will be thrown into disarray. Such a Jacobean domestic nightmare informs the contemporary impact of *Eastward Ho*, in which Quicksilver's transgressions blur the traditional boundaries between master and apprentice, and spread outward to taint every member of the household. There is also the suggestion that the apprentice will dissolve not only social barriers but the means whereby gender and nationality are distinguished. As Touchstone, the master, cries: 'Behind my back, thou wilt swear faster than a French footboy, and talk more bawdily than a common midwife' (I.i.5–7). Using such unofficial languages, Quicksilver rehearses what James C. Scott has called a '"hidden transcript" that represents a critique of power spoken behind the back of the dominant' and threatens, at any moment, to translate himself into a creature beyond the reach of his master's defining powers.[62] Touchstone's hysteria is the stimulus for a host of comic misunderstandings, but it also accords with the play's discovery of a system in disrepair, and even the prim Golding is blighted, behaving in the opening scenes less like an apprentice than a sanctimonious justice.

Eastward Ho pursues its nightmare through dramatizations of the social effects and sexual manifestations of Quicksilver's rebellious predilections. The formation by Quicksilver of a counter-household in which Security, the usurer, takes over from Touchstone as master and father, and in which Sindefy, the prostitute, fulfils the roles of wife, daughter and mistress, has a particularly unsettling aspect. Once Quicksilver has released his materialistic and sexual urges in this new environment, the system he has left behind begins to crumble: economic circumspection is overlooked and doubts are expressed about paternity and filial attachments (V.i.117). As should now be clear, the relationship in English Renaissance drama between the household, the family, economic imperatives and the apprentice's sexuality is of major concern, but the ways in which this is realized are only immediately straightforward. A predicament that crops up repeatedly involves the mistress's lustful desire for her young servant. Brome's *The City Wit*, a play of about 1629 that was revised in 1637–9, partly concerns Josina, a citizen's wife who is attracted to Jeremy, her apprentice and the son of a 'Ferretter', and determines to lie with him. Having failed in her seduction, she curses his 'honest Appetite, sober Ignorance, and modest Understanding'.[63] As the apprentice resists falling in with his mistress's schemes, however, he possesses the moral high ground. By turning from the follies which he is urged to commit, the scene seems to imply, the apprentice will ensure that his innate goodness is eventually rewarded.

An apprentice who is immune to amatory invitations conformed to the ideals promoted by the senior members of the guilds, and Brome's realization gestures towards the virtues of self-denial and sobriety approved by the establishment. The celibacy of apprentices was ratified by law, and they ran the risk of being fined or denied the freedom of the company if they married within the space of their terms.[64] In representations of apprentices' sexuality, however, there was more than one interest at work, and attempted seductions by mistresses carried a dangerously erotic potential and may have encouraged hidden apprentice fantasies. The work of dramatists who, despite associations with the private playhouses, also entertained trading and servant preoccupations, *Eastward Ho* and *The City Wit* are complementary meditations on the controls placed on adolescent desire and on the resistances which those restraints provoked.[65] Official regulations, often flouted, were inadequate to the task of containing acts of sexual incontinence: either apprentices tried to resort to prostitutes or they imitated the example of Richard Wharton, the apprentice of a London ironmonger, who in 1591 locked up his master and mistress in the bedroom so that 'none shoulde interrupte' his 'wickednes' with the maidservant. On another occasion, he, 'in most barberous vigorous & forcible manner', attempted to rape another maidservant, but she scratched him so violently that he desisted.[66] Particularly at risk from apprentices, in material experience and the popular imagination, were widows, as they represented an immediately available capital and the possibility of economic independence.[67]

Echoes of Wharton's deviousness sound in the representation of Quicksilver, while his impatience looks forward to Spendall, the apprentice in Cooke's *Greene's Tu Quoque* (1611–12). Appointed to take care of the shop during his master's absence, Spendall quickly enters an extravagant lifestyle, and is eventually forced to court Widow Raysby to stave off the imminence of disgrace and impoverishment. He exclaims:

> You are rich in Mony, Lands, and Lordships,
> Mannors, and fayre Possessions, and I have not so much
> As one poore Coppy-hold to thrust my head in.
> Why should you not then have compassion
> Upon a reasonable handsome fellow,
> That has both youth and livelihood upon him;
> And can at midnight quicken and refresh
> Pleasures decayed in you?[68]

A popular Red Bull production, *Greene's Tu Quoque* underlines a number of contemporary anxieties: Spendall's proposed exchange substitutes sex for property, and financial gain for lack, in a process of rejuvenation which negotiates apprentices' economic and sexual aspirations and requirements. In view of the immediacy of such representations, it is hardly surprising that schemes in the theatre for the reformation of errant apprentices took on such prominent proportions.

Of course, a reconciliation of separated parties and an attempt to restitute a damaged social order are theatrical conventions; in some English Renaissance dramas, however, the action concludes in such a way as to allow for an ongoing play of apprentice misdemeanours. Even if profligate apprentices realize the error of their ways and are forgiven, their apologies are rarely sincere. Quicksilver's repentance in *Eastward Ho* ensues so suddenly that it becomes absurd, and the mood of levity is heightened when he celebrates his supposed reformation with a song. And, inevitably, as James C. Scott observes, 'an apology may more often represent a comparatively economical means of escaping the most severe consequences of an offence against the dominant order . . . a tactic cynically employed under duress.'[69] 'The ragged colt may prove a good horse' (V.v.65) thinks Touchstone of his apprentice's metamorphosis, a comment that implies suspicion of Quicksilver's sentiments and a lingering distrust of surface appearances. A parodic vitality marks not only the play's final scene but also the epilogue in which Quicksilver asks for audiences to return to the theatre (Epilogus, 1–8): a note of material urgency remote from thrifty patience rings out, and there is a reminder of the apprentice's love of display and wilful acquisitiveness.

Eastward Ho satirically deflates the postures of the civic order and lampoons the redrawing of allegiances; in contrast, the generic anomaly in *Greene's Tu Quoque* is Spendall's more strident refusal to acknowledge his failings and his plan to impersonate, not become, a dutiful citizen. Following the collapse of his impetuous schemes, he is pardoned by his master, Sir Lionel Rash, and declares: 'If through my riot I have offensive beene, / Henceforth I'le play the civil Citizen' (XIX, 2930–1). In these patched and uncertain restorations of authority, there may well be a suggestion of contemporary material practice, and judging from the minutes of some corporations, apprentice misconduct appears to have been surprisingly accepted. On dozens of occasions, after the apprentice apologized for his behaviour, punishment was withheld and pardon granted.[70] Elaborating the precedent set by the livery companies, some dramas entertained the idea that vice was not always the companion of disaster, and that castigation could be circumvented if not wholly subverted. Different voices meet in the representation of the reformed subordinate, but household divisions remain in an imperfect condition and the apprentice's claim to power continues to be asserted.

Even the livery companies, it seems, were not always able to reduce or divert the problem of dissatisfied apprentices, and cases of physical assault represented a more extreme version of the potential collapse of the domestic ideal. A household plagued by unresolved tensions was one in which outbreaks of violence were an ever-present possibility, and ambiguous endings in the drama represented the terminal point of discussions about the implications of the apprentice's rebellious potential. Many cases of breakdown were of a horrific nature: apprentices were trodden upon, kicked in the ribs and belly, beaten with spurs, flogged with cords and rods, flung against posts and stabbed in the arms.[71] Richard Hotchkis, a scrivener's apprentice, was assailed by his master in 1594 'in great outragious & malicious mann[er] in clamorous railinge sort' with 'divers slanderous & obprobrious wordes' and beaten so fiercely that blood poured out of his mouth and ears.[72] But hardship was not always passively endured: a master could be beaten himself if he offered correction and apprentices were, in certain circumstances, given full power to petition their companies, often with favourable results.[73]

Spectacles of apprentice delinquency offered numerous literary opportunities for reinforcing establishment positions, since childhood and youth were conventionally regarded as periods of development which required government. The possibility that masters may have fallen drastically short of a recommended ideal, however, prompted thought about a more rigorous inspection of contemporary hierarchies, and involved the possibility of necessary changes to livery company structures. Perhaps we should not be too struck, therefore, by the relative paucity of indictments of masters who neglected their responsibilities, at least in the drama. By contrast, in popular ballads and pamphlets, specific abuses were highlighted, debate centring on the difficulties of apprentices who were exploited or persecuted, and their efforts to escape intolerable domestic circumstances.[74] A catalogue of employer-related problems was developed in a 1595 pamphlet, the distinctiveness of which resides in its arraignment of the master for having determined the careers of two very different apprentice types. T. I. observes:

> I might heer set before your eyes what mischeifes haue followed to masters by ouer hard vsages of their apprentices & seruants a matter to be looked vnto for some are brought vp to idle to proudely, to wantonly with to much excesse bothe of meat and apparell which brings them to lewdnes, to dycing, to ryoting, to whoredome, to imbeasling of their masters goodes and such like, others on the contrary part want both apparell and sustenance & besides and moste vnreasonable set to taskes to working vppon Sundayes and holy-dayes forbidden, beaten and corrected out of measure and moste vnchristianlike vsed, whereby they are forced for want of further remedie to runne away or to filch & steal to buye victualles orels to runne to a further mischiefe.[75]

Ian W. Archer suggests that this 'poor quality of . . . instruction' contributed to 'the floating population of masterless men about the city supporting themselves by a succession of odd jobs and petty crime.'[76] His comment profitably details the relationship between social conditions and T. I.'s objections, but it does not speculate about the effects which such literature could help to generate. Although popular literature sometimes targeted the master as a possible consumer, it may also have been composed for the apprentice's benefit. Material injustices induced apprentices to defend themselves by seeking redress in the courts; by extension, they could find more than one application in texts instructing employers to be considerate, and a partial justification for continuing to question the powers that ideally ensured their continued obedience.

In an oblique sense, popular texts might be seen as the ideological equivalent of libels, which exhorted apprentices to communicate their frustrations via a more directly political route. Political activity represented, in addition, a public manifestation of violence which, after the 1590s, was most commonly in evidence only at a domestic level. The phenomenon of violence permitted and produced the expression by writers of an anxiety about the undermining of many forms of authority. If representations of insecurity seem to privilege the master's rights, they simultaneously grant the apprentice an implicit licence to resist improving his conduct, and thereby register concerns which affect the members of several social constituencies. For apprentices, moral prohibitions, like the drama, may have worked in more complex and diffuse ways, and may even have become, on occasions, sites for renewed eruptions of conflict.

GENTLE GRIEVANCES

In the early and mid-seventeenth century, representations of apprenticeship acquire a keenly satirical edge. Fresh preoccupations begin to be aired while familiar, older anxieties persist: in drama and prose, questions about the relationship between apprenticeship and gentility are voiced with an intensified urgency, and the figure of the apprentice-gallant makes his first appearance on the stage, developments which have their origins in escalating numbers of gentlemen apprenticed in the livery companies themselves.

Overlapping with each other in the period were the changing composition of theatre audiences and the emergence of a more exclusive theatrical repertoire. While it is difficult to generalize about the public and private traditions in the theatres, it is safe to assume, as Andrew Gurr has argued, that after 1600 gentlemen probably left the citizen amphitheatres, preferring instead the private halls.[77] Audiences could never be homogeneous, of course, but the growing polarization of the theatres almost certainly sharpened social distinctions in the playhouses, contributed to a more sardonically detached representation of apprentices, and helped to shape a critical construction of institutional loyalties. Beaumont's *The Knight of the Burning Pestle* (1607) is poised between two traditions – a set of conventions which flatters popular apprentice tastes, and a newer perspective which places them in a less complimentary light. In its simultaneous celebration and ironization of apprentice aspirations lies a clue to the play's critical fortunes. Its unpopularity in 1607 with the audience at the second Blackfriars theatre may have been related to its indulgent representation of some apprentice interests, while its satirical tone seems to have appealed to spectators in the 1635 and 1636 revivals at the Cockpit and at court.

One indication of the play's acknowledgement of concerns pertinent to apprentices lies in its anatomization of the responsibilities of parents and employers. For the apprentice, Jasper, apprenticeship represents an opportunity to escape the home; for the apprentice, Rafe, it proves too similar to a familial network. The most obviously erring parents are the Merrythoughts who are either too drunk to execute their duties or who are incapable of giving their children their blessing: Old Merrythought's surprise that 'any man will follow a trade or serve, that may sing and laugh, and walk the streets' constitutes a philosophy of improvidence. Their conduct bears out the implied criticism of the play's epistle in which an 'unfortunate child', exposed to 'the wide world', is 'smothered in perpetual oblivion'.[78] The Merrythoughts' shortcomings are contrasted with the actions of the Citizen's Wife who moulds Rafe in the image of the son she has lost (II, 352–7), who urges him to 'call all the youths together in battle-ray' (V, 57–8) in a dangerously militaristic assembly, and who aspires to impress the gentlemen spectators of the play through the apprentice's exploits (Epilogue, 2–12). With these sets of characters, the play emphasizes abnegations or failures of authority, which throws into relief Rafe's investment in a romantic apprentice culture and grants tacit approval to his attempts to combat a restricted or suffocating domestic environment.

For Rafe, a voracious consumer of Iberian tales, the pull of 'adventurous deeds' (III, 320) represents an alternative discipline, a route to mastery and a means of defining himself away from and possibly in opposition to guild controls. As part of its exploration of these tensions, and in a confrontation with the generational and gerontological discourses of the period, *The Knight of the Burning Pestle* addresses adolescent sexual difficulties, which are forcefully communicated in the pursuit by Jasper of his master's daughter, in statements about the insecurity of identity and in a desire for adult autonomy. The giant, Barbaroso, 'shakes a naked lance of purest steel' (III, 236), according to the Host, and 'Without his door doth hang / A copper basin on a prickant spear' (III, 240–1), and the description works powerfully as an expression of fears about castigation by a parental figure and the threat of phallic disempowerment. A particularly heightened attention is drawn to ideas of infantile regression and oral gratification: Old Merrythought sings of being a *'serving-man'* who *'would eat and drink of the best, / And no work would [he] do'* (IV, 336, 342–3), and the Moldavia episode is marked by a stress on food and drink. With such considerations brought to the fore, the play emerges most eloquently as an elaborate fantasy in which repressed needs are articulated in order to be requited. Apprentice ambitions are not too far removed from these fantastic scenarios, since Michael, a younger son, unexpectedly gains an inheritance, and Rafe is promised the hand of the Moldavian princess: younger personalities are favoured, and apprentices can win for themselves a degree of independence.

At the same time, however, *The Knight of the Burning Pestle* dismantles the mythic paradigms it ostensibly approves. Rafe is a knightly apprentice whose elevated language is incommensurate with material realities, whose adventures extend to no more than freeing a barber's syphilitic clients, and whose deeds fail to achieve their paltry object – the recovery of Mistress Merrythought's purse. At one point Rafe even mistakes Mistress Merrythought for a distressed damsel: 'What noise is this?' (II, 112), he asks, 'A gentle lady flying the embrace / Of some uncourteous knight?' (II, 113–14). And, on a later occasion, the incongruity of his rhetoric in the world of commerce is made painfully apparent, his verbal thanks failing to satisfy the more pragmatically-minded tapster, who complains: 'Sir, there is twelve shillings to pay' (III, 149). Elsewhere in the play, Rafe is again rendered materially dependent by the interventions of the Citizen and his Wife. Even the apprentice's extended account of his triumphs is undercut by the stage-direction that accompanies his final appearance: '*Enter* RAFE, *with a forked arrow through his head*' (V, 289). Much of the action is taken up with comic business of this kind, and whatever credence is given in the play to apprentices' anxieties and aspirations needs to be set against its mockery of romantic conventions and its teasing exposure of heroic absurdities.

If Beaumont's text stands as a singular instance of the fusion of a number of apparently incongruous generic elements, later dramatists subject apprenticeship to a more censorious treatment. Scorn is increasingly deployed as a deflationary technique, and even the apprentice seems to suffer from a greater sense of embitterment. Composed in 1626–8, revised in 1648–9 and first performed before a university (Cambridge) audience, Randolph's *Hey for Honesty* features Carion, an apprentice, who notes cynically: 'nothing [is] so hard as to be bound prentice in bedlam, and have a fool to one's master! my very livery is faced with his worship's foolery. Our condition is miserable.'[79] Pride in the institution and an idealistic cultivation of the establishment – the Elizabethan hallmarks of some representations of apprenticeship are revealed as a travesty exciting contemptuous amusement.

The most elaborate formulation of these attitudes is provided by Shirley's *Honoria and Mammon*, in existence in an early version in 1632, enlarged in 1646 and published in 1658. In this work, apprenticeship is a form of employment that is to be actively avoided, as the speech addressed by Squanderbag, a captain, to his soldiers suggests:

Is not this better than a tedious 'prenticeship,
Bound by indentures to a shop and drudgery,
Watching the rats and customers by owl-light?
Tied to perpetual language of, *What lack ye*?
Which you pronounce, as ye had been taught, like starlings.
If any gudgeon bite, to damn your souls
For less than sixpence in the pound? O base!
Your glittering shoes, long graces, and short meals,
Expecting but the comfortable hour
Of eight o' clock, and the hot pippin-pies,
To make your mouth up? all the day not suffered
To air yourselves, unless your minikin mistress
Command you to attend her to a christ'ning,
To bring home plums, for which [she] may relieve
Your teeth, that water, with her next suppository?
You have some festivals, I confess, but when

They happen, you run wild to the next village,
Conspire a knot, and club your groats a-piece
For cream and prunes, not daring to be drunk;
Nothing of honour done.[80]

As Shirley was associated with the Cockpit and the Phoenix theatres, and presented masques at Whitehall, he may have been keen
to distance the leisured society in which he moved, and which
he invariably represented in his drama, from the world of trade
and artisan occupations. It may also have been that the gentlemen of the Inns of Court, many of whom formed part of Shirley's
audience, would have applauded the observation that honour
and riches may be won in the military profession but never by
undertaking an apprenticeship, with its monotony, petty rituals
and obligatory period of servitude.

What is striking about these views is their particularity – their
confinement mainly to a theatrical repertoire. Since the vogue
for Jonsonian humours on the stage, moreover, satire had established itself as an important vehicle for the correction of abuses,
and even as a means of enabling the professions to laugh at themselves, and speculation about satirical constructions of apprenticeship must of necessity take account of and be complicated
by the existence of more typical conventions of complaint. The
satirical representation of the institution also points to the
remoteness of matters of material social urgency. It was only at
times of political crisis that a greater variety and volume of genres
were deployed, reflecting the perceived gravity of apprentice
disturbances. When variations on the attitudes articulated in
Honoria and Mammon find their counterparts in the dramatic *and*
prosaic literature of the period, therefore, issues of potential social
consequence may be at stake. In some ways, Shirley's dispraise
had a venerable lineage. As early as 1586, Sir John Ferne had
written, 'Merchaundizinge, is no competent, or seemelye trade
of lyfe, for a gentleman', and his sentiments both recall the question
of the differences between apprentices and gentlemen, and look
forward to what was to become one of the major discussions of
the seventeenth century.[81]

The situation of the apprentice who was a gentleman was a
crucial aspect of definitions of gentility, nobility and the status
of the professions in general. Quicksilver in *Eastward Ho* (1605)
firmly believes that his social origins are impaired by his

apprenticeship; obsessed with his descent, he is easily roused to defend himself:

> Why, 'sblood, sir, my mother's a gentlewoman, and my father a justice of peace, and of quorum: and though I am a younger brother and a prentice, yet I hope I am my father's son: and by God's lid, 'tis for your worship and for your commodity that I keep company. (I.i.21–5)

It is partly the possibility of being reduced to a servile condition that propels Quicksilver into his fearful pronouncements, but the apprentice is more worried about where precisely he can be located and by what means he is able to define himself. In contrast to Golding, who smugly maintains that 'trade ... taints not my blood' (III.ii.97–8), Quicksilver is anxious to relieve himself of the stigma of the market, and finds comfort in the fact that the gallants, who style him 'cousin Frank' (I.i.35, 36), also recognize his gentle lineage. What was first broached in the early Jacobean drama later found its way into a full-scale debate, and Quicksilver's objections represent only an early instance of a series of exchanges of opinion which was to predominate in pamphlets. An apprentice in a treatise composed by Edmund Bolton in about 1616 despairs: 'I am brought to beleeue, that by being a Prentise, I lose my birth right, and the right of my blood ... which is to be a Gentlemen [sic], which I had rather dye, then to endure.'[82] If, in the later sixteenth century, apprentices assembled on the streets of London to challenge the influence of gentlemen and gallants, by the first and second decades of the seventeenth century, they appear to have acted to align themselves with the groups they previously contested.

Beyond these changes lay several wider social developments. In the earlier seventeenth century, some aristocratic families, suffering a loss of influence, may have apprenticed younger sons in the hopes of reviving waning fortunes. More plausible is the suggestion that there were growing numbers of gentry in the early modern period, and a greater likelihood of their sons entering trade. Whereas in Shrewsbury in the later sixteenth century the Drapers took 20 per cent of their apprentices from the local gentry, by the middle third of the seventeenth century this figure had risen to almost 50 per cent.[83] The London Stationers' Company from 1576 to 1585 enrolled only 15 sons of gentlemen as apprentices;

from 1630 to 1639, however, this figure had increased to 114, and the total number of apprentices bound had not risen dramatically since the earlier period.[84] Similarly, if the figures for the London Fishmongers and Grocers for 1631 to 1660 are compared to those of the late fifteenth century for the Merchant Taylors and Skinners, a movement towards more sons of gentlemen in the larger companies can be noticed. Stephen R. Smith writes:

> These two companies . . . recruited 14.29 per cent of their apprentices from the gentry in the late fifteenth century, whereas the Fishmongers and Grocers in the mid-seventeenth century recruited considerably higher percentages, 26.42 per cent and 36.55 per cent respectively.[85]

Following in the footsteps of the aristocracy, the new gentry committed their sons to professions which were becoming socially acceptable and materially desirable, and it is in anticipation of such a shift in ideology and practice that Edmund Bolton's apprentice delivers his impassioned appeal.

Growing numbers of gentlemen's sons in the livery companies may also account for the appearance on the stage of the apprentice-gallant, of which Quicksilver is a very early example. Companies in the seventeenth century were vexed by the problem of apprentices who dressed above themselves, and allusions to these difficulties inform several dramatic representations. Courtly amusements had probably been available to the apprentice at least since the sixteenth century, and there are frequent references during this period to apprentices attending dancing and fencing schools, consuming their masters' goods, banqueting and holding illicit feasts.[86] The inordinate dress of the apprentice, moreover, was objected to on a number of occasions prior to 1600.[87] However, in the seventeenth century official complaint assumed a particularity and an intensity unrivalled in previous decades. The Merchant Adventurers in 1608 spoke out against apprentices who 'weare . . . apparaile not fytt for [their] . . . Estate or qualitie, but rather becominge some Courtier [or] servinge man'.[88] Orders of a similar kind were issued by the Common Council in 1610 and 1611, and in 1621 a bill was introduced that prohibited apprentices from wearing 'gold or silver' and insisted on 'nothing but cloth or stuff made out of wool'.[89] As the shocked tone of these rulings demonstrates, the bourgeois humility of apprenticeship was being increasingly eroded by a more fashionable and socially distinctive conception of institutional attachment.

It is perhaps partly to apprentices, who may have agitated for an acknowledgement of their gentle status through gallant behaviour, that a number of situations in Caroline drama are directed. In Massinger's *The City Madam* (1632), the apprentices of Sir John Frugal, a merchant, are clearly gentlemen's sons, as the demand of Luke Frugal, his brother, establishes: 'Are you gentlemen born, yet have no gallant tincture / Of gentry in you?'[90] In being treated as clerks and factors, the apprentices are also distinguished from 'Mechanicks' (II.i.52) and lowlier forms of service. Luke proceeds to entice Goldwire, the apprentice, with extravagant possibilities:

> Did'st thou know
> What ravishing lechery it is to enter
> An Ordinarie, *cap a pe*, trim'd like a Gallant,
> (For which in truncks conceal'd be ever furnish'd)
> The reverence, respect, the crouches, cringes
> The musical chime of Gold in your cram'd pockets,
> Commands from the attendants, and poor Porters?
> (II.i.79–85)

Martin Butler has noted that the context of *The City Madam* is aldermanic, and that the audience at the Blackfriars theatre, where the play was first staged, enjoyed numerous city connections.[91] Closely involved in the cultural alliances of their masters, apprentices would have recognized the frustrations inscribed in Luke's temptation, and as the play concludes with the establishment of new links between the citizen and the aristocrat, a celebration of a growing alignment between different social groupings is afforded.

The possibility of a rakish metamorphosis appears again in Brome's *The New Academy* (1635). Strigood, the half-brother to Old Matchil, a merchant, asks Cash, his apprentice, for financial assistance:

> Before I speak too loud, who's money's that
> You use to weare abroad at Feasts and Revels
> In silver lace and satten; though you wait
> At home in simple Serge, or broad-cloth, sir.[92]

Although Cash is only pretending to be a gallant, it would seem that he is one stage nearer to being taken for the genuine article than his dramatic predecessors. Certainly, by the mid-seventeenth century, the apprentice-gentleman was an accepted feature of English society, and efforts to secure status through impersonation were less frequently reported.[93] Sir Edward Coke in the second part of his *Institutes*, completed by 1628, remarked: 'if a Gentleman by birth . . . be bound prentices to arts and trades in London . . . he ought to be named by the degree of a Gentleman.'[94] In a publication of 1652, and as a conclusion to the pamphlet dispute, Sir John Doddridge commented: 'If a Gentleman bee bound an aprentice to a Merchant, or else, &c. he hath not thereby lost his degree of Gentry.'[95] Finally, it would seem, apprentices won the recognition for which they had striven, and found their efforts given an aristocratic and not a bourgeois legitimacy.

CONCLUSIONS

In this chapter, I have discussed representations of apprentices and apprenticeship in terms of their political, domestic and social manifestations. But I have also been concerned to suggest that these categories were not exclusive, and that between them there were points of contact, cross-fertilizations and mutual influences: riots pointed an accusing finger at structures of domestic discipline, and strains in the household were brought into focus by larger social movements and processes. Questions about the exercise of magisterial and institutional power circulated throughout the period and, although most urgently ventilated in the 1590s, were raised with different inflections well into the seventeenth century and even beyond. The political activism of apprentices was a recurring phenomenon. In the 1620s, when pronounced anti-Spanish feeling was running high in the capital, apprentices were quick to make known their nationalistic loyalties. Gondomar, the unpopular Spanish ambassador, was insulted in 1621 as he was carried in his litter through the London streets; an apprentice exclaimed, 'There goeth the devil in a dung-cart', a 'Brickbatt' was thrown and a scuffle broke out. On the point of being whipped, the offending parties were rescued by a crowd of some 300 apprentices.[96] A magician and the supposed originator of malicious prophecies, Doctor Lambe, the physician of the Duke of Buckingham, was spotted at a play in the Fortune in 1628 and set upon by apprentices as he left the theatre. Although he found refuge in the Counter, he died the following day from the injuries he had sustained.[97] In the civil war years, apprentices were a vocal force in lending support to representatives of both the parliamentarian and the royalist causes.[98] It is a measure, perhaps, of the political potential of apprentices that they were represented most commonly in the theatre, an institution which could share an abrasive relationship with authority and articulate subversive ideological tendencies.

Alan Sinfield has remarked that 'Political awareness does not arise out of an essential, individual, self-consciousness . . . but from involvement in *a milieu, a subculture.*' 'It is through such sharing', he states, 'that one may learn to inhabit plausible oppositional preoccupations and forms.'[99] In the English Renaissance, apprentices were at their most dangerous when acting as a group, although this should not take away from the threat posed by their individual misdemeanours. Within the ranks of apprentices, however, there were, at particular conjunctures, different agendas and priorities. Affrays between apprentices, gentlemen and students in the 1580s and 1590s, for instance, sit incongruously next to *Eastward Ho* and Quicksilver's elevation of his gentle lineage. As the gentry sent their sons in greater numbers to join the city companies, attitudes towards social status modified, but this also entailed apprentices themselves changing their perceptions of their supposed 'superiors'. Themselves gentlemen, either by birth or by professional qualification, apprentices stood at the crossroads of a number of uncertain definitions and shifting networks of allegiance.

Emerging from the apprentices' espousal of a number of different political concerns is a clearer picture of divisions among writers, of their cultivation of particular audiences and of their sometimes conflicting professional activities. Brome chose to write for various theatrical companies; Jonson and Marston were also satirists; Massinger used his plays to launch attacks at the court; and Shirley decided to side with Massinger and Randolph against more courtly dramatists in a theatrical dispute of 1629–30. Changing alignments among playwrights and their contrasting identifications had a bearing on representations of apprentices and possibly their material existence. As writers perform balancing acts between sometimes opposed factions and a range of consumers, so do apprentices slip between the polarities of moral rebels and rebellious moralists, support the civic virtues of the city and patronize suburban vices. The powerless and periodically empowered place of apprentices is perhaps the most striking feature of literary texts, which participated in and were determined by social practice.

Culture and ideology were constantly remade and relocated in a turbulent period, and apprentices were viewed as a significant site within which older and new interests could be tested and disseminated. The situation of the apprentice, in particular, was used to ask questions about guild ideals and the ways in which they adapted to fresh conditions and predicaments. In the early seventeenth century, when financial barriers and rising premiums prevented many young men from entering trade, fewer writers promised aldermanic or mayoral glories to the industrious adolescent artisan, while the more outspoken apprentice in Jacobean and Caroline drama may also have been related to a more general anxiety about the falling away of discipline at a time of stress and changing social relations. But representations of apprentices and apprenticeship finally looked ahead rather than at their immediate context. The apprentice's striving for independence, reluctance to remain within the bond of the household and identification with political causes anticipate a later historical moment, another social formation, the irregular enforcement of apprenticeships and the decline of the guilds. The writers who attempted to understand the system of apprenticeship were the prophets of its inescapable collapse and final demise.

NOTES

1. Christopher Brooks, 'Apprenticeship, Social Mobility and the Middling Sort, 1550–1800', in Jonathan Barry and Christopher Brooks, eds, *The Middling Sort of People: Culture, Society and Politics in England, 1550–1800* (Basingstoke and London, 1994), p. 53; Stephen R. Smith, 'The London Apprentices as Seventeenth-Century Adolescents', *Past and Present*, 61, November (1973), p. 150.
2. C.L.R.O., Journals 16, fo. 261^v; *The Ordinances of the Clothworkers' Company* (London, 1881), pp. 66–7.
3. Steve Rappaport, 'Social Structure and Mobility in Sixteenth-Century London: Part I', *London Journal*, 9 (1983), p. 116; Sidney Young,

The Annals of the Barber-Surgeons of London (London, 1890), p. 309.
For apprentices' ability to read and write, see also Edmund Coote,
The English schoole-maister (London, 1627; S.T.C. 5713), sig. A3^r; David
Cressy, *Literacy and the Social Order: Reading and Writing in Tudor
and Stuart England* (Cambridge, 1980), p. 129; James Raine, ed., *York-
shire Diaries and Autobiographies in the Seventeenth and Eighteenth
Centuries*, Surtees Society, 77 (1886), p. 16.

4. Thomas Heywood, *The Four Prentices of London*, ed. Mary Ann Weber
Gasior (New York and London, 1980), p. 2. Richard Norwood wrote
self-critically in his journal in 1639 at the age of 39 of his youth in
London as a fishmonger's apprentice: 'I had a great delight in reading
in vain and corrupt books as *Palmerin de Oliva, The Seven Champions*,
and others like.' See Wesley Frank Craven and Walter B. Hayward,
eds, *The Journal of Richard Norwood* (New York, 1945), p. 17.

5. *The actors' remonstrance, or complaint* (London, 1643; Wing A453),
p. 4; Henry Chettle, *Kind-harts dreame* (London, 1593?; S.T.C. 5123),
sigs E4^{r-v}; Edmund Gayton, *Pleasant notes upon Don Quixot* (London, 1654; Wing G415), p. 271; Stephen Gosson, *The ephemerides of
Phialo, deuided into three bookes* (London, 1579; S.T.C. 12093), fo. 88^v;
Thomas Jordan, *The walks of Islington and Hogsdon* (London, 1657;
Wing J1071), sig. A3^v. The Common Council issued an order to the
Ironmongers' Company in 1582 instructing them to prevent their
apprentices from attending plays and interludes. See C.L.R.O., Journals 21, fo. 196^r, Remembrancia I, fo. 325^v. A group of apprentices
came to the notice of the authorities for staging at a London theatre in 1613 a play in which contemporary political dignitaries were
represented and subjected to ridicule. See Sir Henry Wotton, *Letters of Sir Henry Wotton to Sir Edmund Bacon* (London, 1661; Wing
W3644), pp. 155–6.

6. Gayton, *Pleasant notes*, p. 271. Apprentices and Shrove Tuesday are
more fully discussed in Mark Thornton Burnett, 'Popular Culture
in the English Renaissance', in William Zunder and Suzanne Trill,
eds, *Writing and the English Renaissance* (London and New York,
1996), pp. 115–19; Paul Griffiths, *Youth and Authority: Formative
Experiences in England 1560–1640* (Oxford, 1996), pp. 147–61.

7. Andrew Gurr, *Playgoing in Shakespeare's London* (Cambridge, 1987),
pp. 170–1; K. J. Lindley, 'Riot Prevention and Control in Early Stuart
London', *Transactions of the Royal Historical Society*, 5th ser., 33 (1983),
p. 110; Roger B. Manning, *Village Revolts: Social Protest and Popular
Disturbances in England, 1509–1640* (Oxford, 1988), pp. 211–14; P.R.O.,
PC 2/29/268, SP 14/90/105–6, 135.

8. James C. Scott, *Domination and the Arts of Resistance: Hidden Transcripts* (New Haven, CT and London, 1990), p. 173.

9. Richard Johnson, *The nine worthies of London* (London, 1592; S.T.C.
14686), sigs C4^{r-v}.

10. Ilana Krausman Ben-Amos, *Adolescence and Youth in Early Modern
England* (New Haven, CT and London, 1994), p. 130; Steve Rappaport,
Worlds within Worlds: Structures of Life in Sixteenth-century London
(Cambridge, 1989), p. 311.

11. James Winny, ed., *The Descent of Euphues: Three Elizabethan Romance Stories* (Cambridge, 1957), p. 174. The narrative is more fully explored in Mark Thornton Burnett, 'Henry Chettle's *Piers Plainness: Seven Years' Prenticeship*: Contexts and Consumers', in Constance C. Relihan, ed., *Framing Elizabethan Fictions: Contemporary Approaches to Early Modern Narrative Prose* (Kent, OH, 1996), pp. 169–86.
12. William Chappell and J. Woodfall Ebsworth, eds, *The Roxburghe Ballads*, 9 vols (London, 1871–97), vol. VII, p. 582.
13. Rappaport, *Worlds*, p. 368.
14. B.L., Harleian MS. 2143, fo. 57^v; C.L.R.O., Remembrancia II, fo. 20^r.
15. Manning, *Village Revolts*, p. 206; P.R.O., PC 2/21/8.
16. Ian W. Archer, *The Pursuit of Stability: Social Relations in Elizabethan London* (Cambridge, 1991), p. 7. See also Barbara Freedman, 'Elizabethan Protest, Plague, and Plays: Rereading the "Documents of Control"', *English Literary Renaissance*, 26 (1996), pp. 17–45. In the early modern period, libels took the form of scurrilous writings.
17. Scott, *Domination*, pp. 61–3.
18. Sebastian Giustinian, *Four Years at the Court of Henry VIII*, tr. Rawdon Brown, 2 vols (London, 1854), vol. II, pp. 70–1.
19. C.L.R.O., Repertory 12, 1, fo. 122^r.
20. B. P., *The prentises practise in godlinesse, and his true freedome* (London, 1608; S.T.C. 19057), sig. H3^v.
21. [Samuel Rowlands], *Greenes ghost haunting conie-catchers* (London, 1602; S.T.C. 12243), sig. E3^r.
22. Thomas Rogers, *Leicester's Ghost*, ed. Franklin B. Williams, Jr (London, 1972), p. 18.
23. C.L.R.O., Journals 20, 2, fo. 276^v.
24. Archer, *Pursuit*, pp. 3–4; Bodl. Lib., MS. Eng. hist. c. 474, fo. 99^r; C.L.R.O., Remembrancia I, fo. 98^r; P.R.O., PC 2/13/452; Hyder E. Rollins, ed., *An Analytical Index to the Ballad-Entries (1557–1709) in the Registers of the Company of the Stationers of London* (Chapel Hill, NC, 1924), pp. 179–80.
25. B.L., Lansdowne MS. 41, fo. 31^r.
26. C.L.R.O., Journals 22, fos 417^v, 421^r; Paul L. Hughes and James F. Larkin, eds, *Tudor Royal Proclamations*, 3 vols (New Haven, CT and London, 1964–9), vol. III, p. 60; Manning, *Village Revolts*, p. 203.
27. B.L., Lansdowne MS. 66, fos 241^r-2^r.
28. [Lewis Machin], *Every Woman in Her Humour*, ed. Archie Mervin Tyson (New York and London, 1980), I.i.302–8.
29. Thomas Dekker, *The Dramatic Works*, ed. Fredson Bowers, 4 vols (Cambridge, 1953–61), vol. II, IV.iii.91–2.
30. Archer, *Pursuit*, p. 4.
31. *King Henry VI, Part II*, ed. Andrew S. Cairncross (London and New York, 1988), V.i.166, II.i.58.
32. For complementary readings of the scene, see Craig A. Bernthal, 'Treason in the Family: The Trial of Thumpe v. Horner', *Shakespeare Quarterly*, 42 (1991), pp. 44–54; Ronald Knowles, 'The Farce of History: Miracle, Combat, and Rebellion in 2 *Henry VI*', in Cedric Brown,

ed., *Patronage, Politics, and Literary Traditions in England, 1558–1658* (Detroit, 1993), pp. 192–210.

33. B.L., Lansdowne MS. 71, fo. 28^r; C.L.R.O., Remembrancia I, fo. 341^r; P.R.O., PC 2/19/414, SP 12/243/45.
34. H.H., Cecil Papers, XXXII, fo. 106^r.
35. H.H., Cecil Papers, XXXII, fo. 106^r; John Stow, *A Survey of the Cities of London and Westminster*, ed. John Strype, 2 vols (London, 1720), vol. II, bk V, p. 303.
36. C.L.R.O., Journals 24, fo. 22^v; H.H., Cecil Papers, XXXII, fo. 107^r; P.R.O., SP 12/252/94 III; John Stow, *The abridgement or summarie of the English chronicle* (London, 1607; S.T.C. 23330), p. 499.
37. A. L. Beier, *Masterless Men: The Vagrancy Problem in England 1560–1640* (London and New York, 1985), pp. 93–5.
38. Archer, *Pursuit*, pp. 1–2; John Bellamy, *The Tudor Law of Treason: An Introduction* (London, 1979), p. 78; B.L., Lansdowne MS. 78, fos 159^r, 161^r; C.L.R.O., Journals 24, fo. 25^v; Hughes and Larkin, eds, *Tudor*, vol. III, p. 143; Manning, *Village Revolts*, pp. 209–10; G. W. Prothero, ed., *Select Statutes*, 4th edn (Oxford, 1913), pp. 443–4; Stow, *The abridgement*, pp. 500–1; Stow, *A Survey*, ed. Strype, vol. I, bk I, pp. 65–6; *A students lamentation that hath sometime been in London an apprentice, for the rebellious tumults lately in the citie hapning* (London, 1595; S.T.C. 23401.5), sigs A2^r, B4^v.
39. Thomas Heywood, *The Dramatic Works*, ed. R.H. Shepherd, 6 vols (London, 1874), vol. I, pp. 17–18.
40. Kathleen E. McLuskie, *Dekker and Heywood* (Basingstoke and London, 1994), p. 58.
41. Archer, *Pursuit*, pp. 4–5; B.L., Lansdowne MS. 49, fo. 22^r; C.L.R.O., Journals 22, fo. 54^r.
42. P.R.O., PC 2/20/331.
43. Anthony Copley, *Wits fittes and fancies* (London, 1595; S.T.C. 5738), p. 129.
44. C.L.R.O., Repertory 24, fo. 98^r; G.L., MS. 5570/1, fo. 260^r; P.R.O., Req. 2/213/36. For some preliminary literary examples, see Johnson, *The nine*, sigs D1^r, D4^r, F3^r–4^r; Charles Mackay, ed., *A Collection of Songs and Ballads Relative to the London Prentices and Trades*, Percy Society, 1 (1841), pp. 22–8; William Vallans, *The honourable prentice: or, this taylor is a man* (London, 1615; S.T.C. 24588), passim.
45. Henry Roberts, *Lancaster his allarums* (London, 1595; S.T.C. 21083), sig. A4^v.
46. Anthony Munday and others, *Sir Thomas More*, ed. Vittorio Gabrieli and Giorgio Melchiori (Manchester and New York, 1990), I.i.31–2, I.i.96–7, I.iii.46–7, I.iii.48–50.
47. Scott, *Domination*, p. x.
48. P.R.O., SP 12/261/10 I–II; B.L., Lansdowne MS. 81, fos 72^r, 86^r.
49. Archer, *Pursuit*, p. 8; J. Payne Collier, ed., *Trevelyan Papers, Part II*, Camden Society, 1st ser., 84 (1863), p. 101.
50. Pauline Croft, 'Libels, Popular Literacy and Public Opinion in Early Modern England', *Historical Research*, 68 (1995), p. 272; B.R.H., B.C.B., 1 February 1598–7 November 1604, fo. 228^v.

51. *A students lamentation*, sigs B1ᵛ, B3ʳ. See also Griffiths, *Youth and Authority*, p. 165.
52. For instance, apprentices had access to institutional structures designed to protect their interests; were able to present neglectful masters before the court of assistants or the chamberlain's court; and could take up new placements in extenuating circumstances. See Griffiths, *Youth and Authority*, pp. 307–13; Margaret Pelling, 'Apprenticeship, Health and Social Cohesion in Early Modern London', *History Workshop*, 37, Spring (1994), pp. 33–56; Rappaport, *Worlds*, pp. 234–6.
53. Edward Arber, ed., *A Transcript of the Registers of the Company of Stationers of London, 1554–1640*, 5 vols (London, 1875–94), vol. I, pp. xli–xlii.
54. John Lyly, '*Campaspe*'/'*Sappho and Phao*', ed. G. K. Hunter and David Bevington (Manchester and New York, 1991), III.ii.1–5.
55. B.L., Additional MS. 18913, fo. 32ʳ; C.L.R.O., Journals 21, fo. 356ʳ, Journals 28, fo. 160ᵛ, Repertory 21, fo. 59ᵛ; Hughes and Larkin, eds, *Tudor*, vol. III, p. 60.
56. B.L., Additional MS. 33852, I, fo. 30ʳ; Clothworkers' Co., Court Book 1581–1605, fo. 43ᵛ, Court Book 1605–1623, fo. 251ᵛ; G.L., MS. 8200/1, fo. 146ʳ; Abraham Jackson, *The pious prentice, or, the prentices piety* (London, 1640; S.T.C. 14295), pp. 105–6; P.R.O., Req. 2/174/18; Rappaport, 'Social Structure', p. 115. The unlikelihood of an apprentice ever becoming an alderman had been hinted at as early as the sixteenth century. See *Cyuile and Vncyuile Life* (1579), in W. C. Hazlitt, ed., *Inedited Tracts* (London, 1868), p. 23.
57. G.L., MS. 5570/1, fo. 149ʳ.
58. See B.R.H., B.C.B., 26 April 1559–25 January 1562, fo. 48ʳ, B.C.B., 1 February 1598–7 November 1604, fos 18ʳ, 374ᵛ; B.L., Additional MS. 18913, fo. 146ʳ, Lansdowne MS. 74, fo. 55ʳ; Clothworkers' Co., Court Book 1623–1636, fo. 112ᵛ; C.L.R.O., MC6/94, Remembrancia I, fo. 57ʳ; Goldsmiths' Co., Court Book K, 1, fo. 51ʳ; G.L.R.O., MJ/GDR 2/109ᵛ, MJ/SBB 21/10; G.L., MS. 4655/1, fo. 65ᵛ, MS. 5570/1, fo. 280ʳ; P.R.O., C2/Eliz. I/A4/8, C2/Eliz. I/B14/30, PC 2/30/153, Req. 2/102/36, Req. 2/163/104.
59. Chappell and Ebsworth, eds, *Roxburghe*, vol. VIII, p. xxviii; [Sir William Denny], *Pelecanicidium: or the Christian adviser against self-murder* (London, 1653; Wing D1051), pp. 4–5; Daniel Tuvil, Sᵗ. *Pauls threefold cord* (London, 1635; S.T.C. 24396.5), p. 289.
60. Ben Jonson, *The Complete Plays*, ed. G. A. Wilkes, 4 vols (Oxford, 1981–2), vol. II, II.i.122–3.
61. Goldsmiths' Co., Court Book O, 3, fo. 473ʳ.
62. Scott, *Domination*, p. xii.
63. Richard Brome, *The Dramatic Works*, ed. John Pearson, 3 vols (London, 1873), vol. I, I.i.p. 288.
64. Clothworkers' Co., Court Book 1605–1623, fos 86ᵛ, 132ᵛ; C.L.R.O., Repertory 10, fo. 71ᵛ; G.L., MS. 4655/2, fo. 169ʳ; P.R.O., Req. 2/39/95; Tyne and Wear Joint Archives Service, Newcastle, GU/Ma/4, p. 40.

65. Divisions between the popular and private theatrical traditions were not rigid or constant. The middling sort were recorded as attending some fashionable theatres while, in the 1580s and 1600s, tradesmen and servants went to Paul's where Marston's plays were performed. See Martin Butler, *Theatre and Crisis 1632–1642* (Cambridge, 1984), pp. 303, 334.

66. P.R.O., Req. 2/283/38. For apprentices resorting to prostitutes or attempting the chastity of their mistresses or masters' daughters, see B.R.H., B.C.B., 7 May 1576–19 November 1579, fos 77ᵛ, 287ᵛ; C.L.R.O., MC6/66; G.L.R.O., MJ/SR 1004/194; Griffiths, *Youth and Authority*, pp. 213–21.

67. See William Lilly, *A History of his Life and Times, from the Year 1602–1681*, 2nd edn (London, 1826), p. 25.

68. J. Cooke, *Greene's Tu Quoque*, ed. Alan J. Berman (New York and London, 1984), XVII, 2533–40.

69. Scott, *Domination*, pp. 57–8.

70. B.R.H., B.C.B., 26 April 1559–25 January 1562, fos 1ʳ, 51ʳ, 76ᵛ; Clothworkers' Co., Court Book 1581–1605, fos 162ᵛ, 184ᵛ, 199ᵛ; G.L., MS. 4655/1, fos 12ʳ, 21ʳ, 103ʳ, MS. 5570/1, fos 396ʳ, 595ʳ.

71. C.L.R.O., Repertory 28, fo. 239ᵛ, 316ᵛ, Repertory 30, fo. 87ᵛ, MC6/66, MC6/96; G.L., MS. 4329/4, fo. 169ʳ.

72. P.R.O., Req. 2/48/26. Cf. G.L.R.O., MJ/SBB 148/41.

73. B.R.H., B.C.B., 1 February 1598–7 November 1604, fo. 52ᵛ, B.C.B., 1 March 1627–7 May 1634, fo. 106ᵛ; Clothworkers' Co., Court Book 1558–1581, fos 132ʳ, 245ʳ; C.L.R.O., Repertory 29, fo. 181ᵛ; G.L., MS. 4655/1, fo. 35ᵛ. Parents could also petition if the treatment given to their children-apprentices was deemed objectionable. See North Yorkshire County R. O., QSM 2/10 MIC 97, fo. 145ʳ; Alfred Plummer, *The London Weavers' Company 1600–1970* (London and Boston, 1972), p. 88; P.R.O., Req. 2/414/21.

74. Thomas Dekker, *Foure Birds of Noahs Arke* (1609), ed. F. P. Wilson (Oxford, 1924), p. 9; Hyder E. Rollins, ed., *A Pepysian Garland: Black-Letter Broadside Ballads of the Years 1595–1639* (Cambridge, 1922), pp. 223–8; Richard West, *The court of conscience or Dick Whippers sessions* (London, 1607; S.T.C. 25263), sig. F4ʳ.

75. T. I., *A world of wonders. A masse of murthers. A couie of cosonages* (London, 1595; S.T.C. 14068.5), sig. F4ʳ.

76. Archer, *Pursuit*, p. 207.

77. Gurr, *Playgoing*, p. 67.

78. Francis Beaumont, *The Knight of the Burning Pestle*, ed. Sheldon P. Zitner (Manchester, 1984), IV, 330–1; Dedicatory Epistle, 2, 4–5, 9.

79. Thomas Randolph, *The Poetical and Dramatic Works*, ed. W. C. Hazlitt, 2 vols (London, 1875), vol. II, I.i.p. 385. For the play's provenance, see Martin Butler, 'The Auspices of Thomas Randolph's *Hey for Honesty, Down with Knavery*', *Notes and Queries*, 35 (1988), pp. 491–2.

80. James Shirley, *The Dramatic Works*, ed. William Gifford and Alexander Dyce, 6 vols (London, 1833), vol. VI, V.i.p. 70.

81. Sir John Ferne, *The blazon of gentrie* (London, 1586; S.T.C. 10824), p. 72.

82. Edmund Bolton, *The cities advocate, in this case of honor and armes; whether apprentiship extinguisheth gentry?* (London, 1629; S.T.C. 3219), sig. B1ᵛ. For the date of this work, see J. P. Cooper, *Land, Men and Beliefs: Studies in Early-Modern History* (London, 1983), p. 71. Bolton's pamphlet was one of the few kept by the Goldsmiths of London in their library. See Brooks, 'Apprenticeship', p. 241.

83. T.C. Mendenhall, *The Shrewsbury Drapers and the Welsh Wool Trade in the Sixteenth and Seventeenth Centuries* (London, 1953), pp. 88–9.

84. Cyprian Blagden, 'The Stationers' Company in the Civil War Period', *The Library*, 13 (1958), p. 2.

85. Stephen R. Smith, 'The Social and Geographical Origins of London Apprentices, 1630–1660', *Guildhall Miscellany*, 4 (1973), p. 200. See also Brooks, 'Apprenticeship', p. 61.

86. B.R.H., B.C.B., 26 April 1559–25 January 1562, fos 90ʳ, 99ᵛ, B.C.B., 7 May 1576–19 November 1579, fos 346ʳ, 348ʳ; C.L.R.O., Journals 20, 1, fo. 32ʳ; Goldsmiths' Co., Court Book K, 1, fo. 35ʳ.

87. B.R.H., B.C.B., 1 February 1598–7 November 1604, fo. 53ᵛ; Sylvia Lettice Thrupp, *A Short History of the Worshipful Company of Bakers of London* (Croydon, 1933), p. 90.

88. B.L., Additional MS. 18913, fo. 32ʳ.

89. C.L.R.O., Journals 28, fos 119ʳ, 161ʳ, P. D. 10. 211; N. B. Harte, 'State Control of Dress and Social Change in Pre-Industrial England', in D. C. Coleman and A. H. John, eds, *Trade, Government and Economy in Pre-Industrial England: Essays presented to F. J. Fisher* (London, 1976), p. 150. See also Brooks, 'Apprenticeship', p. 80; Griffiths, *Youth and Authority*, pp. 221–34; Pelling, 'Apprenticeship', p. 54.

90. Philip Massinger, *The Plays and Poems*, ed. Philip Edwards and Colin Gibson, 5 vols (Oxford, 1976), vol. IV, II.i.51–2. See Martin Butler, 'Massinger's *The City Madam* and the Caroline Audience', *Renaissance Drama*, 13 (1982), p. 164.

91. Butler, 'Massinger's *The City Madam*', pp. 162, 166.

92. Brome, *Works*, vol. II, I, p. 4.

93. See *The petition of the weamen of Middlesex* (London, 1641; Wing P1838), sig. A4ʳ; *H.M.C., Various*, 8 vols (London, 1901–14), vol. II, p. 204; James Howell, *Epistolae Ho-Elianae* (London, 1650; Wing H3072), pp. 213–14; Paul Seaver, 'Declining Status in an Aspiring Age: The Problem of the Gentle Apprentice in Seventeenth-Century London', in Bonnelyn Kunze and Dwight D. Brautigam, eds, *Court, Country and Culture: Essays on Early Modern British History in Honour of Perez Zagorin* (Rochester, NY, 1992), pp. 129–47.

94. Sir Edward Coke, *The second part of the Institutes* (London, 1671; Wing C4952), pp. 668–9.

95. Sir John Doddridge, *Honors pedigree* (London, 1652; Wing D1793), p. 150.

96. Thomas Birch, ed., *The Court and Times of James I*, 2 vols (London, 1848), vol. II, pp. 247–8; C.L.R.O., Repertory 35, fos 141ᵛ–2ʳ; D. N., *Londons looking-glasse. Or the copy of a letter, written by an English travayler, to the apprentices of London* (London, 1621; S.T.C. 18327), passim; P.R.O., SP 14/187/59.

97. B.L., Egerton MS. 784, fo. 138^r; John Lambe, *A briefe description of the notorious life of J. Lambe* (London, 1628; S.T.C. 15177), pp. 20–1; Rollins, ed., *A Pepysian*, pp. 276–82.
98. Stephen R. Smith, 'Almost Revolutionaries: The London Apprentices during the Civil Wars', *The Huntington Library Quarterly*, 42 (1979), pp. 313–28.
99. Alan Sinfield, *Faultlines: Cultural Materialism and the Politics of Dissident Reading* (Oxford, 1992), p. 37.

2

Crafts and Trades

Once the apprentice had successfully passed through training, a new phase in his career presented itself. Most often, he was immediately employed as a journeyman, a member of a livery company qualified to earn wages but disallowed from setting up as a master or a householder in his own right.[1] Only through the accumulation of capital could the journeyman eventually employ servants and gain admittance to the senior positions of his company. As the only writers in the English Renaissance who gave imaginative expression to the journeyman's conditions, Thomas Dekker, who worked mainly within the drama, and Thomas Deloney, who confined himself to prose fiction and ballads, occupy a unique place.

It might be useful to speculate about the limited space devoted to journeymen in contemporary literary representations. Certainly, in general terms, they failed to excite the same degree of political anxiety as apprentices, which may suggest a separateness from the culture of their youthful associates. Because they were placed at a brief stage in a longer progress, journeymen may not have presented to writers an immediately identifiable audience. In Dekker and Deloney's work, perhaps not surprisingly, therefore, other servants as well as journeymen are an important presence. For Dekker, the chief concern is the shoemaker's fraught partnership with his journeymen, whereas Deloney's area of enquiry expands to encompass the clothier's treatment of his 'factory' hands, some of whom work in domestic service.

In this chapter, I discuss Dekker and Deloney's representations of the master or mistress's relations with their journeymen and servants in a craft and trading context. In spite of the differences between them, I argue, the writers unite in their shared ideological response to the changes that were overtaking crafts and trades in the later sixteenth century. Utilizing the household as a trope, they explore shifting centres of power within the domestic unit, at a time when new economic structures moved manufacture away from the home and into larger industrial arrangements. Transformations in the contemporary economy were exacerbated by concomitant factors, such as dearth and the influx of foreign workers, and it is these forces that animate Dekker and Deloney's complementary representations of masters who struggle to protect their households from the threat of upheaval. In showing the employers' cultivation of hospitality, I conclude, the writers offer an answer to the problems engendered by a diversifying economy, but these answers are themselves complicated by representations of alternative allegiances that go against the ideal of masters and servants supporting each other in profitable harmony. Throughout, Dekker and Deloney alternately face and retreat from the increasing complexity of social and economic developments, taking comfort in nostalgic fictions of employment while confronting the growth of a more specialized market. In this way, their writing constitutes an attempt to form a bridge between disintegrating conceptions of service and the demands of competitive enterprise.

THE INDUSTRIAL FAMILY

Nowhere are the tensions between residual and emergent forms of service better exemplified than in the opening stages of Deloney's prose fiction, *Jack of Newbury* (c. 1597). A debate about men and women's roles encourages reflections upon the nature of authority and its traditional functions. In the first chapter, the Dame, a clothier's widow who is attracted to the 'good gouernment' of Jack, her foreman, gives him responsibility for all 'hir Workefolkes'.[2] What lies behind her decision, however, is the belief that Jack's experience of service will make him an obedient husband, and she rejects her older, wealthier suitors on the grounds of their independent spirit. When they eventually marry, Jack's fears that the Dame will disdain 'to be gouerned by him' (p. 12) are dramatically realized.

The respective duties of husband and wife, specifically regarding the management of the household, are subjects on which Jack and his new wife cannot agree. Despite Jack's commands, the Dame intends to continue as a mistress rather than assuming the mantle of a meek spouse, as exemplified in her refusal to abandon 'her ordinarie custome' of setting 'forth in the morning among her gossips . . . and not . . . [returning] home till night, without any regarde of her houshold' (p. 22). It is the unstable territory between the obligations prescribed by gender and class that the fiction negotiates. Caught in a limbo between foreman and husband, Jack attempts to assert himself by barring his wife from the house, only to find that she craftily gains readmittance, locking him out in the process. The lines of demarcation between the master, who was a householder, and the servant, who could only aspire to a similar status, fluctuate alarmingly in this scene. The Dame reclaims her territorial rights; Jack is reduced to sleeping 'among his Prentices' (p. 24); and the 'natural' inferiority of service begins to re-establish itself.

In the battle for the material signs of household supremacy, however, the Dame's victory cannot last. Her wilfulness is cut short by her untimely death; Jack is free to become undisputed master; and, following his late wife's example, marries a servant 'tried in the guiding of his house' (p. 26). This 'excellent good huswife' (p. 26) throws the Dame's shortcomings into relief and, through her submissiveness to the clothier, authorizes the relinquishment of Jack's servant identity. He is now able to assume full masterly status. But this inversion of the opening scenario fails to cancel out the confusions which the fiction has created. Unanswered questions about the first wife's power linger; patriarchal government is revealed as dependent upon women's support; and the categories of husband and wife, and master and servant, have not yet settled into tidy arrangements.

Questions about the exercise of authority are granted a more contemporary urgency in the treatment of Jack's relations with his workforce. In particular, the representation of a household whose basic form is still evolving is seen as part of the wider phenomenon of an expanding industrial sector – the disappearance of the independent producer system and the shift to centralized modes of manufacture run on a 'capitalistic' basis.[3] By the late 1540s, as Steve Rappaport notes, 'London's merchants shipped overseas each year more than three times as many cloths as they had half a century earlier.'[4] Thanks to the boom in the export trade and increased demand, some manufacturers, notably in rural areas, responded by becoming large-scale employers in a single premises. The 'real' Jack of Newbury, John

Winchcombe, was a successful Berkshire clothier with London merchant connections, and he was joined by William Stumpe, a Wiltshire clothier, who converted the abbey of Malmesbury into a factory where his workers operated the looms.[5] Judging from contemporary accounts, these early industrial operations met with considerable success. If a later antiquary is to be believed, Stumpe, like Jack of Newbury, entertained Henry VIII in his house, while the Springs of Lavenham, Suffolk clothiers, patronized their parish church, built up associations with the gentry and bought property in their own county, in Norfolk, Essex and Cambridgeshire.[6]

However, such cases were the exception rather than the rule, and cloth manufacture was usually conducted in one of two ways.[7] Most common was the 'domestic' or 'putting-out' system whereby the clothier bought wool from the wool-grower, cleaned and mixed it, and distributed it for carding and spinning to women working at home. The wool was then passed on to a weaver and later to other independent craftsmen, such as dyers and finishers. Finishing processes were often carried out by the clothier himself. Equally common was a family engaging in cloth production, the children carding wool, the wife spinning it into yarn and the husband weaving the fabric and finishing the material.

At the heart of Deloney's fiction is a verse description of Jack's factory-like establishment, which merges traditional manufacturing methods and gains energy from the impact of new technologies. The ways in which the factory is described illuminate initially the clothier's attempts to impress his prospective father-in-law, the 'olde man' (p. 28) of Aylesbury, through demonstrations of patriarchal authority and industrial power:

> Within one roome being large and long,
> There stood two hundred Loomes full strong:
> Two hundred men, the truth is so,
> Wrought in theese Loomes all in a rowe,
> By euery one a pretty boy,
> Sate making quils with mickle ioie.
> And in another place hard by,
> An hundred women merrily,
> Were carding hard with ioyfull cheere,
> Who singing sate with voices cleare.
>
> (pp. 26–7)

The 'men' are clearly seen as the more important members of the workforce, outnumbering the 'women' who labour in the factory's peripheral areas. The 'prety' boys who attend the loom-workers suggest both social harmony and the perpetuation of the system through the involvement of the younger generations. In the song, moreover, is a further expression of contentment, the musical chorus articulating the united endeavour of Jack's employees: the clothier, it seems, is still driven to control women's economic contributions.

At the same time, the description anticipates a more developed form of industrial organization and a less personal relationship between the employer and his workforce, even if the language in which it is couched evokes an earlier, but still active stage of the economy. Jack is conceived less as a business entrepreneur than as a paternalistic master, governing according to practices that had long been in existence. The work of the factory is registered as a family activity: the male loom-workers and boys are followed by women and maidens, and the 'children' of locals pick wool for a penny a day. Despite a workforce which numbers over 1000 persons, Jack presides over a domestic unit, a working household, and is additionally traditional in his manufacture of kersies (coarse narrow cloth), not the 'new draperies' that contemporary consumers found more attractive. It is not coincidental, therefore, that Jack shows the old man of Aylesbury 'euery office in his house' (p. 26) and the butcher, brewer and baker who 'stood his houshold in good stead' (p. 28). The establishment is finally summed up in the words, 'this great houshold and familie' (p. 28), a striking means of referring to a clothier who is childless.

In this respect, Deloney translates the proto-industrial implications of his material into an essentially puritan model of contractual relations in which the functions of employer and head of household were synonymous, and in which 'family' connoted wife, children and all other domestic dependants. In *Jack of Newbury*, however, the conjunction of the two economic polarities of factory and family, and the idealized attempt to reconcile these conflicting modes of production, serve only paradoxically to expose the differences between them and the uncertain relationship between Jack's many guises. The great lengths taken by the clothier in his efforts to impress suggest an insecurity about the roles he is obliged to fill – master and son-in-law, husband and metaphorical father to his employees. The fiction's sensitivity to new economic configurations is a shaping force in the representation of Jack, who finds confusions over his position as a servant replaced by more pressing questions about his filial, paternal and managerial attachments.

FOREIGN INTRUSIONS, FAMISHED FAMILIES

In Deloney's fiction and Dekker's *The Shoemaker's Holiday*, the relationship between the master's power and an 'other' is elaborated at a number of levels. As women are figured as a locus of anxiety, so are aliens and the threat of famine. Both the latter joined forces to aggravate the already tense social climate of the 1590s. The introduction of the new draperies in the later sixteenth century had revived the cloth industry: attracted by their skills and labour potential, the government welcomed the Huguenot artisans of the Low Countries and France, fleeing from religious persecution at a moment when the Counter-Reformation was in one of its most violent phases.[8] Patronized by the crown, aliens were encouraged to settle in England and revitalized the cloth trade in Norwich, Colchester, Canterbury and Southampton, and a number of other urban centres.[9]

In London, however, as chapter 1 has demonstrated, the strangers were often a focus for discontent. The question of whether or not they should enjoy trading privileges, and be able to sell their goods by retail, was debated in the House of Commons in 1593. Arguing against immigration, Sir Walter Ralegh approved the proposal that the strangers should be expelled. Speaking in favour of England's acceptance policy, Sir Robert Cecil, concerned to maintain the momentum of the economic upsurge, claimed that honour had come to the country through the charity that the foreigners had received. A bill against the strangers' retailing of foreign wares was passed by 162 votes to 82, only to be rejected in the House of Lords, which may point to ties between aristocratic and mercantile interests.[10]

Beyond the corridors of Whitehall, popular petitions from the early 1590s onwards challenged the refugees in a provocative vein, as a 1593 libel posted by apprentices and journeymen suggests:

you ... drunken drones ... fainthearted Flemings; and ... fraudulent ... Frenchmen, by your cowardly flight from your own ... countries, have abandoned the same into the hands of ... proud, cowardly enemies, and have, by a feigned hypocrisy and counterfeit show of religion, placed yourselves here ... under a most gracious and merciful prince.[11]

As a professional weaver as well as a writer, Deloney was alive to the implications of such protests, and in June 1595 joined with other members of his livery company to issue an extended complaint:

There are many [strangers] ... that vse the trade of Weaving, whoe ... vnkindly vse themselues towards vs, ... the[y] onely seeke their owne private lucre w[i]thout ... respect of ... liberties and priviledges ... the lawes of our Lande the[y] regard not ... many of them kepe Apprentices and Loomes twyce or thryce as many as they ought ... what can we call this but plaine theft ... They haue opened and discovered the secretes of our Occupac[i]on ... by this meanes many a poore English man is ... brought to ... miserye.[12]

On the point of delivering copies of the document to the French and Dutch churches, however, the ringleaders were foiled in their plot, and Deloney briefly imprisoned.[13]

From an inspection of these materials, a number of quite different charges emerges. Indicting the aliens for their personal failings, such as greed and disrespect, shades into an anxiety about the effects of their conduct on craft and trading interests. Illicit business practice and competition, it is feared, will imperil English monopolies and, eventually, undermine the security of the state itself. It is in the light of the diversity of such grievances that several narratives involving foreigners in Deloney's fiction acquire a subversive potential.[14] In *Jack of Newbury*, Benedick, a young Italian merchant, desires Joan, the clothier's servant and the wife of one of his weavers. He begins his seduction by attempting to inveigle himself into the good graces of Joan's husband, tempting him with 'a hundreth pound, wishing him to be a seruant no longer' (p. 63), thereby threatening social as well as sexual priorities. His next step is to flatter Joan with fantasies of becoming a lady. Having realized the deception, Joan plots with her husband to revenge herself upon the treacherous Italian, whose unsettling intrusions now take on almost all of the features of the popular alien stereotype. Instead of the woman he lusts after, Benedick embraces a sow in bed and, still smarting from the bestial flavour of his punishment, departs 'from *Newbery* before day' (p. 68). In the face of the infiltration of alien forces, servants rally to act upon a community's principles: economic and sexual property is defended, and the hierarchical structures which maintain Jack's power are triumphantly validated.

As meditations on Elizabethan preoccupations, however, Deloney's prose is rarely unproblematic, and the choice of a visiting Italian for a satirical target plays down the dangers of too close an identification with the London immigrant population. Nevertheless, in what was probably his next fiction, *The Gentle Craft, Part I* (c. 1597), Deloney permits himself a greater specificity, which may explain the apparently more accommodating solution proposed to the question of the foreigner's slippery influence. Once again, a formulaic plot device serves an ideological purpose: John, a Frenchman, and Haunce, a Dutchman, both journeymen of shoemaker Simon Eyre, compete for Florence, their master's maidservant. Each journeyman attempts to expose the other, revealing their mutual deviousness: Haunce broadcasts the fact that John is already married, and, in revenge, the Frenchman tricks his fellow-servant into losing his wine and meal. The situation only begins to resolve itself when Florence, appalled by their antics, chooses instead to marry Nicholas, a journeyman with impeccably English credentials. Narrative logic demands that Eyre enters to approve the proceedings, and it is perhaps partly due to his new position as an alderman that he is able to seal the match 'with great credit', to do 'very much' for '*Iohn* Frenchman', and to show 'himselfe a good Master to his man *Haunce*, and to all the rest of his seruants' (p. 166).

Whereas in *Jack of Newbury* the threat to English hierarchies is expelled, in *The Gentle Craft, Part I* it is absorbed into a paradigm of household relations, which is predicated upon the master's munificence. The expected punishments fail to materialize, a manoeuvre which dampens the inflammatory potential of contemporary tensions, while Eyre himself evokes the merciful prince described in libels and parliamentary pronouncements. The conclusion, in fact, gestures in several directions at one and the same time. It is both equitable and discriminatory, a ratification of the powers of English authority and a recognition of the economic importance of a new labour market. But even this movement betrays a residual antagonism. The process of cultural integration is never completed, since the foreigners fail to win the object of their attentions: it is only the possibility that is made visible.

The experience with the authorities in 1595 had not diminished Deloney's zest for controversy, however, and the following year it was anxieties about food shortages that led him to deploy a popular literary form to broadcast dangerous political opinions. On 26 July, 1596, Stephen Slany, the Lord Mayor of London, wrote to William Cecil, Lord Burghley, about a 'certein ballad . . . w^{ch} . . . prescribeth orders for ye remedying of [the] dearth . . . in [a] vaine & vndiscreet manner [so] that . . . the poor may aggravate their grief & take occasion of soom discontentment'. The 'maker', Slany added significantly, 'is on Delonie . . . an idle fellowe'.[15] Poor harvests from 1594 to 1597 had created, in some areas, conditions of near famine.[16] Dearth-related riots broke out during the period, and many clothiers, apprehensive about dwindling sources of revenue, were forced to lay off their workers or drastically to reduce their wages.[17] The effects of dearth on the cloth trade could not have escaped Deloney's notice, nor may he have been unaware of parliamentary legislation in 1597 and 1598, which increased their incomes and made provisions for the relief of textile workers in times of economic catastrophe.[18]

Although the ballad is lost, the prose narratives survive to deliver their uncompromising judgement on contemporary events. In *Jack of Newbury*, which pre-dates the emergency measures of the 1598 parliament, the clothier devises an elaborate pageant to introduce the fictionalized Henry VIII to the children of his 'poore' wool-pickers (p. 49), to Diana, the goddess of chastity, and to Bellona, the goddess of war. Invariably represented as one of the Furies, riding in a chariot and holding a spear in her hand, Bellona works as an anxious extension of tensions that, in other forms, were played out in artisan protest and civil strife.[19] Traditionally, Diana functioned as a fertility deity who protected the lower orders, especially slaves, which invites speculation about the mechanisms available to relieve the children's straitened circumstances. But Diana is also associated with Elizabeth I's cult of chastity; in addition to Cynthia and Belphoebe, Diana was the goddess the queen particularly favoured.[20] In this sense, Diana's presence has an allusive political dimension. Through the goddess's associations, doubts are raised about overpopulation and illegitimacy, the twin evils animating the social nightmare of late Tudor authorities. More obliquely, a metaphorical embodiment of Elizabeth implicitly reprimands Henry VIII for the laxity of his economic programme. By implicating Henry VIII, the sovereign's father, in the spectacle of distress, Deloney questions the workings of royal power and, by extension, centralized administration itself.

By far the longest and certainly the most vivid passage in the pageant is reserved for 'Famine', who is personified as 'a tall Woman, so leane and ill fauoured, that her cheek bones were ready to start out of the skinne, of a pale and deadly colour, her eyes sunke into her head: her legges so feeble, that they could scantly carrie the body' (p. 48). With 'Famine' and her sisters, the 'Sword' and 'Fyre', as eloquent representatives, Jack reveals the stretched resources of his benevolent practice. Constrained by his powerlessness, the clothier is realized as a force of potential retribution, even as the possessor of quasi-divine powers: plague, famine and the sword were frequently interpreted as the three arrows with which God would communicate wrath and vengeance.[21] If the fiction mediates a dissatisfaction with the efficiency of existing systems of poor relief, however, the clothier is never allowed clearly to articulate his frustrations. In contrast, *Jack of Newbury* finally settles upon scenes in which faithful subjects offer a generous monarch their allegiance. The King, Queen and nobility take on the poor children as their personal servants, a gesture which pacifies Jack, delights his employees and dilutes the discontent attendant upon crises of subsistence. It is through service that an escape route from the poverty trap is advanced. But such localized answers, the fiction also suggests, are of limited use in addressing larger, nation-wide distresses, which, beyond Newbury, still remain. Three chapters later, for instance, there are references to clothiers 'in most places' in England 'abating the poore workemens wages' and expelling 'their people; Weauers, Shearemen, Spinners and Carders' (p. 56). Already a figure of some notoriety, Deloney diffuses the implications of his material, even as he highlights the need for economic policies less dependent on a monarch's whimsical largesse.

The anxieties that activate *Jack of Newbury* equally bear upon Dekker's play, *The Shoemaker's Holiday* (1599), which offers a contrasting exploration of a master who is unable to protect his servants from harsh vicissitudes. Simon Eyre, the titular shoe-maker, is convinced that he will be able free Ralph, his journey-man, from military service. 'I'll get thy husband discharged, I warrant thee... Stand by, with your pishery-pashery, away! I am a man of the best presence,' he tells Jane, Ralph's wife.[22] Accompanying the assurance of this opening, however, are darker suggestions about the fragility of family relations. The potential gravity of the situation is stressed by Firk, another of Eyre's jour-neymen, who argues that, without her husband's support, Jane will be forced to 'beg' (I, 141) as a prostitute. Gradually the buoyant note is replaced by a knell which sounds the collapse of Eyre's household illusions. Having botched his attempts to bribe the officers into allowing him to keep Ralph 'at home' (I, 133), Eyre can only reflect bitterly on his lack of success: 'You will not release him? Well, let him go... let him vanish!' (I, 164–5). The drums of war now drown the shoemaker's boastful, but ill-founded rhetorical ebullience.

In revealing the circumstances of a household cracking beneath external pressures, the play's opening forms part of a larger contemporary narrative in which the effect of deprivation on employers was a major theme. From 1595 to 1596, when the dearth was reaching its peak, mayoral correspondence and privy coun-cil minutes complained about less privileged London householders who relinquished their trades or abandoned their domestic dependants.[23] As *The Shoemaker's Holiday* progresses, the refrain of 'want', an oblique comment on famine, points to a thinly veiled criticism of the implementation of social responsibilities. The officer, Roland Lacy, promises Ralph, 'Thou shalt not want, as I am a gentleman' (I, 180), but, in retrospect, officers and masters must stand accused of failing to provide for their charges. Although Eyre and his wife, Margery, agree to care for Jane while Ralph is away, she is allowed mysteriously to leave and later appears as a seamster's drudge. Through these criticisms, more penetrating analyses of the operations of social privilege are conducted. The elevated position of the careless Lacy means that he can desert the army and escape the consequences of his actions; as he muses, 'Thou canst not want – do Fortune what she can' (III, 23). For Ralph, who, in common with other sol-diers of the period, returns from battle penniless, such indiffer-ence is incomprehensible, and he must turn to work to re-establish himself: 'Since I want limbs and lands, / I'll to God, my good friends, and to these my hands' (X, 110–11), he states.[24] In the image of the injured journeyman, the material advantages of social standing are made forcibly apparent. Money, the play suggests, takes second place to status in the exercise of authority, and in this process the vulnerabilities of masters as well as servants are exposed. Compared to Eyre, Jack's confrontation with adversity is superficially more successful. For the clothier and the shoemaker, however, who respond to crises with a similarly misplaced confidence in their abilities, the final discovery is that want is the unwelcome spirit that refuses to be banished from their midst.

HOSPITABLE PERFORMANCES

In Deloney's fiction and Dekker's drama, a debate about social responsibilities continually threatens to interrupt the narrative. Witnesses to the dissolution of households, the craftsmen and tradesmen in these texts practise a combination of generous hospitality and prudent financial management, in ways which ultimately indict the aristocracy and call into question its execution of traditional functions.[25] Hospitality had a venerable lineage. As Felicity Heal has demonstrated, the early modern Christian householder was expected to engage in shows of beneficence, and was invariably realized according to classical principles of magnanimity, gentility and honourable entertainment. Most often, it was in the behaviour of the aristocrat or gentleman that the virtues of hospitality found their ideal expression.[26] Cast in a similar mould is Jack of Newbury, whose extended wedding celebrations contribute to the 'great reliefe of the poore' (p. 29), who keeps an open house for his friends and neighbours, and whose kitchen is a cornucopia of good things to eat. With Simon Eyre in *The Shoemaker's Holiday*, the affirmation of hospitality is developed more slowly. By the close, however, with his household fortuitously reconstituted, Eyre can announce his plan to feast the apprentices. Anticipating the Shrove Tuesday festivities, Hodge, the foreman, exclaims, 'Let's feed and be fat with my lord's bounty' (XVIII, 192–3), and he is answered by Firk whose roll-call of foodstuffs resembles the menu of an exclusive restaurant.

But the meanings attached to hospitality evolved in relation to important material pressures as well as prevailing moral attitudes. By the end of the sixteenth century, manufacturing and commercial interests had transformed the fortunes of a number of families. For the Periams in Exeter and the Ishams in North-amptonshire, for example, trade was a route to the acquisition of estates and the establishment of noble connections through marriage.[27] While Jack and Eyre do not follow an identical tra-jectory in their careers, they cultivate aristocratic conduct in com-parable ways, and their hospitality, in particular, accords with W. K. Jordan's findings that during this period the London mer-cantile community was responsible for the greatest number of charitable endowments.[28] At the same time, the hospitable per-formances staged by the clothier and the shoemaker draw atten-tion to lapses in aristocratic observances, and thereby open further gaps between contemporary social groupings. Although Lawrence Stone's thesis that the aristocracy suffered from a crisis in the sixteenth and seventeenth centuries due to infertility, incompe-tent land management and reckless expenditure has been con-tested, it is certainly the case that some noble families suffered a major decline and found themselves incapable of meeting their customary obligations.[29] In 1576, George Gascoigne complained that the 'stately lord, which woonted was to kepe / A court at home, is now come up to courte, / And leaves the country for a common prey', and his verse typifies a wider anxiety about the social repercussions of the abandonment by the upper gentry and aristocracy of hospitality on a lavish scale.[30]

In their writing, Deloney and Dekker reflect upon these devel-opments, considering the ways in which master and mistress' relations with their servants are informed by aristocratic para-digms, and exploring the territory shared by hospitable prac-tices and prodigal expenditure. Members of the aristocracy in Deloney's fiction are invariably victims of financial and sexual profligacy who descend the social scale, and present, therefore, perilous role models. In *Jack of Newbury*, Sir George Rigley and his brother, due to 'scarcity in their purses' and weakening 'cred-its . . . in the Citie', are forced 'to ride into the country, where at their friends houses they might haue fauourable welcome, with-out coyne or grudging' (p. 82). An abuse of hospitality occurs when one of Jack's maidservants falls pregnant to the feckless Sir George, and the clothier reprimands him for the offence: 'had you no mans house to dishonor but mine?' (p. 86). Tricked into marrying the servant, Sir George is obliged to live with the clothier in a position of dependency; only when the King hears of the humiliation is the knight delivered and his wife advanced. As the fiction's conclusion, however, the episode introduces more questions than it resolves. While the transgressions of the nobility are rectified, this can only be facilitated through the promotion of the maidservant, who now stands above Jack in the hierarchical scheme. The reassembly of class barriers muddles their distinguishing features, so that accident dictates the restoration of the social order, and doubts are raised about the ability of the aristocracy to weather its self-inflicted impoverishment.

Through such episodes, Deloney casts a cynical eye over the failings of the landed classes, even as he also indicates the attraction that aristocratic influences continue to exercise. Although aristocratic virtues are objects of bourgeois cultivation, most often, the texts suggest, it is the vices that exert an appeal. The master can fall prey to these temptations, but the mistress is seen to be the more susceptible, as her behaviour suggests a parody of the emphasis on hospitable entertainment. *Jack of Newbury* mocks the actions of the former maidservant, Mistress Winchcombe, who economizes on her 'great house keeping' (p. 71), giving her servants 'shorter commons' (p. 73) so that she can the better maintain her new wardrobe. With such measures, she runs dangerously close to a form of aristocratic wastefulness, and the equilibrium that sustains the competing interests of the household members is upset. As *The Shoemaker's Holiday* demonstrates, the master may impersonate an alderman successfully, but the mistress presents a ridiculous spectacle if she attempts a similar subterfuge, reflecting inconsistencies in patriarchal ideology and the anxieties that women continue to stimulate.

Between the need to save and the will to spend, both of which can be detrimental to household relations, there are troubling parallels. In *The Shoemaker's Holiday*, Margery learns that her husband has been promoted to the position of a sheriff, which means that she adopts a tone more suitable to her newly elevated circumstances. Playing the role of a benefactress, she imagines herself bestowing attention on a feudal dependant:

Good morrow, good [Hodge]. I thank you, my good people all. Firk, hold up thy hand, here's a threepenny piece for thy tidings.

(X, 126–8)

The gift to Firk notwithstanding, Margery's magnanimity is a sham, and it underscores her failure to honour her promise to care for Jane as well as introducing a number of epistemological questions. While the master may aspire to establish a hospitable household, the mistress is seen to be incapable of managing a comparable set of aristocratic conventions. For Dekker, there is no language within which the mistress's elevation can be easily accommodated, and what finally emerges from Margery's affectations is a nuanced sense of representational limitations.

The logical development of a failure to provide properly for servants is a household in which hospitality is prostituted, and in which money cannot function as a bonding instrument. In Deloney's *Thomas of Reading* (c. 1597–c. 1600), the implications of the mistress's abnegations of responsibility are pushed to extreme conclusions. With this fiction, the underside of an aristocratic ideal is exposed: prodigality percolates downwards, and the hospitable household threatens to become the pauper's grave. Tom Dove, the clothier, is dedicated to 'pleasure' (p. 337). The generosity which he originally extended to a workforce taken from the vagabond classes has been gradually replaced by improvidence, echoing the sequence described in a treatise first published in 1555: 'ignoraunce' of 'good house keping . . . tendeth towardes such maisters, as neither know the right vse of worship nor liberalitie', and 'robbeth maisters of such duties as their seruantes oughte by obedience to owe'.[31] The clothier's excesses have, indeed, destabilized household relations, as he is deserted by his servants on becoming bankrupt. One of them, moreover, becomes particularly disrespectful: 'if you be poore, you may thanke your selfe, being a iust scourge for your prodigalitie . . . to stay with you, is the next way to make vs like you' (p. 338). A servant usurping his master's authority was an ideological anomaly in the English Renaissance, and a form of *rapprochement* occurs when, thanks to the good offices of other clothiers, Dove recoups his losses and readmits his servants into employment. But the reunions are hesitant, for 'albeit [Dove] seemed to forgiue [his servants] . . . he would neuer trust them for a straw' (p. 340). Once again, the bourgeois household has been disrupted by a form of aristocratic mismanagement. Although the crafts come together to exorcize the threat of ruin, the fellowship is only an emergency measure, and in the uneasy reunion with the servants are the signs of new strains and differences.

For Deloney and, to a lesser extent, for Dekker, then, the bourgeois investment in hospitality as a mode of organizing master and servant relations generates unexpected ideological tensions. What separates a sensitivity to the welfare of others from a damaging extravagance cannot always be distinguished, and the fiction and the drama show them to be intimately associated. In a variation on the preoccupation with expenditure, however, Dekker offers a form of compromise. By dramatizing the uses of money in a number of aristocratic and bourgeois contexts, *The Shoemaker's Holiday* endorses an ideal in which fellowship is promoted and the master's authority validated through a carefully constructive deployment of resources. As part of its representation of these practices, the first scene airs a debate about the nature of prodigality. Sir Hugh Lacy, the Earl of Lincoln, describes his nephew, Roland, as an 'unthrift' (I, 17) and a 'bankrupt' (I, 28). Although the portrait is unjust, the sentiments expressed sit comfortably with the play's dominant motifs, for many of the characters dispense money to bring kudos upon themselves or to develop strategic enmities. When Lincoln bestows 'thirty portagues' (I, 90) on his nephew, for instance, it is a thinly disguised bribe. In return for the money, the younger Lacy is to transfer his affections from Rose, the mayor's daughter, before exiling himself. In a similar category is Sir Roger Oatley, the mayor, who promises his servant, Dodger, reimbursement if he will 'rid' Lacy 'into France' (IX, 96). At the same time, he attempts to persuade Rose to marry Hammon, a gentleman, enticing her with the prospect of a 'thousand marks' (XI, 29). In these exchanges, money and a lust for power consort with each other in divisive ways. Integrity and morality, it is thought, are goods to be bought and sold in the market. Cash serves as a mechanism to produce familial estrangement, and all social interactions bear the print of a material attitude.

Where Deloney hesitates in his realization of fellowship and its redemptive properties, Dekker eventually adopts a more affirmative attitude. When Ralph departs for the war, he is offered monetary gifts. The journeyman takes leave respectively of Eyre (the master), Hodge and Firk (the foreman and the journeyman) and his wife, in a scene that visually dramatizes the unity and structure of the corporate shoemaking enterprise. Previously, the familial household had shown itself to be deficient in its provision of support, throwing into relief the non-familial household over which Eyre presides and whose communal activities he now endorses; he exclaims:

> Hold thee, Ralph, here's five sixpences for thee. Fight for the honour of the Gentle Craft, for the Gentlemen Shoemakers, the courageous cordwainers . . .
>
> (I, 213–16)

Firk gives 'three twopences' (I, 221) and Hodge, a 'shilling' (I, 224). In the place of the acrimony that expenditure can aggravate, *The Shoemaker's Holiday* suggests that money, administered wisely, bolsters the interests of masters and servants, strengthens their contractual relationship and confirms their mutual dependence. Of course, since Eyre has already failed in his attempt to retain Ralph, his conduct in this scene is not entirely convincing. Conspicuous, too, is Margery, who, on this occasion, neglects to dip into her purse. The approval of a socially responsible attitude towards money, however, is clear, even if the execution of the principle falls short. At various points, the play details hospitable and economic ideals to which some of the characters aspire, but it also reveals a battered economy and social privilege as the barriers that prevent these ideals from being successfully realized.

ALTERNATIVE ALLEGIANCES

For Deloney and Dekker, the practical application of communal practices is further jeopardized by the competing claims of alternative allegiances. The different forms that loyalty can assume (to the self, to factions within the household and to the master) have a dislocating effect, revealing conflicts of interest and gaps in the recommendations that the writers elaborate. In Deloney's *The Gentle Craft, Part II* (c. 1597–c. 1598), Tom Drum, a Sussex journeyman described as 'a very odde fellow' and a 'boasting companion' (p. 219), puts his own welfare first. An example of what social historians have termed the 'betterment migrant' (a servant who travelled for purposes of social and economic improvement), he leaves his shoemaker master and sets off for the capital in search of a less onerous and more materially advantageous professional placement.[32] Nor is this the first time that he has elected to desert his work. As he explains to a dispossessed knight in a cynical construction of his trade, 'if I should have grieved at the Ill will of every Master that I have serued, I verely thinke I had kild a proper man long ere this; for I am sure I have had as many Masters, as there are Market townes in *England*' (p. 232). Forced to join the army, appropriately as a drummer, Drum eventually arrives in London, but his wanderlust brings no significant material compensations. His masters come to despair of him, and 'his daily vaunts' (p. 264) about military service brand him an unregenerate charlatan.

Despite the conclusion of the Drum episode – that the cultivation of individualistic behaviour goes unrewarded – servant allegiances remained vexed issues, as the labour disputes of Dekker's *The Shoemaker's Holiday* demonstrate. There are two moments when Eyre's servants attempt to establish a solidarity from which their master is deliberately excluded. The first is provoked by Eyre's refusal to agree to Firk's request that he take on Hans as a journeyman: at this point, none of the characters recognizes the Dutchman as Lacy in disguise. Values of fraternity lend the dispute its critical edge, as Firk and Hodge, dismayed by the poor reception granted to so 'fine' (IV, 59) a fellow-worker, threaten to leave in protest. Cries Firk:

> If [Hodge] remove, Firk follows. If Saint Hugh's bones shall not be set a-work, I may prick mine awl in the walls and go play. Fare ye well, master.
>
> (IV, 63–6)

In the place of anti-alien feelings, the scene substitutes codes of camaraderie, which also involve redistributions within the power network.[33] The crisis is temporarily averted when Eyre accepts Hans into his service, but his authority has been compromised and his servants have staked a claim to rights with powerfully disruptive implications.

On the second occasion, Eyre insults not a member of the shoemaking fraternity but his wife, Margery, whom he calls a 'bombast-cotton-candle-quean' (VII, 39), 'rubbish' and 'kitchen-stuff' (VII, 48). This new crisis extends the previous argument. Firk leaps to Margery's defence, declaring:

> Nay, dame, you shall not weep and wail in woe... Master, I'll stay no longer. Here's a venentory of my shop-tools. Adieu, master. Hodge, farewell.
>
> (VII, 51–3)

Hodge makes immediate preparations to accompany him: if they cannot work as brothers in service, they must unite as brothers in exile. But this time, the servants are easily placated with a gift of beer, which enables Eyre to continue to humiliate his wife in public. Loyalty among the members of a fraternity, it appears, is more precious than the ties that bind them to their mistress, and it is by overruling Margery's authority that Eyre can prevent the threatened walkout. The scene opened with a discussion about holiday entitlements; it closes with the affirmation of Eyre's masterly status, bringing the conflicts full circle. A steady application to employment under one master emerges as the moral lesson of these scenes, and, indeed, Hodge and Firk are ostensibly rewarded for their efforts. On ascending to the mayoralty, Eyre ensures that Hodge, who becomes a master, and Firk, who becomes a foreman, share in his success. The play's conclusion, however, is undercut by the realization that the promotion has been achieved through Eyre's manipulation of demonstrations of authority, as when he impersonates an alderman in order to possess a ship's merchandise. In *The Shoemaker's Holiday*, servants rise coincidentally through participation in their master's economic skulduggery, which contrasts unfavourably with the view that hard work is the only route to material preferment.

Perhaps most unsettling are those moments in the texts when allegiances form with the master rather than against him: the household unites to create a particularly resilient force, and this is highlighted in Deloney's representation of Jack of Newbury's private army. As Laura Caroline Stevenson has noted, when Jack prepares to defend his country against the invading Scottish forces, he copies his superiors in dressing his servants as liveried retainers.[34] The clothier 'had made readie fiftie tall men well mounted in white coates . . . [with] Demilances in their hands . . . fiftie armed men on foot with Pikes, and fiftie shot in white coats' (p. 30). More striking, perhaps, is the fact that in the late sixteenth century there can be imagined a clothier powerful enough to assemble retainers at all. Tudor authorities became particularly concerned when magnates used their followings of servants and tenants for private warfare, as the 1504 Statute of Liveries, which had placed restrictions on the practice, suggests.[35] Further attempts to curtail retaining were made as late as 1572, when a statute was introduced which attempted to control the size of aristocratic followings.[36] In view of the anxieties that a local militia aroused, it is not coincidental that Jack and his retainers are committed to faithful service on their sovereign's behalf. Although 'fewe better [soldiers] were found in the field' (p. 30), at the critical stage, they do not enter battle, for the Scots are defeated by the Earl of Surrey, whose claim to noble blood is indisputable. At once a wistful evocation of the retinues of the past, Jack's creation of an impeccably drilled army is a forceful demonstration of his industrial ascendancy: it is as if the soldiers, who have identical appearances, originate in the same mould, and represent, therefore, the finest of the clothier's factory productions.[37] In addition, although Deloney sidesteps the prospect of servant victory on the battlefield, the clothier's ability to raise such a retinue suggests possibilities for alternative ties of loyalty and forms of political involvement, the purposes of which may not only be patriotic. The work of Jack's servants is subsumed into his desire for honour, in ways which challenge the mechanisms whereby military glory could be achieved and raise dangerously meritocratic questions.

CONCLUSIONS

As new markets were established in the early modern period, so were there created opportunities for professional advancement, and, in this connection, Dekker's *The Shoemaker's Holiday* and Deloney's fiction are pertinent reflections on the acquisition of status. In the wake of the changes in fortune described by the writers, fresh allegiances form and power relations modify, although this is a process that differs across the servant, mistress and master categories. At first sight the bias is conservative. Humiliation is reserved for those journeymen and mistresses who refuse to remain in their allotted places, whereas ambitious masters enjoy a freedom from ridicule or censure. It would be a mistake, however, to reduce these representations to validations of authority; as we have seen, a political criticism is at work in Deloney's construction of aristocratic practices and government policy, and related insecurities, particularly about the capabilities of masters, inform the treatment of social responsibilities and the management of crises of subsistence.

Given the mobility between the categories of master and servant in the texts, a lively sense of the permeability of social identity emerges. As *Jack of Newbury* demonstrates, the role of the servant slips and slides according to the employer's commercial successes. The servant can become or impersonate a soldier, and a master who works as a clothier may behave as an aristocratic magnate. Together these fluctuations and confusions articulate wider uncertainties about the languages of occupational classification at a critical moment in England's economic history. Even the bewildering mixture of asseverations and colloquialisms with which Eyre attempts to contain his wife's excesses in *The Shoemaker's Holiday* can be seen as Dekker's imaginative response to a society facing the obligation newly to define itself. More threatening, perhaps, is Eyre's mode of address. By associating himself with a 'Prince' (VII, 46) and calling his servants 'gentlemen of the Gentle Craft' (XXI, 146–7), the shoemaker creates his own noble status: if members of a household may assume new places in society purely through linguistic aptitude, then gentility is robbed of its innate qualities. Only fragile, learned systems can remain in place to distinguish occupational groupings, and class, in turn, will become one of many negotiable cultural constructions.

As the instability of identity is so crucial a preoccupation in their work, it is perhaps not surprising that the writers should also be concerned to fix social roles more precisely, to impose upon situations of conflict forms of closure. Aliens are relocated to the margins of the narrative, and the aristocracy, although erring in several respects, is usually permitted to recover from social displacement. While the classes merge in unexpected combinations in Deloney's fiction, at times it appears as if existing arrangements remain impervious to intrusions. A 1559 draft of the Statute of Artificers proposed that the 'artificer' and 'clothier' should be debarred from the purchase of lands, and it was joined in 1576 by an act which aimed to introduce similar measures.[38] Despite his aristocratic pretensions, Jack of Newbury never aspires to the acquisition of estates, and while the Springs of Lavenham, the Suffolk clothiers, formed gentry associations, he does not extend his influence in similar directions.

Ultimately, therefore, neither writer elected to press his materials to radical conclusions. After 1600, Deloney fell silent, while Dekker moved in his later work towards satire, masques and civic entertainments. Only in *Match Me in London* (1620–1) did the dramatist return to the more familiar territory of *The Shoemaker's Holiday*, but in this play Bilbo, the former servant of Malevento, a nobleman, is an unwilling journeyman. Little remains to offset his disdain for his new calling, as he reflects upon the days when he had 'both men Seruants and maid Seruants vnder' him and resents having 'to weare a flat cap here and cry what doe you lacke'.[39] With Deloney's fiction and Dekker's *The Shoemaker's Holiday*, in fact, we witness the slow death of a distinctive literary landscape. The fecundity of Eyre's rhetoric and the magnitude of Jack's family notwithstanding, the shoemaker and the clothier inhabit a world that is decaying even as it is being extolled. One indication of the process, perhaps, is the fact that Eyre, like Jack, never becomes a biological parent, despite declarations about his 'lusty' potency (XXI, 31). The representations of crafts and trades that flourished in the 1590s described an order, like the writing itself, already in a process of dissolution, slipping into oblivion, approaching its inescapable extinction.

NOTES

1. Steve Rappaport, *Worlds within Worlds: Structures of Life in Sixteenth-century London* (Cambridge, 1989), p. 221.
2. Thomas Deloney, *The Novels*, ed. Merritt E. Lawlis (Bloomington, IN, 1961), pp. 7, 5. For a complementary reading, see Joan Pong Linton, '*Jack of Newbury* and Drake in California: Domestic and Colonial Narratives of English Cloth and Manhood', *English Literary History*, 59 (1992), pp. 26, 31–3; Mihoko Suzuki, 'The London Apprentice Riots of the 1590s and the Fiction of Thomas Deloney', *Criticism*, 38 (1996), pp. 190–2.
3. Sybil M. Jack, *Trade and Industry in Tudor and Stuart England* (London, 1977), pp. 67–77; Norman Lowe, *The Lancashire Textile Industry in the Sixteenth Century*, Chetham Society, 3rd ser., 20 (1972), pp. 31, 42, 55, 100; D. M. Palliser, *The Age of Elizabeth: England under the Tudors 1547–1603* (London and New York, 1983), p. 250.
4. Rappaport, *Worlds*, p. 89.
5. Literary tradition has tended to conflate the two Winchcombes, father and son, into one individual. See S. T. Bindoff, *The House of Commons 1509–1558*, 3 vols (London, 1982), vol. III, pp. 632–3; Eric Kerridge, *Textile Manufactures in Early Modern England* (Manchester, 1985), pp. 16–17. John Winchcombe the elder's will is at the P.R.O., PROB 11/19/27. On Stumpe, see John Leland, *The Itinerary of John Leland in or about the Years 1535–1543*, ed. Lucy Toumlin Smith, 5 vols (London, 1907–10), vol. I, p. 132.
6. Bodl. Lib., MS. Aubrey 2, fo. 143ʳ; David Dymond and Alec Betterton,

Lavenham: 700 Years of Textile Making (Woodbridge, 1982), pp. 9, 26, 32, 53.

7. See G. D. Ramsay, *The Wiltshire Woollen Industry in the Sixteenth and Seventeenth Centuries*, 2nd edn (London, 1965), pp. 6–30; John T. Swain, *Industry Before the Industrial Revolution: North–East Lancashire 1500–1640*, Chetham Society, 3rd ser., 32 (1986), pp. 108–62.

8. C. W. Chitty, 'Aliens in England in the Sixteenth Century', *Race*, 8 (1966), pp. 130–1.

9. Peter J. Bowden, *The Wool Trade in Tudor and Stuart England* (London, 1962), p. 51.

10. Sir Simonds D'Ewes, *A compleat journal of the votes* (London, 1693; Wing D1247), pp. 508–11; Laura Hunt Yungblut, *Strangers Settled Here Amongst Us: Policies, Perceptions and the Presence of Aliens in Elizabethan England* (London and New York, 1996), p. 41. For an alternative reading, which stresses Lord Burghley's protection of the strangers' interests, see Andrew Pettegree, *Foreign Protestant Communities in Sixteenth-Century London* (Oxford, 1986), pp. 291–2.

11. John Strype, *Annals of the Reformation*, 4 vols (Oxford, 1824), vol. IV, p. 234. See similar artisan complaints in Arthur Freeman, 'Marlowe, Kyd, and the Dutch Church Libel', *English Literary Renaissance*, 3 (1973), pp. 44–52; P.R.O., PC 2/19/384.

12. G.L., MS. 4647, fos 125^r–8^r.

13. C.L.R.O., Remembrancia II, fo. 20^v, Repertory 23, fo. 406^v.

14. For useful related discussions, see Julia Gasper, *The Dragon and the Dove: The Plays of Thomas Dekker* (Oxford, 1990), pp. 18–19; Suzuki, 'The London Apprentice Riots', pp. 195–6.

15. B.L., Lansdowne MS. 81, fo. 76^r.

16. W. G. Hoskins, 'Harvest Fluctuations and English Economic History, 1480–1619', *Agricultural History Review*, 12 (1964), p. 32.

17. Mark Thornton Burnett, '"Fill gut and pinch belly": Writing Famine in the English Renaissance', *Explorations in Renaissance Culture*, 21 (1995), p. 29; Buchanan Sharp, *In Contempt of All Authority: Rural Artisans and Riot in the West of England, 1586–1660* (Berkeley, Los Angeles and London, 1980), pp. 18–21; John Walter and Keith Wrightson, 'Dearth and the Social Order in Early Modern England', *Past and Present*, 71, May (1976), p. 32. On the reduction of clothiers' wages, see P.R.O., PC 2/21/30.

18. Michael Frederick Roberts, 'Wages and Wage-Earners in England: The Evidence of the Wage Assessments, 1563–1725', unpublished D Phil thesis, University of Oxford, 1981, pp. 34–7.

19. Pierre Grimal, *The Dictionary of Classical Mythology* (Oxford, 1986), pp. 75–6.

20. Frances A. Yates, *Astraea: The Imperial Theme in the Sixteenth Century* (London, Boston, Melbourne and Henley, 1985), pp. 29, 76, 80, 110, 216.

21. William Gouge, *Gods three arrowes: plague, famine, sword* (London, 1631; S.T.C. 12116).

22. Thomas Dekker, *The Shoemaker's Holiday*, ed. Anthony Parr (London and New York, 1990), I, 118–19, 124–5.

23. *H.M.C., Hatfield House*, 24 vols (London, 1883–1976), vol. VI, pp. 534–5; P.R.O., PC 2/22/75. See also Henry Arthington, *Prouision for the poore, now in penurie* (London, 1597; S.T.C. 798), sig. C4ʳ.
24. Mark Thornton Burnett, 'Tamburlaine: An Elizabethan Vagabond', *Studies in Philology*, 84 (1987), pp. 316–17.
25. My argument in this paragraph has been stimulated by Laura Caroline Stevenson, *Praise and Paradox: Merchants and Craftsmen in Elizabethan Popular Literature* (Cambridge, 1984), pp. 154, 190–2.
26. Felicity Heal, *Hospitality in Early Modern England* (Oxford, 1990), pp. 3–4, 23–4, 392. See also Lena Cowen Orlin, *Private Matters and Public Culture in Post-Reformation England* (Ithaca, NY and London, 1994), pp. 148, 159–61, 170, 173, 224.
27. Mary E. Finch, *The Wealth of Five Northamptonshire Families 1540–1640*, Northamptonshire Record Society, 19 (1956), pp. 4–25; W. G. Hoskins, 'The Elizabethan Merchants of Exeter', in S. T. Bindoff, J. Hurstfield and C. H. Williams, eds, *Elizabethan Government and Society: Essays Presented to Sir John Neale* (London, 1961), p. 176.
28. W. K. Jordan, *Philanthropy in England 1480–1660: A Study of the Changing Pattern of English Social Aspirations* (London, 1959), pp. 335–6.
29. Lawrence Stone, *The Crisis of the Aristocracy 1558–1641* (Oxford, 1966), passim. More detailed accounts may be found in Lawrence Stone, *Family and Fortune: Studies in Aristocratic Finance in the Sixteenth and Seventeenth Centuries* (Oxford, 1973), passim. For studies which challenge Stone's theories, see Barry Coward, *The Stanleys Lords Stanley and the Earls of Derby 1385–1672: The Origins, Wealth and Power of a Landowning Family*, Chetham Society, 3rd ser., 30 (1983), p. 192; Anthony Fletcher, *A County Community in Peace and War: Sussex 1600–1660* (London and New York, 1975), p. 25.
30. George Gascoigne, 'The Steele Glas' (1576), in *The Complete Works*, ed. John W. Cunliffe, 2 vols (Cambridge, 1907–10), vol. II, p. 154. See also John Barlow, *An exposition of the second epistle to Timothy, the first chapter* (London, 1625; S.T.C. 1434), p. 83; Felicity Heal, 'The Crown, the Gentry and London: The Enforcement of Proclamation, 1596–1640', in Claire Cross, David Loades and J. J. Scarisbrick, eds, *Law and Government under the Tudors: Essays Presented to Sir Geoffrey Elton* (Cambridge, 1988), pp. 211–26.
31. *The institucion of a gentleman* (London, 1568; S.T.C. 14105), sig. Eiʳ.
32. Peter Clark, 'The Migrant in Kentish Towns 1580–1640', in Peter Clark and Paul Slack, eds, *Crisis and Order in English Towns 1500–1700* (London, 1972), pp. 137–8.
33. As David Bevington points out, Firk's initial motive in urging that Hans be employed is satiric. See his 'Theatre as Holiday', in David L. Smith, Richard Strier and David Bevington, eds, *The Theatrical City: Culture, Theatre and Politics in London, 1576–1649* (Cambridge, 1995), p. 111.
34. Stevenson, *Praise*, p. 114. For a comparable instance of the tensions discussed in this paragraph, see Henry Roberts, *Haigh for Devonshire* (London, 1600; S.T.C. 21081), sigs G1ʳ–2ʳ.

35. G. R. Elton, ed., *The Tudor Constitution: Documents and Commentary*, 2nd edn (Cambridge, 1982), pp. 34–7.
36. Paul L. Hughes and James F. Larkin, eds, *Tudor Royal Proclamations*, 3 vols (New Haven, CT and London, 1964–9), vol. II, pp. 350–52.
37. For such an evocation, see John Stow, *A Survey of London*, ed. Charles Lethbridge Kingsford, 2 vols (Oxford, 1908), vol. I, pp. 87–91.
38. R. H. Tawney and Eileen Power, eds, *Tudor Economic Documents*, 3 vols (London, 1924), vol. I, p. 326; Ramsay, *Wiltshire*, pp. 45–6.
39. Thomas Dekker, *The Dramatic Works*, ed. Fredson Bowers, 4 vols (Cambridge, 1953–61), vol. III, II.i.10–11.

3

Carnival, the Trickster and the Male Domestic Servant

In English Renaissance drama, the male domestic servant or 'servingman' is a familiar type, albeit one whose presence is not always singled out for critical treatment. Among the many varieties of the type, Brainworm in Jonson's *Everyman in His Humour* (1598) and De Flores in Middleton and Rowley's *The Changeling* (1622) are well-known examples. Invariably dramatic texts associate the male domestic servant with a set of recurring features. Deflating lofty attitudes with bawdy and skilled in disguise, he often takes delight in declaring physical needs, hatching ingenious schemes and confounding magisterial authorities. The appeal of the type also reached beyond the stage, with moral treatises, satires and ballads all contributing to keep the male domestic servant at the forefront of the popular imagination.

In this chapter, my discussion of the male domestic servant divides into three sections, each of which adopts a different but complementary emphasis. The first section maintains that the comedies of Plautus and Terence constituted a repository of dramatic conventions, which dramatists in the sixteenth and seventeenth centuries were able to adapt in their representations of the male domestic servant's trickster-like abilities. English Renaissance plays, in particular, establish that the type was extended to meet a new variety of dramatic functions. These appropriations, the second section argues, took on more precise, localized meanings at certain historical junctures. Above all, the male domestic servant lent himself to a range of metaphorical uses. Across a variety of literary forms, the representation of this type facilitated an exploration of a perceived crisis in service, as well as providing a means of addressing broader insecurities.

With many of these representations, it is impossible to ignore the carnival component. This is evident in several ways, most obviously in an emphasis on a 'holiday' spirit and the inversion of roles, and an attention to the rituals whereby the lower orders could step out of place. The third section focuses on this preoccupation, arguing that 'carnivalesque' inversion provided a medium through which anxieties about the status quo could be articulated. Concentrating on the figure of the male domestic servant in a number of dramas, chiefly *The Changeling*, this section builds upon recent theoretical work to contend that, as a dramatic device, inversion is erratic in its effects. The male domestic servant's antics in the plays suggest that inversion neither affirms the inviolability of the social order nor supports new hierarchies based upon misrule. Instead, the tension between these two tendencies generates negotiations about the exercise of power, which have overtly political dimensions.

DRAMATIC PRECEDENTS

The male domestic servant in English Renaissance drama represented the logical development of a long-standing theatrical tradition. The type's earliest incarnation was in the form of a slave in Plautus and Terence's Roman comedies, where he served the function of providing humour and assisting in impersonation and tricksy intrigues, invariably for a young master's benefit.[1] Two versions of the slave are described by the playwrights, the 'clever trickster' and the 'faithful servant', but there was little attempt to distinguish between these essentially formulaic characters, and even less sense of their contemporary historical conditions. As George E. Duckworth notes, the slaves unite in their mutual 'boastfulness and self-glorification, their impudence and insolence, their inquisitiveness, indiscretion, and love of gossip, [and] their fondness for moralizing'. 'They are often lazy and indifferent', he adds, 'and they do not hesitate to lie, cheat, and steal when it seems necessary.'[2] Crucially, the slaves are motivated by their fidelity to their masters, even when their actions take on cunning and unscrupulous forms.[3]

Of course, the classical *servus* filtered into the popular repertoire by way of a host of later adaptations. Contributing to the evolution of the male domestic servant in Renaissance drama were medieval miracle plays, mystery cycles and early sixteenth-century interludes, in which tempting attendants and faithful, wordly-wise servants either corrupt their masters or advise them on how best to develop a romantic attachment.[4] Contemporary sources were also important. The Italian *novella* and comedy, themselves indebted to Roman models, offered a wealth of situations involving servants disguising themselves, helping their masters to woo, and conducting love affairs with their employers' wives.[5] The 'fools', 'saucy boys' and tricksters of the English urban mummings, masques and folk plays were an equally rich influence, and, as Robert Weimann has suggested, their antics, in turn, echo the 'inverted conceptions' of Roman Saturnalian festivals.[6]

Given the richness of this lineage, it is not entirely surprising that the male domestic servant in English Renaissance drama should reveal marked differences from his classical predecessors. During this period, the servant's functions are increased: his fidelity and trickery are distinguished from each other or reduced, and there is a more obvious attempt to encourage audience involvement in his schemes. Emerging from these changes is a firmer sense of the servant's historical particularities. In Jonson's *Every Man in His Humour*, Brainworm is an example of the servant as a trickster. Disguised as a soldier, he pauses between tricks outside the city walls to articulate his rationale:

> 'Slid, I cannot choose but laugh, to see myself translated thus, from a poor creature to a creator; for now must I create an intolerable sort of lies, or my present profession loses the grace: and yet the lie to a man of my coat is as ominous a fruit as the *Fico*. Oh sir, it holds for good polity ever, to have that outwardly in vilest estimation, that inwardly is most dear to us. So much for my borrowed shape.[7]

In his behaviour, Brainworm resembles the folkloric trickster, who is a *bricoleur*, transforming materials at hand to produce creative solutions, and a vagabond, living, as Barbara Babcock-Adams states, 'beyond all bounded communities and . . . not confined . . . to any designated space'.[8] As the servant acts to delay his old master's pursuit of his errant son, he is also akin to the trickster in his classical manifestation. But Brainworm begins to move away from both traditions in consistently deriving pleasure from his own inventiveness. Terms such as 'translation', 'creature' and 'shape' have a self-conscious 'literary' aspect, suggesting that Brainworm has turned trickery into an art form, and that his function is to promote reflections upon the exercise of artistry, even upon Jonson's own status as a dramatist. He dictates and supervises the action, and the play as whole centres around his amorally attractive manipulation of a range of creative devices.

In his role as a commentator, Brainworm is similar to Adam, the old domestic servant in *As You Like It* (1599). Adam is distinguished from the classical slave in that he is devoid of trickery; instead, he is represented only in terms of his faithful qualities. These work to raise questions about familial responsibilities and to illuminate the servant's instructive influence. Adam's centrality to the play's concerns is best illustrated when he warns Orlando of the evil intentions of his brother, Oliver:

> Your brother, no, no brother, yet the son –
> Yet not the son, I will not call him son –
> Of him I was about to call his father,
> Hath heard your praises, and this night he means
> To burn the lodging where you use to lie
> And you within it.[9]

Vacillating between the fraternal and the filial, the speech functions to introduce some of the play's central confusions.[10] Adam's fidelity as a servant authorizes the provision he promises as a substitute father, as exemplified in his willingness to give Orlando his thriftily treasured pension fund (II.iii.38–47). The servant is never tempted to spend his money, and his attitude is that, as a 'foster-nurse' (II.iii.40), it has maternal properties. In these episodes, Adam has his Plautine and Terentian role extended, since he fills the vacant shoes of Orlando's parents, and practises a form of generosity that shows up Oliver's failure to respect his father's injunctions.

On several occasions, Adam is able, through his fidelity, to instruct the brothers in the patience which they so conspicuously lack, as when he counsels: 'Sweet masters be patient. For your father's remembrance, be at accord' (I.i.63–4). At his first appearance, Orlando complains to Adam about the servitude in which he is placed, apparently unaware of the irony of his choice of audience. The remainder of the play reveals Orlando's education in social graces – what he must learn is the endurance prescribed by his trusty manservant. Once again, the male domestic servant is established as the locus of values integral to the healing of familial differences. Not only do these scenes modify the Roman slave's functions, they also play significant variations upon the fidelity which is one of his unwavering characteristics. Adam's conduct is virtuous only from a particular vantage-point. His fidelity is never in doubt, but he chooses to exercise it according to his own subjective and selective criteria. In order to follow Orlando, Adam must be unfaithful to Oliver, which suggests that loyalty, a quality to be earned, can never be taken for granted.

Even with those male domestic servants who exhibit trickery and faithfulness in equal measure, the classical slave type is reinvented for specific purposes. In *King Lear* (1604–5), Kent, the earl who poses as a servant in order to escape banishment, represents a particularly intriguing figure. At first sight, his actions merge the trickster's role with that of the faithful servant. By tripping up Oswald, for instance, the steward who refuses to acknowledge royal authority, Kent displays a trickster-like athletic versatility and devises measures to protect the king from one of his more offensive subjects. On other occasions in the play, one of the two roles has a greater dominance. As Caius, Kent embodies the discourses of the faithful servant, notably when he attempts to demonstrate to Lear the extent to which he has usurped the 'differences' of degree.[11] While also in disguise, Kent is allied with the clever trickster in his imitated accents and witty companionship, as his joking responses to questions about his age indicate; he is 'Not so young . . . to love a woman for singing, nor so old to dote on her for anything' (I.iv.37–8). However, the trickster finally cedes place to a faithful servant whose loyalty is expressed in Kent's revelatory divestiture, in his rejection of dissimulating stratagems. At the end, Kent declares, ''Tis noble Kent . . . I am the very man' (V.iii.267, 285). To Kent's admission of identity Lear fails to respond, and the servant's perfect services are qualified in this supremely anti-climactic moment. Although the conventions enlisted in the *dénouement* are comic, therefore, the play places a tragic slant upon them. The legacy of Roman comedy is appropriated to suit generically incongruous materials, and the slave's entertaining intrigues are reformulated as part of a discussion about the nature of self-sacrifice and the forms of conduct that ideally guarantee monarchical allegiance.

With these three plays, the possibilities inherent in the classical slave type are abundantly evident. Through the servants' behaviour, the plays are able to develop their aesthetic, moral and political observations, while also unfolding the narrative. But representations of the male domestic servant, while meeting dramatic functions, harboured social dimensions and performed ideological work. As a clever trickster and as a faithful servant, the figure proved useful in introducing but not necessarily resolving a number of contemporary preoccupations.

SERVICEABLE METAPHORS

On the English Renaissance stage, and in a smaller sample of prosaic representations, the male domestic servant assumes peculiar historical inflections. Most obviously, it is implied that the values of domestic service are under threat and that the institution itself is in flux. By considering a range of contexts, I attempt to account for the particularities of these constructions and argue that their social dimensions are more elusive than it might initially appear.

As You Like It offers an eloquent instance of this instability in contemporary master-servant relations. Adam is elevated by Orlando into the pantheon of an endangered species:

> in thee appears
> The constant service of the antique world,
> When service sweat for duty, not for meed.
> Thou art not for the fashion of these times,
> Where none will sweat but for promotion,
> And having that, do choke their service up
> Even with the having.
>
> (II.iii.56–62)

As the organic metaphors of the speech indicate, Adam's paradisial landscape is being eroded by the product-oriented mentality of a market economy. But Adam's 'constant service', despite being marked out for praise, is recognized as a transient phenomenon. Almost as soon as he enters Arden, Adam declines and presumably dies, which suggests that the virtues of his 'antique world' are unsustainable. The forest of Arden, like Adam, a nostalgic construction, is similarly exposed as untenable, since it neglects the more pragmatic requirements of a return to court and the recovery of political favour. Adam and Arden are finally constituted as the mythic objects of fantastic projections. Nor are Adam's circumstances a unique phenomenon. His sufferings, which stem from dispossession and a lack of 'food' (II.vi.1), link him to Corin, the abandoned shepherd whose 'fortunes' (II.iv.75) come to 'nothing' (II.iv.83). Through these associative connections, the uncertainties facing Adam dissolve into reflections upon the predicament of a number of oppressed social groupings. It is not exclusively servants who are vulnerable to the pressures of material exigency.[12]

In *As You Like It*, it is only suggested that service is unstable – the ubiquitous male domestic servants against whom Adam's exceptional qualities are measured never make an appearance. *King Lear*, however, dramatizes what *As You Like It* bypasses, and represents male domestic servants caught up in a crisis of authority, the effect of which is to precipitate service into a highly visible predicament. Of course, *King Lear* has often been instanced as a work which utilizes master–servant relations to mediate the collapse of 'feudalism' and the decline of the landed aristocracy.[13] While such arguments err on the side of generality, it is certainly the case that the play debates conflicts in political loyalty, and includes a servant's conduct that is catastrophic in its ramifications. These questions are crystallized when Kent, not yet disguised as a servant, takes exception to Lear's behaviour. He protests, unsolicited, against the fate visited upon Cordelia, making his first act as a subject one of resistance: 'Royal Lear, / Whom I have ever honour'd as my King, / Lov'd as my father, as my master follow'd . . . check / This hideous rashness' (I.i.138–40, 149–50). When Kent disguises himself as Caius and argues with Oswald, the debate is widened. The dispute between the two servants underscores their uncertain positions in the royal household, and is additionally complicated in that, from one perspective, Oswald, the steward of Lear's daughter, is behaving as a 'good' servant, in contrast to Kent who assumes that being the king's 'man' qualifies him to be offensive.

But it is in the actions of Cornwall's nameless servant that the debate about political loyalty has its most graphic illustration, and the play is tipped towards certain crisis. His attempt to prevent

Gloucester's blinding shows the self-restraint necessary for a servant stretched to its breaking-point:

> *First Servant.* Hold your hand, my Lord.
>   I have serv'd you ever since I was a child,
>   But better service have I never done you
>   Than now to bid you hold.
> *Regan.*   How now, you dog!
> *First Servant.* If you did wear a beard upon your chin
>   I'd shake it on this quarrel.
> *Regan.*   What do you mean?
> *Cornwall.* My villain!   [*They draw and fight.*
>   (III.vii.70–6)

The exchange replays Lear and Kent's initial conflict in a more violent form, and it advances to a ritualized climax in which Regan stabs to death the 'peasant' servant who dares to 'stand up thus' (III.vii.78). Despite the indignation of Gloucester's tormentors, they act to preserve rather than to damage the social order. They respond not so much to the servant's interference in their plans but to his challenge to his master's authority, succinctly registered in the status-laden terms, such as 'dog' and 'villain', which pepper their protestations. The gravity of this servant's actions is fully realized when a messenger, in a later scene, reports that the Duke of Cornwall has died from his wounds (IV.ii.70–1). As Richard Strier observes, the news confirms the servant as guilty of 'petty treason', and stresses the importance of keeping a tight rein on explosive emotions.[14] From this outcome, a startling conclusion presents itself. A humble servant, it seems, is limited in his uses, whereas a good servant can only be militantly aggressive.[15] In its representation of master–servant relations and hierarchical structures, *King Lear* reveals a profoundly paradoxical stance.

In *King Lear*, then, authority questions are figured in terms of the pressures placed upon male domestic servants as they attempt to determine the practical application of their allegiance. As the servant's conscience collides with the master's overweening will, the male domestic servant becomes ensnared in larger crises over which he has little control. In contrast, in several prose texts of the period, there is a contrary diagnosis, and blame is laid at the door of the servants themselves rather than wider social forces. Texts ranging from jest-books to social treatises suggest that servants are less the casualties of social crisis than its most likely instigators, and that they engage in the active promotion of conflict for their own ends. Anthony Copley relates an interchange between a master and a steward in a 1595 jest-book:

> Certain Seruing-men complain'd to their niggardlie maister how that his Steward allow'd them but only Sallades and Cheese to their Suppers a nightes: Whereupon the Gentleman call'd the Steward before him, and in a great chafe saide vnto him: Is it true . . . that you giue my men sallades and Cheese to their suppers? I charge you doe no more so, but giue them their Sallades one night, and their Cheese another, and so in order.[16]

The jest privileges the master's witty economizing, giving him the last word. Censure is reserved for the servants whose appetite is translated into a form of domestic rebellion, which, in keeping with the logic of the joke, can only be comically suppressed.

For Henry Crosse, writing in *Vertues common-wealth* in 1603, domestic service is characterized not only by disloyalty but by vices which have alarming social repercussions. The author casts his polemic in the guise of a reforming programme:

> Many idle persons drop out of Gentlemens houses, who with a frowne of their maister, are turned out of all preferment, not able to get their own liuely-hood, but constrained through want to follow bad courses, & being out of seruice, fall into offence of lawe, and are many times eaten vp by Tyborne.
>
> And yet some heires of good possibilities, vnder colour of learning ciuilitie, humanitie, and some commendable qualities, are by their parents made Seruing-men, and their young wits so pestered with vice, that they sildome proue good members in the Common-wealth.
>
> To conclude, euery one ought to betake himselfe to some honest and seemely trade, and not suffer his sences to bee mortified with idlenesse.[17]

Crosse posits a connection between being 'out of seruice' and criminal offences, and his claim might be usefully read alongside A. L. Beier's findings that servants and apprentices accounted for almost three-quarters of the Londoners whose occupations were listed in the 1597 to 1608 Bridewell records.[18] But such criminal consequences are only incidental to the main thrust of Crosse's argument, which condemns service as inherently and irredeemably flawed. The profession is realized as a disruptive power, one antithetical to the 'work' principle upon which a healthy social body depends. According to Crosse, the crisis has worsened to such an extent that the stability of the commonwealth itself is at risk, jeopardized by one of its most important social institutions.

In drama and prose, then, male domestic servants are respectively the victims of or the prime movers behind a perceived breakdown in the social order. Such a disparity in perspective has a number of explanations. Generic requirements are obviously an element, but readers and audiences might be more influential factors. Anthony Copley, a court satellite, dedicated his jest-book to George, the Earl of Cumberland, and to 'the Gentlemen READERS', which furnishes a clue to its field of circulation.[19] The landed orders made a habit of collecting *facetiae* and *joco-seria* in English, Latin, French and Italian versions, and would surely have approved a joke which stimulates laughter with the master at the expense of his hungry retinue.[20] Henry Crosse elects to determine his audience by addressing *Vertues common-wealth* to 'the Right Honourable *Robert Lee*, Lord Maior of the honorable Citie of *London*: And ... *the Right worshipfull the Aldermen his brethren*', establishing a municipal provenance for himself which bears out his preoccupation with crime and idleness.[21] Of course, while these dedications shed light on the texts' contents, they do not explain them. Intended readership is never a guarantee of actual readership, and texts were as diverse in their consumers as in their ideological orientations.

If writers differed in their analyses of the service crisis, there was no disagreement over its unsettling implications. It was a matter of general concern that society and servants were critically interrelated. The material circumstances underpinning these fears, however, are less easy to determine. Certainly, English society in the late sixteenth and early seventeenth centuries was witness to rapid changes at a variety of levels. As Keith Wrightson has suggested, a developing national market in the early modern period encouraged a pronounced polarization in the living standards between rich and poor, a redistribution of income towards the upper social ranks, and setbacks for the residue of less privileged, labouring wage-earners.[22] At the same time, as Ian W. Archer observes, upward and downward social mobility in towns and cities (one effect of population growth, inflation and an intensification of commercial enterprise) steadily established itself as a familiar characteristic and was reflected in a heightened legislative concern with regulative offences, particularly in years of economic catastrophe.[23] Obviously, these developments contributed to general insecurities, but it cannot be assumed that they extended to the crisis in service described so eloquently on the contemporary stage. What might be suggested is that other anxieties about related dependent groups were channelled through representations of the male domestic servant. As the ensuing pages argue, these representations allowed several voices to be heard in the theatre, including those belonging to the elderly and to rebellious soldiers. Perhaps most intriguing for writers was the facility with which the male domestic servant could tap into and stand for a range of social constituencies.

There are several reasons for the servant type's ability to function as symbolic property, as a barometer of fluctuation and change. First, with a greater visibility than other dependants, the male domestic servant was implicated in hierarchical arrangements, and could therefore be used to illuminate the nature of related 'service' networks. Secondly, the category of 'male domestic servant' was a fluid one. In practice and in the popular mind, there were links between servants and criminals, and between soldiers (who may have been ex-servants), vagrancy and other forms of domestic employment. It was not always easy to recognize where male domestic service ended and other forms of social attachment began.

The metaphorical deployment of the male domestic servant can be apprehended at the level of a recurring dramatic scenario. A common narrative involves a servant who, after being maltreated or abandoned by his employer, is forced into extreme measures in order to survive.[24] This works to address more than one anxiety and draws attention to a number of social predicaments, besides those that affect the servant himself. In Shirley's *Love Tricks* (1626), the action centres upon Gorgon, an innocent male domestic servant arbitrarily rejected by his master, who

dresses as a soldier recently returned from service in the Low
Countries to beg for alms. Beyond the servant's disguise lies the
more pressing problem of the threat posed by a disgruntled militia.
Disbanded soldiers were seen as a social plague in the 1620s, a
period of industrial decline and intensified migration in which
underemployment and unemployment were chronically apparent. From 1626 to 1628, unpaid soldiers and sailors who had
fought in the French and Spanish campaigns rioted in the capital. In November 1626, six captains from the Irish expedition
broke into the Duke of Buckingham's chambers while he was at
dinner in an unsuccessful attempt to gain compensation, an
indication of the desperation of their circumstances.[25] *Love Tricks*
quickly shifts attention away from these events when Gorgon is
met by Gasparo, a gentleman, who proposes that the servant
should leave off his soldier's garb and travel with him to the
country in search of an idyllic retirement:

> *Gasparo.* Excellent! We'll turn shepherds presently; thou shalt
> be Phillis and I'll be Corydon . . . they say there is good hospital-
> ity in the woods, and songs and pastimes upon Sylvanus' day.
> *Gorgon.* But that were pretty! shall I be a woman?[26]

The changes of sexual identity and class location that Gorgon
experiences – from itinerant to classical victim and heroine – places
his military disguise at a remove from its Caroline contexts. In a
similarly recuperative fashion, a fantasy on the theme of pastoral camaraderie is played as a panacea for abnegated responsibilities, social divisions and the disturbances affecting the
metropolis. The exchange is less closed than this schema allows,
however. One of the 'tricks' of *Love Tricks* is Gorgon's practice
of a provisional, metamorphic prowess, as he can impersonate
an usher in a school of compliments, a soldier and a shepherd-
ess, thus raising the possibility that the military profession, too,
could transgress its allotted role. In this sense, Gorgon, true to
his name, encapsulates the dangers inherent in the classical
Medusa, an agent of monstrous transformations. Denied rein-
statement with his master, Gorgon is eventually thrown back
upon his own resources. His final 'trick' is to win 'twenty pieces'
(V.iii.p. 96) from a gull, a move which recalls but again limits
the failure of the soldiers of contemporary London legitimately
to secure their own financial reward.

By the conclusion of *Love Tricks*, Shirley has elaborated Gorgon's imitations to effect a broader critique. Because the play merges the soldier's conditions with those of the male domestic servant, it encourages its audience to ponder the relationship between economic necessity and social unrest in general. Through the servant's unstable career patterns, it goes on to question the powers, embodied in masters or even officers, that exacerbate forms of geographical and professional displacement. For Shirley, the servant-trickster is a register of a system in which structures of reciprocity may be falling into disrepair.

It is possible to see the male domestic servant figure, therefore, as the prompt for discussion about the ways in which society was able to provide for some of its more vulnerable members. Such a case could certainly be argued for the popular figure of the old servant in numerous contemporary plays and pamphlets.[27] With these literary examples, anxieties take the form of speculation about the fate of almost 10 per cent of the population in the period who were aged over 60 years.[28] Means for supporting the elderly were riven with inadequacies. More fortunate older servants may have been accommodated by their masters, although it is difficult to establish if this was a common occurrence.[29] In addition, an expectation that the family would care for its poorer relatives must often have proved impossible to put into practice. As David Thomson notes: 'English households were not normally large or multi-generational', and 'one in every two . . . of those living into old age would have had no surviving children with whom they might even conceivably have lived'.[30] If these measures failed, the official situation was no less bleak. Since male domestic servants lacked an equivalent guild structure which might have made pensions available, their position, when elderly, was especially fragile. The Poor Law acts of 1598 and 1601 outlawed begging and authorized cash payments to the old, blind, lame and feeble, but the uneven enforcement of the statutes meant that they met with only partial success.[31]

In the drama, there is frequent recourse to a narrative in which an older servant is obliged to rely upon his ingenuity to ensure material support. Arnold is the old servant in Brome's *The English Moore; or The Mock-Mariage* (1636–7). Already separated from his first master, he is sacked for laughing about the plight of his new master's lover. (She has just fled from an enforced marriage to a usurer.) Alone on stage, Arnold broods upon his new circumstances:

> tis proper to old Servingmen,
> To be soe seru'd. What course now must I take?
> I am too old to seeke out a new Master.
> I will not beg: because I'll crosse the prouerbe
> That runs vpon old Serving creatures. And
> Stealing's a hanging matter. I haue noe mind to't.
> Wit & Invention helpe me wth some shift
> To helpe a cast off now at a dead lift.
> Sweet Fortune heare my sute.[32]

Notable by its absence is any mention of recourse to poor relief. For Arnold, begging and theft are the only available options, and the familiarity of his situation is reinforced by his allusion to proverbial wisdom. He refers, of course, to the widely circulating proverb that a profligate servant in youth became a beggar in old age. Through Arnold's plight, the inadequacy of welfare structures at the parish level is highlighted. But while Brome brings these issues into play, he does not dramatize the old servant's worst nightmare. His slippery descent into beggary is never witnessed. Instead, a miraculous intervention comes to the servant's rescue. He is engaged to play the yokel father of a supposed 'natural fool' in order to humiliate the philandering usurer. In so doing, Arnold is reconciled with his original master, who conveniently witnesses the performance. As in *Love Tricks*, the manservant dons a disguise to avoid ruin, a manoeuvre which points up the derelictions of those responsible for his maintenance. At the same time, the result of the disguise in both plays is to ensure the male domestic servant's return to relative prosperity, thereby smoothing over the previous criticism of failing support mechanisms. *The English Moore; or The Mock-Mariage* has a conventional 'happy ending', but some questions linger unresolvedly. Since the temperamental tendencies of Arnold's masters have not been reformed, further troubles appear imminent. Arnold has only wit and invention to thank for being able to resume a perhaps tenuous employment. He represents a uniquely fortunate case in a society in which the problem of the elderly still remains.

Over the previous pages, I have suggested that the mapping of anxieties onto the male domestic servant reveals the ways in which this type functions as a trope, as a conductor for divergent interests. Because the drama concentrates upon servants who are out of place, or who face the prospect of having to assume new social roles, they touch upon anxieties about upward and downward social mobility. Although these anxieties are only hinted at in the theatre, they are more fully elaborated in popular verse, in which a wider spectrum of social groupings have their concerns mediated through a vicarious contact with male domestic service. A paradoxical figure, simultaneously slipping in and out of categories and fixed to a hierarchical order, the male domestic servant proved a convenient vehicle for testing the stability of early modern social formations.

A 1617 satire by Henry Fitzgeffrey, in which a scholar muses on the recent completion of his studies, brings these mobility questions into an immediate focus:

> What bred a *Scholler*: borne a *Gentleman*,
> Of 5. yeares *standing* an *Oxonian*.
> Of person *Proper*: of a *comely Feature*:
> And shall I basely now turne *Seruing-Creature*?

In their starkly antithetical conjunctions, the lines rehearse the increasingly common view that service and gentility are too far removed to be likely companions. Education, social graces and refinement sit uneasily with the male domestic servant's menial status. Very quickly, however, the speaker stages an abrupt turnabout, finding in the profession hidden advantages:

> (*Foole!*) hug thy fortune. S'fut't may be thy making
> A *Ladyes* proffered *Seruice* not worth taking?
> Who her *serues* (sure) shall be well *Borne*: (and
> *One* knowne sufficient for the *Turne before*. (more)
> The more thy *Standing*, greater (*Foole*) thy *Grace*.
> And thou farre fitter to supply the place.
> For men in seruing *Ladyes* much may *get*,
> Then men of *Best-parts* soonest they'l admit.[33]

The satire eventually dwindles into a masturbatory and misogynist fantasy in which the role of the servant blurs with that of a male prostitute. As such, it traces the prospect of downward social mobility through a sequence of puns, culminating in the final joke about the phallic rise. In this way, 'service', a yardstick against which the scholar measures his own value, is elaborated into an interchangeble social and sexual experience. For university audiences, such a playful scenario may well have been materially suggestive. According to some commentators, by the early seventeenth century there were more scholars than the state could place in employment.[34] Mark H. Curtis goes further and identifies a type which he terms the 'alienated intellectual', a young graduate who despaired at being able to gain a secure clerical position in the straitened circumstances of patronage at the Jacobean court.[35] Given Fitzgeffrey's associations with Lincoln's Inn, and request for '*Braue Gallants* . . . [his] Poesie [to] *peruse*', it may have been that the verse spoke also to students at the Inns of Court.[36] Even for this professional group, it seems, the male domestic servant brought together anxieties about the disappointment of social ambitions. The figure could serve both as an incentive to work hard and as a powerful deterrent against self-indulgence.

If Fitzgeffrey's satire consoles itself with the enticing possibilities of domestic service, in *A pleasant new dialogue: or, the discourse between the serving-man and the husband-man*, a 1626 ballad, an affirmative construction of the institution is ultimately denied. The ballad features two speakers, a 'servingman' and a ploughman, who debate the advantages of their respective professions. Once again, the male domestic servant is the basis for a comparison of professional standards, while also facilitating a more detailed assessment of downward social mobility. Initially, the servant is allowed the dominant voice, extolling his undemanding existence:

> Why should I labour, toyle, or care,
>   since I am fed with dainty fare?
> My Gelding I have for to ride,
>   my cloake my good sword by my side,
> My bootes and spurres shining like gold,
>   like those whose names are high inrold:
> What pleasure more can any crave,
>   then such content as I now haue?[37]

Although the reference to the 'fencing-schoole' may have been appreciated by domestic servants, the ballad is only incidentally concerned with their leisure activities.[38] Instead, it translates material possessions, clothes and diet into charged indicators of power and civility, elevating the servant into aristocratic echelons. But the speaker's complacency is short-lived. By the final verse, his accomplishments have been undercut, and they emerge as only imperfect markers of status and prestige. For, with his stubborn pride, earthy aphorisms and homiletic emphases, the ploughman wins the dispute, to the extent that the servant abandons his occupation altogether:

> Thus to conclude and make an end,
>   let none with Husband-men contend:
> You see here yeelds a loftie mind,
>   and to good counsell is inclin'd.
> Thus will we all like lovers grée,
>   the painfull man shall pressed be,
> For by the labour of the hand,
>   we doe receive fruits from the land.[39]

In the light of the divorce between the ballad and the material elements of economic distress in the 1620s, this celebratory note must have seemed incongruous. The real value of an agricultural labourer's wages was at its lowest point in the second decade of the seventeenth century, only 44 per cent of its fifteenth-century value.[40] Only in 1622–4, furthermore, harvest failures caused widespread dearths, which threatened the livelihoods of smallholders and labourers alike.[41] With these contexts in mind, the ballad's location in a metaphorical realm is confirmed. It alternates between two occupations to underscore general observations, invoking modes of economic management to promote industry and prudence. Even downward mobility is to be embraced if it preserves a dedication to and the social importance of 'labour', a 'loftie' virtue with which 'true' nobility can be achieved. Behind this emphasis lie conservative interests, anxieties about idleness and an inappropriate and potentially disruptive display of symbolic social forms. Ultimately, servants as well as ploughmen play only subsidiary parts to a grander moral and political imperative.

To recapitulate, I have argued that representations of the male domestic servant were chronologically specific and dictated, in part, by particular economic crises. I have also suggested that the servant could work in a metaphorical capacity to discharge broader anxieties and pass social comment. Implicit in my account has been the assumption that literary texts answered the needs of a multiplicity of audiences, one aspect of the different meanings which they brought into play. Some dramas, notably those by Brome and Shirley, were written for more privileged companies and exclusive theatres such as the Phoenix or the Salisbury Court. Other plays, such as Shakespeare's, were given popular and royal performances. None of the dramatists, however, spoke for identical agendas or interests. In addition, the mixed composition of some theatre audiences ensured that the same drama could take on different meanings in a variety of playing locations.[42] As the servant attracted the greatest interest in the theatre, it may have been that actors and dramatists, who were themselves 'servants' and bound to an uncertain economic matrix, looked to the type as a coded representative of their own material experience.

What was true for the theatre may also have applied to the non-dramatic forms in which the male domestic servant was so rich a resource. *Ephemerides*, in particular, were increasingly popular, with a survey of inventories initially establishing the landed orders as prominent consumers. In 1585, Thomas Marshe, a London bookseller, sued Edward Wingfield, a Huntingdonshire gentleman, for unpaid items, including chapbooks, ballads, romances and newsbooks, while Sir Roger Townshend entered murder pamphlets in his 1625 library catalogue.[43] Judging from other materials, however, the popularity of *ephemerides* was both socially broad and geographically diverse. A list compiled in 1575 by Captain Cox, a Coventry mason, consisted of over 60 satires, merry tales and almanacs, and invites comparison with Nicholas Bownd's 1595 remark that 'you shall sooner see one of these newe Ballades' in 'the shops of Artificers, and cottages of poore husbandmen'.[44] In a developing literate culture, moreover, servants may have been able to share in the masters' reading pastimes, and even to find in apparently conservative constructions of their lives subversive implications. It is clear that a number of domestic servants were able to read, which would explain the following comment passed in a 1603 treatise.[45] The 'Seruing-man', it complains, spends his 'whole life in vaine reading' of 'the Court of *Venus*, the Pallace of Pleasure, *Guy* of *Warwicke*, *Libbius* and *Arthur*, *Beuis* of *Hampton*, the wise men of *Goatam*, *Scoggins* Ieasts, *Fortunatus*, and those new delights that haue succeeded these'.[46] These observations would have had made little sense if some servants, at least, were not readers, and they confirm that the escalating consumption of texts cannot be underestimated.

As these comments suggest, ephemeral literary forms were found wanting in some quarters as they neglected 'serious' concerns in favour of frivolous, comic escapism. Throughout this account, however, I have stressed laughter's importance as a mediating device, and the social dimensions implicated in its deployment. In several plays, a humorous, usually last-minute intervention serves to blur a logic which might otherwise push the discussion through to a realignment of fractured master and servant parties. With a smaller group of texts, such as jest-books, a comic twist dissipates anxieties, relocating them to sites of ridicule. Through laughter, injuries could be healed and differences forgotten in reconcilement. Laughter, of course, is also intimately linked to carnival, a period of release in which the reconciling of differences took an institutionalized form.[47] One of the most common scenarios in the theatre, and in a smaller number of pamphlets, involves a male domestic servant who usurps his master's position, a familiar carnival manoeuvre.[48] It was in carnival where anxieties about the social order were granted their ultimate release.

SERVANT INVERSIONS, CARNIVAL MANOEUVRES

In this section, I direct my discussion mainly towards dramas in which the male domestic servant's inversive behaviour occupies a central place. As the narrative of the servant changing roles unfolds, conflicting energies become apparent – subversive tendencies, claims to power and efforts to institute closure. A comparison suggests itself here with Richard Wilson's assessment of carnival, which, he argues, 'was never a single, unitary symbolic system in the Renaissance, but a discourse over which constant struggle was waged by competing social groups'.[49] It is in the 'carnivalesque' moments enjoyed by the male domestic servant, I suggest, that a critique of the social order assumes its most elaborate articulation.

Expressions of institutionalized inversion were central to festive practices in England in the late sixteenth and early seventeenth centuries. At particular times of the year, inversion could be engineered through gender reversals and cross-dressed performances.

Over Hocktide, women were permitted to bind the men of the parish, only releasing them for a fee, while men disguised themselves as Maid Marian during the annual May games.[50] Primarily, it seems, normally subordinated youth groups played important parts on such occasions, and delighted in their levelling, mocking impulses. Over the 'Twelve Days' of Christmas, for instance, town and church corporations appointed a 'lord of misrule', sometimes from the ranks of domestic servants, and sponsored the provision of meals for local children as part of the so-called 'feast of fools'.[51] Between the broad outlines of these festivals and representations of the male domestic servant's activities, there are some tantalizing parallels. Most often, the servant's inversive antics involve not only a brief mastery but also a change of identity, leading, in some cases, to promotion and the enjoyment of a new authority. To facilitate his affair with a smith's wife, a prior in *The Cobler of Caunterburie*, a 1590 jest-book, dresses himself as a scullion. On one occasion, he is ill and Tom, the prior's kitchen-boy, takes his place. In the darkness the unfaithful wife cannot tell the difference between the master and the servant, and Tom enjoys her favours: 'the Scull . . . entred Commens [he has sex with the smith's wife] . . . and with that got him away without saying one worde'.[52] Like other pamphlets of the period in which a male domestic servant takes on a metonymical sexual mastery, woos his lady and sexually displaces his employer, humour arises from the wife's lack of discrimination, the refusal to respect the master's superior status and the possibilities inherent in the servant's slippery impersonations.[53]

In the drama, the male domestic servant's inversions, in contrast, are discovered as a more openly parodic imitation of the master's lifestyle. Cooke's play, *Greene's Tu Quoque* (1611–12), compares the situation of Staines, a gentleman who falls upon hard times, with that of Bubble, his servant, who is the surprised recipient of his uncle's fortune. Staines solicits Bubble for service, and the servingman-turned-gentleman, resplendent in new finery, replies in grandiloquent terms that bear a suspicious similarity to those once used by his master:

> I wil not stand with you for such a matter, because you have beene my master, but otherwise, I will entertaine no man without some Knights or Ladies Letter for their behaviour. *Gervase* I take it is your christen name.[54]

The use of the first name insists even further upon Staines's debasement. Coupled with the reference to convention in the form of a recommendation, it draws attention to Bubble's increasingly inflated vision of himself. Such servant behaviour assumes a more exaggerated cast in Massinger's *The Great Duke of Florence* (1627), which replays the inversive scenario in a higher social setting. Calandrino, servant to the nephew of the Duke of Florence, accompanies his master to court, where he feels obliged to take account of his new circumstances by instructing himself in 'correct' behaviour. But his lessons are to little avail, for he is soon posturing in a gauche attempt at *politesse*. He so mangles a message to the Duchess of Urbin that she gives him ten ducats for entertaining her with his ineptitude. Whether these servants agitate to be accepted as gentlemen or as courtiers, their actions are framed in terms of deviations from or reinventions of a masterly code of conduct.

At first sight, the effects of such inversions betray a conservative bias. A familiar formula of dislocation and subsequent reintegration serves the purpose of underlining the differences between social groupings. Derelictions in the male domestic servant's behaviour are absorbed into a drive towards conformity and obedience, and in his impersonations lie the seeds of an eventual reacceptance into society. Although *The Cobler of Caunterburie* concludes with the scullion being appointed to the prior's position, the essential features of the hierarchy are unaffected: the religious order still exercises a far-reaching influence, and Tom is incorporated into the *status quo* after having opposed it. With the drama, the male domestic servant's return to order is often accompanied by scenes of ritualistic humiliation. In *Greene's Tu Quoque*, Bubble finally learns that there is more to being a gentleman than clothes and rhetorical extravagance. His awkward courtship of a gentlewoman is greeted with hilarity, which implies that women are the standard against which the servant's lack of civility can be ultimately appreciated. When his master recovers his wealth, an event coinciding with Bubble's bankruptcy, the tables are turned once more, and the servant is brought back to his original starting-point. The balance of power is restored, and the social order is affirmed by countenancing the prospect of the male domestic servant's temporary release from restricting obligations.

In these scenes, therefore, anxieties about the instability of the social order are introduced only to be dispelled. The conclusions disentangle the confusions that have brought the 'high' and the 'low' into an unexpected proximity, and ratify distinctions of place and position, thereby exorcizing the threat of the servant's disruptive interventions. These are also among the imperatives of Massinger's *The Great Duke of Florence*, particularly in its closing moments. In the final scene, Calandrino, the male domestic servant, despairing of his campaign to become a courtier, informs the Duke of the rationale behind his impending marriage to an oafish waiting-woman:

> the whole race
> Of such as can act naturally fooles parts,
> Are quite worne out, and they that doe survive,
> Doe onely zanie us; and we will bring you,
> If we die not without issue, of both sexes
> Such chopping mirth-makers, as shall preserve
> Perpetuall cause of sport, both to your Grace,
> And your posterity, that sad melancholly
> Shall ne're approach you.[55]

Only the nobly born can master courtly manners, it is suggested, and Calandrino's failure to secure an elevated place in an unfamiliar environment offers corroboration of his lowly status. The impending union is the most eloquent confirmation of the male domestic servant's decision not to move out of his class, and, once married, he will establish himself as the breeder of a future race of buffoons. As the speech's emphasis on the theatrical tradition of folly implies, Calandrino's potency, and the 'natural fools' that his marriage promises to produce, will ensure that society remains unchanged. Its hierarchical arrangements will find legitimation in the antics of Calandrino's children for several generations.

As these moments of 'carnivalesque' abasement demonstrate, the spectacle of inversion could have a recuperative effect. One of the functions of festive inversion, it might be argued, was to discharge tensions and to channel aggression into laughter, reinforcing the social fabric in the process. In this connection, the conclusions of *Greene's Tu Quoque* and *The Great Duke of Florence* have a discursive similarity to expressions of 'charivari'. This serenade of French origins, known in England as the 'riding' or the 'skimmington', involved cacophonous music and demonstrations against moral transgressors. The object of the community's mockery, normally a husband who had been humiliated or cuckolded by his more unruly wife, was obliged to ride backwards on an ass as part of his punishment.[56] An example of the community taking the law into its own hands, 'charivari' reveals the anxieties aroused by challenges to patriarchal government: as in the drama, humiliation and inversion join forces to reconstitute abandoned hierarchical principles.

Festive occasions in England, of course, worked in various ways dependent upon their form and context. It cannot be assumed that either 'charivari' or festivity in general always pushed in similar directions. In the case of 'charivari', wives as well as husbands could bear the brunt of local opprobrium. Because communities were inconsistent in the targets they selected for ridicule, it is difficult to generalize about the effects of popular justice in practice.[57] Far from shaming errant personalities, 'charivari' may have exacerbated an awareness of inequalities, and the relationship between festive release and social protest suggests that this was a constant possibility.[58] As chapter 1 argued, Shrove Tuesday offered an opportunity for apprentices to object to changes in the repertory of the London theatres, and these occasions were often an excuse for violence. The cacophonous 'rough music' of pipes, drums and tabors could also be used as insurrection calls. In protests against disafforestation and enclosure in the west of England in 1626–32, the sound of drums accompanied the rioters, whose leaders went under the title of 'Lady Skimmington', a crossed-dressed carnival anomaly.[59] From these perspectives, it is clear that, in their festive manifestation, inversions opened spaces within which social abuses and government policy could be criticized, and in so doing encouraged the development of an antagonistic political consciousness.

A clear-cut link between appropriations of carnival practice and literary representations cannot be readily assumed. Nevertheless, it is striking that the male domestic servant's inversive conduct invariably points up flaws in hierarchical relations, in such a way as to suggest a social critique. Across a range of genres, images of the servant 'on top' have the effect of debunking authority in all its manifestations, thereby subjecting the dominant order to a particularly exacting scrutiny.[60] In *The Cobler of Caunterburie*, the scullion, by virtue of his liminal status, is able to blur the categories that keep the priory and the smithy distinct, and his easy movement between the two is part of a larger satirical treatment of established religion.[61] Punished by the prior when his deceptions come to light, the scullion plots with the smith to gain revenge. The prior is bundled into a sack to be whipped, and, as the scene moves towards its climax, Tom reveals the deception to the crowd, explaining: 'I was once a scholler . . . and then I learned . . . Liue charily, if not chastly: Bee not so forwarde . . . that you discouer your faults to the whole worlde.'[62] The revelation has a dramatic effect, to the extent that the role-reversals which have informed the narrative assume a permanent cast:

> the people that heard this collation said, *Tom* scull was worthy to be Prior: wherupon the Abbot and the Fryars . . . turned away the old Prior and made *Tom* scull Prior in his roome: thus was the Prior punisht for his Lechery, the Smith reuengde for his Cuckoldry, and the scull for his blowes stumbled on a good promotion.[63]

On the one hand, it would appear as if Tom's promotion is entirely appropriate, since a scholar is able to take up his rightful place. On the other, the conclusion is complicated by the fact that a scullion assumes power through wit and deviousness. More unsettling still, perhaps, is that Tom is allowed to continue to recommend his brand of private skulduggery to his audience. One questionable figure has been replaced by another, which perpetuates the priory's participation in forms of local injustice. The moral flaws of the religious order have yet to be rectified.

From the conclusion of *The Cobler of Caunterburie*, therefore, it is clear that the male domestic servant's inversive behaviour is the prompt for a range of criticisms of the failings of central social institutions. In the drama, however, this critical voice assumes less obvious forms, and reveals itself in a nuanced interrogation of the languages and behaviours essential to the maintenance of hierarchical niceties. One expression of Calandrino's attempt to become a courtier in *The Great Duke of Florence* is his inflated rhetoric, as his greeting to his master indicates: 'My grand Signior / Vouchsafe a *bezolus manus*, and a cringe / Of the last edition' (III.i.392–4). But a chance encounter with his old country companions signals an end to the male domestic servant's charade. The ease with which he drops his pretensions and harmony is re-established highlights the durability of friendship as opposed to court attachments. If, in *The Great Duke of Florence*, civility prevents authentic social intercourse, in *Greene's Tu Quoque*, it is the pursuit of a gentlemanly lifestyle that has a damaging effect. In this play, an inversive scenario is instrumental in establishing both the master and the servant as butts of ridicule. Throughout, their common linguistic mannerisms suggest their shared predilection for extravagance, as when Staines regrets having 'spent' (II, 163) and 'consumed' (II, 164) his fortune, only to be echoed by Bubble, who desires to cultivate a 'brave' (VII, 732) and 'Gentleman-like' appearance (VII, 783). At the close, when he returns to service, Bubble still speaks in the language of his betters, and tells an officer, 'I will take his worships offer without wages, rather then come into your clutches againe' (Sc. XIX, 2899–2901). In addition to mocking Staines and Bubble's excesses, the conclusion offers a more challenging proposal. Although order is reasserted, the distinctions between Bubble and Staines remain blurred, which emphasizes the arbitrary nature of social divisions. *Greene's Tu Quoque* pushes the implications of the inversive scenario to its furthest extent. Masters and servants, it is implied, depend upon the economy and their conduct to ensure their positions. They do not belong to a set of 'natural' relations.

However these three examples manifest the male domestic servant's inversions, they share a number of mutually enriching preoccupations. In the drama and the jest-book can be detected forces which pull in contrary directions, and they illuminate, at different times, both attempts to institute control and pockets of power or resistance. The servant's experience of mastery exposes cracks in the façade of constituted authority, to the extent that the return to order is often inconclusive. Closure appears an uncertain prospect.[64] One play, however, offers a complementary perspective. *The Changeling* is a distinctive case in that it features a male domestic servant who manages to escape his domestic role altogether. De Flores is the male domestic servant of Vermandero, an Alicant nobleman. Over the course of the play, he succeeds in seducing Beatrice Joanna, his master's daughter, wresting her from Alsemero, her husband. The drama takes a 'carnivalesque' moment of inversion and expands it into a broader trajectory, so that the entire action turns into a slow festive movement. In a self-conscious fashion, *The Changeling* describes the gradual process whereby De Flores comes to dominate and even to reform the society that has held him in thrall.

As *The Changeling* develops, it becomes clear that inversion is a central motif. Even the first scene harbours suggestions about the reversals in status that the rest of the play goes on to anatomize. In a powerful statement of the sexual desire that he entertains, De Flores fantasizes about the gloves that Beatrice Joanna has cast upon the ground: 'She had rather wear my pelt tanned in a pair / Of dancing pumps than I should thrust my fingers / Into her sockets here'.[65] The speech works at several metaphorical levels. It conjures up the prospect of cross-dressing, with Beatrice Joanna and De Flores assuming each other's clothes. In so doing, it hints at the likelihood of gendered inversions, which also entail the possibility of a switch in class locations. The passage therefore functions to introduce a discussion about the uncertainty of ascribed social roles and to fulfil a proleptic purpose. Mistress and servant change places in a preview of their approaching union and the transgressions that will consequently be enacted.

Before De Flores and Beatrice Joanna begin their relationship, their positions in the Alicant hierarchy are elaborated in some detail. Elevation and rectitude mark Beatrice Joanna at the start: she boasts about her 'Virginity' (I.i.192), treats De Flores contemptuously and scolds him for his neglect of social proprieties (I.i.225). In contrast, De Flores's lowly status is registered in the demeaning language with which he is invariably associated. He is, for instance, tied to 'troughs', 'deformity' and the 'slimy and dishonest eye' (II.i.43, 45). To adopt Mikhail Bakhtin's reading of carnival, social hierarchies in the play have affinities with the 'classical' body, 'grotesque' lower bodily strata and 'billingsgate' abuse.[66] Once their relationship has commenced, however, and their roles threaten to become inverted, Beatrice Joanna and De Flores's language undergoes one of several transformations. It is as if their words as well as their roles are exchanged. The loss of her virginity means that Beatrice Joanna can no longer maintain her 'classical' pretensions, and a reduction to the 'grotesque' is implied when she alludes to the 'common sewer' that has robbed her of 'distinction' (V.iii.153). As Beatrice Joanna begins to slip in the hierarchy, De Flores advances. It is perhaps not coincidental that Beatrice Joanna promises to make the increasingly commanding servant 'master / Of all of the wealth' (III.iv.155–6) in her treasury. Accompanying De Flores's rise to power are suggestions that the servant will come to enjoy the material trappings of mastery as well as its rhetorical and sexual possibilities.

Inversion, in fact, is not so much a characteristic of De Flores's conduct in the play as the strategy he exploits in his drive to secure dominion. At different points, De Flores compares his situation to that of 'an ass' (II.i.77) and his features to those of a 'swine' (II.i.43), and the associations that gather about these totemic creatures recall the importance of animals not only to inversive processional rituals but to festivity in general. Peter Stallybrass and Allon White, for instance, understand the 'symbolic importance' of the pig in terms of 'carnival... "low" discourses, the body and the fair'.[67] The effect of these references is to suggest that De Flores is the animal victim of a court system that would punish him for his transgressions. This is further confirmed when, in an echo of the bull-baiting spectacles that marked church ales, De Flores sees himself as a 'Garden-bull' that takes 'breath to be lugged again' (II.i.80–1).[68] But it becomes increasingly obvious that animals in the play have subtler symbolic functions. They betoken not so much the servant's powerlessness as his imagined manipulation of inversive forms to secure his own ends. A later allusion to the 'stag's fall' and the 'keeper who has his fees' (III.iv.3–40) implies that De Flores will cuckold Alsemero, and it is precisely such a scenario that is borne out by the succeeding narrative. The central stages of the play map Beatrice Joanna's infidelities and De Flores's growing sexual influence.[69] Once secure in the inversion that he has devised for himself, De Flores can, with the confidence of a 'charivari' crowd, humiliate Alsemero in public, as his boast to the court suggests: 'I coupled with your mate... her honour's prize / Was my reward, I thank life for nothing / But that pleasure' (V.iii.162, 168–70). As well as assuming a master's prerogatives through his inversions, De Flores manages to replace Alsemero, Beatrice Joanna's husband, in his mistress's affections.

I suggested earlier that the male domestic servant's festive inversions are the constituent parts of a social critique. Growing out of De Flores's actions in *The Changeling* is a critical assessment of the differences inherent in the categories of master and servant. In revealing flaws in the ruling élite and dangerous possibilities in De Flores's role, the play undoes the distinctions that normalize 'service'-centred mentalities and institutions. One aspect of the play's assessment is its representation of the limitations of mastery. Changeableness, incomprehension and hypocrisy mark the élite, communicated neatly in Alsemero's recollection of his first sight of Beatrice Joanna: ''Twas in the temple where I first beheld her, / And now again the same. What omen yet / Follows of that? ... The place is holy, so is my intent' (I.i.1–3, 5). Beyond Alsemero's vacillating efforts to justify his emotions lie suggestions about the fallibilities of the aristocratic order, and an inability to distinguish between immediate impressions and material realities. If the aristocratic order is vulnerable, then it is in its most obvious manifestation, the castle, that these suggestions receive their clearest statement. Vermandero maintains that he is loath to show 'our chief strengths to strangers: our citadels / Are placed conspicuous to outward view / On promonts' tops, but within are secrets' (I.i.162–4), which points to a fear that his defences are susceptible to leakage and exposure. At any moment, it seems, the stronghold may be penetrated, revealing the inadequacy of its claims to impregnability. To adopt Bakhtin's terminology, the 'classical' body of the castle threatens to become, like Beatrice Joanna, open and 'grotesque', and therefore at the mercy of a servant's invasive ambitions.[70] No less important to the play is its consideration of the opportunities which service affords.[71] In contrast to the closed conditions of aristocratic Alicant, De Flores enjoys clear-sightedness and freedom of movement. He exploits the practical features of his office to say more than would usually be permissible, and recognizes that his role as messenger can be utilized to his own advantage. With the 'keys' (II.ii.164) that have been entrusted to him, he is able to unlock the castle's most closely fortified entrances and exits. Making use of legitimate behaviour for illegitimate ends, De Flores reveals weaknesses in the material domain of the aristocracy as well as in the symbolic forms essential to its survival.

Even as the categories of master and servant are being interrogated, so does the drama allude to the points of contact that bring them into unexpected conjunctions. The play's critique of the artificial divisions that separate masters and servants gains in intensity since it is conducted through De Flores, a servant whose status is ultimately ambiguous. De Flores is no stereotypical subversive. Instead, as Beatrice Joanna's assessment of him establishes, 'he's a gentleman / In good respect with my father, and follows him' (I.i.133–4). One of the notable features of *The*

Changeling is that the aristocratic order is not invaded from below or from without: it is penetrated from the inside. The ascription of gentility to De Flores has several implications. First, it establishes that the play goes beyond a simple conflict involving different class groupings; rather, the action focuses upon an insidious struggle between members of a similar social constituency who have roughly equivalent credentials. Secondly, it works to question the category of 'gentleman', showing it up as multivalent. As the play dismantles the conventions that dictate master and servant relations, so does it suggest that gentility, too, is an imperfect guarantee of either social standing or ideal behaviour.

In the central stages of *The Changeling*, these interrogations are hinted at in the inversions which form so integral a part of De Flores's actions. But inversions themselves are dependent upon a complex of related factors, and are sometimes achieved only through discussion and argument. In fact, inversion is one result of negotiation, and it would seem to be scenes involving the practice of negotiation that dominate the play most completely. Many forms of demonstration are conservative in origin, and the early modern period was no exception to this rule. They entail codes of reciprocity, and are often structured and restrained in their execution. Petitions may take the place of crowd action, and even protest can be expressed with a ceremonial detachment.[72] As Theodore B. Leinwand observes, the 'lower orders' are not 'limited to a choice between quietism and insurrection'.[73] In March 1629, in the Essex port of Maldon, over 100 women assembled with their children, boarded a Flemish ship and filled their caps and aprons with grain, a sequence of events related to dearth, to a decline in the cloth industry and to a crisis in European trade markets. What clearly emerges from the disturbance, as De Flores's machinations in *The Changeling* will similarly reveal, is the measure of power enjoyed by the participating parties. Villagers seem to have been well schooled in legislation concerning the grain trade: they realized that the authorities were obliged to prevent the export of foodstuffs in periods of adversity, and that they could make their voices heard at the vice-admiralty court. The women who provoked the dispute exploited their ambiguous status in the community for their own purposes. For their part, the authorities declined to press charges against the five leaders, possibly fearing reprisals. Forced to remember their responsibilities, the magistrates withdrew permission to export and contributed substantial amounts of their own resources towards grain for the local population.[74] The Maldon crisis illustrates the flexibilities and balances involved in power relations. Governors and governed, ruled and rulers, joined in theoretical dialogue and ritual encounter to represent competing and compatible social prerogatives.

Although there are no obvious connections between the Maldon crisis and representations of the male domestic servant, *The Changeling* produces something approximating to its effect. The play's major rhythms are those of demand and return, retirement and forward movement. In many ways, it explores the strategies enlisted by characters who seek to secure personal benefits, and negotiation is a useful model with which to understand their transactions. Most obviously, it is De Flores's role as a negotiator upon which the play concentrates. At first, Beatrice Joanna assumes that De Flores will dispatch Alonzo, her fiancé, unquestioningly, establishing himself as the obedient agent of her 'employment' (II.ii.94). What ensues quickly becomes a familiar pattern of petition and counter-response, as De Flores begins to 'sue' for his mistress's 'service' (II.ii.117, 120), and it dawns upon Beatrice Joanna that services are never rendered without a request for payment. By the time Alonzo has been murdered, autocratic commands have given way to bargain-oriented exchanges. These are inaugurated when De Flores shows his mistress the severed finger of her fiancé, still bearing its jewel, a move which places Beatrice Joanna first in her servant's debt and later in his power. In a rejection of the 'three thousand golden florins' (III.iv.61) which Beatrice Joanna offers, De Flores threatens to abandon petitioning if his kisses are refused: 'I will not stay so long to beg 'em shortly' (III.iv.93). The servant is now able to claim the full benefits of his mastery – 'The last is not yet paid for' (III.iv.106) – as he drives Beatrice Joanna to acknowledge their mutual responsibilities for the murders and equal status: 'You must forget your parentage to me' (III.iv.136). Distinctions of blood dissolve with this climactic declaration, and, in the act of kneeling (III.iv.155), Beatrice Joanna becomes the play's final petitioner. No longer can it be assumed that lineage and rank ensure the male domestic servant's subjection.

Emerging from De Flores's seduction is a critique of the ways in which power is managed and distributed. The play assumes its most radical stance, perhaps, in suggesting that the male domestic servant can achieve power, not in acts of open revolt but through a gradual, persistent weakening of aristocratic defences. In this endeavour, negotiation becomes a vital weapon in the servant's arsenal. It is difficult to see a match between a negotiation model and the play's final stages, however. Bent upon securing Beatrice Joanna for his own use, De Flores employs negotiation as a tactic, but the results hardly resemble a negotiated settlement – the servant has reduced his mistress to a form of sexual enslavement. If, in the last scene, moreover, it seems as if society is in tatters, the characters are also pressed to own that it has undergone some productive transformations, highlighting the dependency of the aristocratic order on those it would ostensibly dominate. De Flores might be a subversive, but he is equally a force for the reassertion of order. Subversion, according to the play's paradoxical logic, promotes progress. The ramifications of the servant's relationship with Beatrice Joanna mean that Tomazo, Alonzo's brother, no longer requires revenge; that Antonio and Francisco, disguised in the madhouse, confess their follies; and that Alsemero speaks with a degree of insight absent from his early utterances. 'Man and his sorrow at the grave must part' (V.iii.219), he states, assuming a new tone of confident authority. Unlike his male domestic servant counterparts, De Flores acts in such a way as to strip a pervasive blindness and to propel Alicant into a pyschologically revitalized phase of its development. The social order has a servant to thank for its reformation.

CONCLUSIONS

It is therefore clear that dramatic precedent played only a supportive role in the evolution of the male domestic servant in English Renaissance theatre. Contemporary social forces exerted a more pressing influence, and they shaped the servant's metaphorical utility as well as the anxieties with which he came to be associated. Because the male domestic servant was a ubiquitous figure in the early modern landscape, the type could be adapted to meet different functions and to generate speculation about forms of social identification and even political allegiance. For a range of audiences, these adaptations therefore involved crucial material and ideological questions. Linked in the popular mind to social mobility, and in his manifestation as a trickster to artistic practice, the servant may also have signalled anxieties familiar to contemporary players. Early sixteenth-century accounts suggest that some actors were employed as male domestic servants in noble households, and it is certainly the case that the King's Players worked as tailors and glaziers during their tenure as troupe members.[75] Well-versed in social mobility, the acting profession was perhaps drawn to the predicament of a servant type such as Brainworm or Gorgon, particularly since rulings of 1572 and 1597 condemned as vagabonds 'all idle persons going about . . . using . . . unlawfull Games and Playes'.[76] Even the old servant in plays and pamphlets, it might be argued, had a theatrical aspect. Adam, adrift in a newly commercial world, can be read as a romantic evocation of a previous economic phase of actor and patron relations.

Questions about the social order took on an additional intensity at 'carnivalesque' moments, and they find their fullest expression in the drama with the male domestic servant's inversion of hierarchies. As mediated through representations of the servant, such inversions functioned as a sensitive register of social anxieties. Of course, the connections between festivity and service were of classical origin, and a common Plautine situation describes a slave who, as Erich Segal observes, engages in 'saturnalia', 'misrule' and '"playing holidays"'.[77] Although there are areas of correspondence between classical conventions and English Renaissance theatrical practice, however, divergences are equally apparent. Stuart Hall argues that 'the overflowing of libidinal energy' accompanying 'the moment of "carnival" . . . makes it . . . a potent metaphor of social and symbolic transformation', and it may have been that these metaphorical properties were perfectly suited to the representation of a male domestic servant type invariably associated with mobility and shifts in fortune.[78] 'Carnivalesque' inversions, it seems, presented themselves as the most suitable rhetorical mode within which the servant's conditions and actions could be expressed. At the same time, a political dimension informs the dramatic representation of inversive situations, for they create spaces within which servant voices, usually circumscribed by hegemonic powers, are allowed to agitate for acknowledgement.

As the discussion of *The Changeling* confirms, no play shared a transparently mimetic relationship with communal festivities.

One result of the Reformation was the prohibition of many forms of popular culture. May Day holidays were virtually policed out of existence, shaming rituals declined in importance and even in Elizabethan London very few instances have been found of 'riding' and 'skimmington' punishments.[79] While it may have been restricted in practice, festive inversion was still a viable tool of discourse, an ephemeral phenomenon with an established history and an active scenario in the theatre. Its presence in the drama of the period is testimony to its continuing valency. A manifestation of shared interests, it answered to more than one contemporary imperative, working to relax tensions and quell discontent even as it also gave rein to potentially explosive social tendencies.

In general, master and servant inversions in the theatre reveal the diverse and unpredictable purposes which festive and group behaviour could be made to serve. These are evident in the ways in which male domestic servants perform balancing-acts between challenges to existing social arrangements and a submission to hierarchical requirements. The inversive scenario may not discover servants as members of a political sub-culture, but it does point to faults in the fabric of control and fissures that were vulnerable to exploitation. If De Flores in *The Changeling* is typical of the male domestic servant in the drama, then he represents a threatening property indeed. For his macabre victories highlight the role of the underprivileged in continuing negotiations, which confirm the English Renaissance theatre, in particular, as one site among many where ritualized conflicts could be enacted and where the ownership of power could be disputed.

NOTES

1. George E. Duckworth, *The Nature of Roman Comedy*, 5th edn (Princeton, NJ, 1971), p. 250.
2. Duckworth, *Roman Comedy*, p. 249. See also G. Kenneth G. Henry, 'The Characters of Terence', *Studies in Philology*, 12 (1915), pp. 84–5.
3. Duckworth, *Roman Comedy*, p. 251.
4. On servants in miracle plays and mystery cycles, see Mirth in *The Pride of Life* (c. 1350), in Peter Happé, ed., *Tudor Interludes* (Harmondsworth, 1972), ll. 263–74, and Garcio/Pikeharnes in *Mactatio Abel* (c.

1400–*c*. 1450), in A. C. Cawley, ed., *The Wakefield Pageants in the Towneley Cycle* (Manchester, 1958), ll. 48–52, 419–32. On servants in interludes, see Sempronio and Parmeno in *Calisto and Melebea* (printed *c*. 1525), in Richard Axton, ed., *Three Rastell Plays* (Cambridge, 1979), ll. 164–70, 251–4, 281–7, 416–71, 535–41.

5. Victor Oscar Freeburg, *Disguise Plots in Elizabethan Drama: A Study in Stage Tradition* (New York, 1965), pp. 45, 49–51; Richard Hosley, 'The Formal Influence of Plautus and Terence', in John Russell Brown and Bernard Harris, eds, *Elizabethan Theatre*, Stratford-upon-Avon Studies 9 (London, 1966), pp. 130–45.

6. Robert Weimann, *Shakespeare and the Popular Tradition in the Theater: Studies in the Social Dimension of Dramatic Form and Function*, tr. Robert Schwartz (Baltimore and London, 1987), pp. 20–1.

7. Ben Jonson, *The Complete Plays*, ed. G. A. Wilkes, 4 vols (Oxford, 1981–2), vol. I, II.iv.1–7. For further instances of the trickster in English Renaissance drama, see Mark Thornton Burnett, '"For they are actions that a man might play": Hamlet as Trickster', in Peter J. Smith and Nigel Wood, eds, *'Hamlet': Theory in Practice* (Buckingham and Philadelphia, 1996), pp. 24–54; William R. Dynes, 'The Trickster-Figure in Jacobean City Comedy', *Studies in English Literature*, 33 (1993), pp. 365–84.

8. Barbara Babcock-Adams, '"A Tolerated Margin of Mess": The Trickster and His Tales Reconsidered', *Journal of the Folklore Institute*, 11 (1975), p. 155; William J. Hynes, 'Mapping the Characteristics of Mythic Tricksters: A Heuristic Guide', in William J. Hynes and William G. Doty, eds, *Mythical Trickster Figures: Contours, Contexts, and Criticisms* (Tuscaloosa and London, 1993), p. 42.

9. *As You Like It*, ed. Agnes Latham (London and New York, 1991), II.iii.19–24.

10. On some of these confusions, see Louis Adrian Montrose, '"The Place of a Brother" in *As You Like It*: Social Process and Comic Form', *Shakespeare Quarterly*, 32 (1981), pp. 37, 40.

11. *King Lear*, ed. Kenneth Muir (London, 1975), I.iv.87.

12. For a contextual account of the play's economic dimensions, see Richard Wilson, *Will Power: Essays on Shakespearean Authority* (Hemel Hempstead, 1993), pp. 63–82.

13. Rosalie L. Colie, 'Reason and Need: *King Lear* and the "Crisis" of the Aristocracy', in Rosalie L. Colie and F. T. Flahiff, eds, *Some Facets of 'King Lear'* (London, 1974), pp. 185–219; Paul Delaney, '*King Lear* and the Decline of Feudalism', *Publications of the Modern Language Association of America*, 92 (1977), pp. 429–440.

14. Richard Strier, *Resistant Structures: Particularity, Radicalism, and Renaissance Texts* (Berkeley, Los Angeles and London, 1995), p. 193. See also Frances E. Dolan, *Dangerous Familiars: Representations of Domestic Crime in England, 1550–1700* (Ithaca, NY and London, 1994), pp. 21–2.

15. On these questions, see Strier, *Resistant Structures*, p. 194.

16. Anthony Copley, *Wits fittes and fancies* (London, 1595; S.T.C. 5738), p. 123. For a similar joke, see R. C(hamberlain), *Jocabella, or a cabinet of conceits* (London, 1640; S.T.C. 4943), no. 44.

17. Henry Crosse, *Vertues common-wealth* (London, 1603; S.T.C. 6070), sig. S3ᵛ.
18. A. L. Beier, *Masterless Men: The Vagrancy Problem in England 1560–1640* (London and New York, 1985), p. 44. See also Paul Griffiths, *Youth and Authority: Formative Experiences in England 1560–1640* (Oxford, 1996), pp. 327–34, 359–66.
19. Copley, *Wits fittes*, sigs A2ʳ, A3ʳ.
20. Sir Robert Gordon of Gordonstoun (1580–1656), sometime gentleman of the privy chamber, owned a 1617 edition of Copley's work. See T. A. Birrell, 'Reading as Pastime: The Place of Light Literature in some Gentlemen's Libraries of the 17th Century', in Robin Myers and Michael Harris, eds, *Property of a Gentleman: The formation, organisation and dispersal of the private library 1620–1920* (Winchester, 1991), pp. 115, 122.
21. Crosse, *Vertues*, sig. A2ʳ.
22. Keith Wrightson, *English Society 1580–1680* (London, 1982), pp. 13–14, 140.
23. Ian W. Archer, *The Pursuit of Stability: Social Relations in Elizabethan London* (Cambridge, 1991), pp. 242–3.
24. For an example of servants in receipt of low wages who are pressed to steal to support themselves, see Thomas Middleton, *The Phoenix* (1603–4), ed. John Bradbury Brooks (New York and London, 1980), III.i.129–41. The play explodes the contemporary myth that theft was the province of organized professional groups, but eventually chooses to invest in a comic exposure of justice rather than worrying at the links that could make poverty and crime close associates. See also Archer, *Pursuit*, p. 206.
25. K. J. Lindley, 'Riot Prevention and Control in Early Stuart London', *Transactions of the Royal Historical Society*, 5th ser., 33 (1983), pp. 112–13.
26. James Shirley, *The Dramatic Works*, ed. William Gifford and Alexander Dyce, 6 vols (London, 1833), vol. I, IV.v.p. 73.
27. See Ben-Arod Gad, *The wandering-jew, telling fortunes to English-men* (London, 1640; S.T.C. 11512), pp. 32–4; *Mery Tales and Quick Answers* (1567), in W. Carew Hazlitt, ed., *Shakespeare Jest-Books*, 2 vols (London, 1864), vol. I, pp. 70–1; Anthony Nixon, *A straunge foot-post, with a packet full of strange petitions* (London, 1613; S.T.C. 18591), sigs C3ᵛ–4ᵛ; *Pasquils Jestes* (1609), in Lena Cowen Orlin, ed., *Elizabethan Households: An Anthology* (Seattle and London, 1995), pp. 51–2; George Wilkins, *The Miseries of Enforced Marriage* (1607), ed. Glenn H. Blayney, Malone Society (Oxford, 1963 [1964]), ll. 1353–71, 1560–71, 1606–12, 2530–5.
28. E. A. Wrigley and R. S. Schofield, *The Population History of England 1541–1871* (London, 1981), pp. 216–17.
29. See Arthur Collins, ed., *Letters and Memorials of State*, 2 vols (London, 1746), vol. II, p. 44.
30. David Thomson, 'Welfare and the Historians', in Lloyd Bonfield, Richard M. Smith and Keith Wrightson, eds, *The World We Have Gained: Histories of Population and Social Structure* (Oxford, 1986), p. 363.

31. Paul Slack, *Poverty and Policy in Tudor and Stuart England* (London and New York, 1988), pp. 29, 84, 126–7.
32. Richard Brome, *The English Moore; or The Mock-Mariage*, ed. Sara Jayne Steen (Columbia, 1983), III.iv.4–12.
33. Henry Fitzgeffrey, *Satyres: and satyricall epigram's* (London, 1617; S.T.C. 10945), sigs D1ᵛ–2ʳ. See also the views expressed in Thomas Whythorne, *The Autobiography*, ed. James M. Osborn (London, New York and Toronto, 1962), p. 28.
34. J. A. Sharpe, *Early Modern England: A Social History 1550–1760* (London, 1987), p. 256.
35. Mark H. Curtis, 'The Alienated Intellectuals of Early Stuart England', *Past and Present*, 23, November (1962), pp. 25–43.
36. Fitzgeffrey, *Satyres*, sigs A2ʳ, G6ʳ.
37. Richard Climsell, *A pleasant new dialogue: or, the discourse between the serving-man and the husband-man* (London, c. 1640; S.T.C. 5427), fo. 1ᵛ. The ballad is dated 1626 in Natascha Würzbach, *The Rise of the English Street Ballad, 1550–1650*, tr. Gayna Walls (Cambridge, 1990), p. 295.
38. The servingman, Thomas Whythorne, mentions visits to dancing and fencing-schools in his autobiography. See Whythorne, *Autobiography*, pp. 11, 12.
39. Climsell, *A pleasant new dialogue*, fo. 1ᵛ.
40. Margaret Spufford, *Contrasting Communities: English Villagers in the Sixteenth and Seventeenth Centuries* (Cambridge, 1974), p. 48.
41. Wrightson, *English Society*, pp. 33, 136–8.
42. For 'servingmen' at the theatres (the public amphitheatres rather than the hall playhouses), see Andrew Gurr, *Playgoing in Shakespeare's London* (Cambridge, 1987), pp. 65–6, 119–20, 133, 155, 208–9, 217.
43. R. J. Fehrenbach and E. S. Leedham-Green, eds, *Private Libraries in Renaissance England*, 4 vols (Binghamton, 1992–5), vol. I, pp. 85, 134; Henry R. Plomer, 'Some Elizabethan Book Sales', *The Library*, 7 (1916), pp. 328–9.
44. Robert Langham, *A Letter*, ed. R. J. P. Kuin (Leiden, 1983), pp. 131–43; Nicholas Bownd, *The doctrine of the sabbath* (London, 1595; S.T.C. 3436), p. 242.
45. For additional writing activities by male domestic servants, see John Bradford, *The copye of a letter* (Wesel? 1556?; S.T.C. 3504.5); W. R., *The most horrible and tragicall murther of John lord Bourgh* (London, 1591; S.T.C. 20593); Nathaniel Wickins, *Woodstreet-compters-plea, for its prisoner* (Amsterdam, 1638; S.T.C. 25587); James Yates, *The castell of courtesie, whereunto is adioyned the holde of humilitie: with the chariot of chastitie* (London, 1582; S.T.C. 26079).
46. Crosse, *Vertues*, sigs O1ᵛ–2ʳ. See also Barnaby Rich, *Faultes faults, and nothing else but faultes* (London, 1606; S.T.C. 20983), fos 39ᵛ–40ʳ.
47. See Keith Thomas, 'The Place of Laughter in Tudor and Stuart England', *The Times Literary Supplement*, 3906, 21 January (1977), pp. 77–81.
48. For examples not explored here, see Aston Cokayne, *The Obstinate Lady* (1629–31), ed. Catherine M. Shaw (New York and London, 1986),

I.i.224–6; John Fletcher, *Women Pleased* (1619–23), in Francis Beaumont and John Fletcher, *The Dramatic Works*, ed. Fredson Bowers, 10 vols (Cambridge, 1966–96), vol. V, I.iii.1–7, 73–5; and Thomas Heywood and Richard Brome, *The Late Lancashire Witches* (1634), ed. Laird H. Barber (New York and London, 1979), I.i.403–19 and V.i.2595–7. Carnival and the drama are most fully discussed in Michael D. Bristol, *Carnival and Theater: Plebeian Culture and the Structure of Authority in Renaissance England* (New York and London, 1985); François Laroque, *Shakespeare's Festive World: Elizabethan Seasonal Entertainment and the Professional Stage*, tr. Janet Lloyd (Cambridge, 1991).

49. Wilson, *Will Power*, p. 61.

50. Ronald Hutton, *The Rise and Fall of Merry England* (Oxford and New York, 1996), pp. 26, 118, 158.

51. Hutton, *Rise and Fall*, pp. 9–10, 53–4.

52. 'The Cobler of Caunterburie' and 'Tarltons Newes out of Purgatorie', ed. Geoffrey Creigh and Jane Belfield (Leiden, 1987), p. 28.

53. See John Davies, *Wits Bedlam* (London, 1617; S.T.C. 6343), sig. D7^v; William Goddard, *A satirycall dialogue or a sharplye-invective conference* (London, 1616?; S.T.C. 11930), sig. A4^v; Samuel Pick, *Festum voluptatis, or the banquet of pleasure* (London, 1639; S.T.C. 19897), p. 31. See also B.L., Additional MS. 28003, fos 173^{r-v}.

54. J. Cooke, *Greene's Tu Quoque*, ed. Alan J. Berman (New York and London, 1984), Sc. II, 272–6.

55. Philip Massinger, *The Plays and Poems*, ed. Philip Edwards and Colin Gibson, 5 vols (Oxford, 1976), vol. III, V.ii.228–36. For additional examples of a similar scenario, see *Old Fortunatus* (1599), in Thomas Dekker, *The Dramatic Works*, ed. Fredson Bowers, 4 vols (Cambridge, 1953–61), vol. I, III.i.390–497; *A Maidenhead Well Lost* (1632–3), in Thomas Heywood, *The Dramatic Works*, ed. R. H. Shepherd, 6 vols (London, 1874), vol. IV, III.i.p. 132; *The Rare Triumphs of Love and Fortune* (1582), ed. John Isaac Owen (New York and London, 1979), III, 738–45, IV, 989–95, V, 1831–2.

56. Martin Ingram, 'Ridings, Rough Music and the "Reform of Popular Culture" in Early Modern England', *Past and Present*, 105, November (1984), pp. 81–3. Paul Griffiths has found a number of instances of youth groups engaging in 'charivari', although, as he himself admits, the evidence is rather thin. See his *Youth and Authority*, pp. 169–75.

57. On 'charivari', see David Underdown, *Revel, Riot, and Rebellion: Popular Politics and Culture in England, 1603–1660* (Oxford and New York, 1987), pp. 39, 55, 100–1, 178, 254.

58. It is clear that authorities feared seasonal holidays as occasions for political insurgence. See C. W. Chitty, 'Aliens in England in the Sixteenth Century', *Race*, 8 (1966), p. 134; Anthony Fletcher, *Tudor Rebellions* (London, 1968), p. 111.

59. Ingram, 'Ridings', p. 91; Roger B. Manning, *Village Revolts: Social Protest and Popular Disturbances in England, 1509–1640* (Oxford, 1988), p. 83.

60. I am, of course, adapting the phrase, 'Women on Top', employed

in Natalie Zemon Davies, *Society and Culture in Early Modern France* (Stanford, CA, 1975), pp. 124–51.

61. Occupying himself with the washing of dirty linen, the scullion is a mediator between the 'high' and the 'low', between, in Bakhtin's terms, the 'classic canon' of the priory and the 'grotesque realism' of sexual intrigue. See Mikhail M. Bakhtin, *Rabelais and His World*, tr. Hélène Iswolsky (Cambridge, MA, 1968), pp. 19, 21, 26, 29, 39, 202, 281, 317, 320; Mark Thornton Burnett, 'Tamburlaine and the Body', *Criticism*, 33 (1991), pp. 31–47.

62. 'The Cobler', p. 31.

63. 'The Cobler', p. 32.

64. An earlier generation of historians tended to see carnival working in either a subversive or a recuperative capacity. See Peter Burke, *Popular Culture in Early Modern Europe* (London, 1978), pp. 178–204; Bernard Capp, 'Popular Literature', in Barry Reay, ed., *Popular Culture in Seventeenth-Century England* (London and New York, 1988), pp. 210–11, 217, 231; R. W. Scribner, *Popular Culture and Popular Movements in Reformation Germany* (London and Ronceverte, 1987), pp. 71–101. As my argument suggests, I understand festive inversions to function in contrary directions, invariably at one and the same time. For a useful theoretical discussion, see Peter Stallybrass and Allon White, *The Politics and Poetics of Transgression* (London, 1986), pp. 1–26.

65. Thomas Middleton and William Rowley, *The Changeling*, ed. Joost Daalder (London and New York, 1990), I.i.230–2.

66. See Bakhtin, *Rabelais*, pp. 19, 21, 26, 29, 39, 281, 317, 320; Stallybrass and White, *Politics*, pp. 1–26. De Flores's predilection for dismembering his victims would also seem to reinforce his connections with the 'grotesque'. See Bakhtin, *Rabelais*, p. 202.

67. Stallybrass and White, *Politics*, p. 44.

68. On bull-baiting, see Hutton, *Rise and Fall*, p. 157; Laroque, *Festive*, pp. 48, 291–2, 296.

69. On the significance of antlers to carnival processions, see Hutton, *Rise and Fall*, p. 62; Laroque, *Festive*, pp. 266–7, 285.

70. For a complementary reading, see Michael Neill, '"Hidden Malady": Death, Discovery, and Indistinction in *The Changeling*', *Renaissance Drama*, 22 (1991), pp. 95–121.

71. For brief but insightful remarks on the place of service in the play, see Lisa Jardine, *Reading Shakespeare Historically* (London and New York, 1996), p. 122; Scott Wilson, *Cultural Materialism: Theory and Practice* (Oxford, 1996), pp. 169–96.

72. A. J. Fletcher and J. Stevenson, 'Introduction', in Antony Fletcher and John Stevenson, eds, *Order and Disorder in Early Modern England* (Cambridge, 1985), p. 38; J. A. Sharpe, *Crime in Early Modern England 1550–1750* (London and New York, 1984), pp. 138–9; Wrightson, *English*, pp. 175–6.

73. Theodore B. Leinwand, 'Negotiation and New Historicism', *Publications of the Modern Language Association of America*, 105 (1990), p. 480.

74. John Walter, 'Grain Riots and Popular Attitudes to the Law: Maldon and the crisis of 1629', in John Brewer and John Styles, eds, *An Ungovernable People: The English and their Law in the Seventeenth and Eighteenth Centuries* (London, 1980), pp. 48–9, 51–2, 59–64.
75. Paul Whitfield White, *Theatre and Reformation: Protestantism, Patronage, and Playing in Tudor England* (Cambridge, 1993), p. 43.
76. Beier, *Masterless*, p. 97; R. H. Tawney and Eileen Power, eds, *Tudor Economic Documents*, 3 vols (London, 1924), vol. II, pp. 328, 355.
77. Erich Segal, *Roman Laughter: The Comedy of Plautus* (Cambridge, MA, 1970), pp. 164, 167.
78. Stuart Hall, 'Metaphors of Transformation', in Allon White, *Carnival, Hysteria, and Writing: Collected Essays and Autobiography* (Oxford, 1993), p. 7.
79. Archer, *Pursuit*, pp. 78, 94; Martin Ingram, '"Scolding women cucked or washed": A Crisis in Gender Relations in Early Modern England?', in Jenny Kermode and Garthine Walker, eds, *Women, Crime and the Courts in Early Modern England* (London, 1994), pp. 48–80; Sharpe, *Crime*, p. 178.

4

Women, Patriarchy and Service

In early modern England, women took up serving positions in a variety of household situations and across a spectrum of social classes. Collectively known as 'maidservants', and usually younger and unmarried, they performed such diverse tasks as milking, cooking, cleaning and assisting in childcare. They could work, in addition, in several capacities – as apprentices, as chambermaids, and as companions and attendants.[1] It was through the exercise of a number of these professional functions that women servants made a vital contribution to the contemporary labour force.

The processes whereby women became servants were shaped by social and economic considerations. At upper social levels, personal recommendations and family connections were influential. Women could be passed from one family to another when particular positions became vacant. 'I have sente you[r] wiffe a dearie mayde', wrote Agnes Throckmorton, a Warwickshire gentlewoman, to her son in 1611, continuing, 'I hope shee will prove a good serva[u]nt [for] shee hath a good Reporte.'[2] On occasions, poor or elderly relations worked as waiting-women or ladies' companions.[3] Women from lower social levels pursuing employment, however, may not have been able to rely upon such exchange networks. For both the elderly relative and the younger woman entering service, economic necessity dictated a move away from the parental home. In her demographic study, Vivien Brodsky Elliott uncovers a high level of mobility among London's female servant population. Parental death, she argues, was an important element in determining young women's migration patterns. Most of those women arriving in the capital were in their late teens and over half were technically orphaned. Of female servants travelling to London in the period from 1597 to 1619, Elliott estimates, 62 per cent had lost their fathers by the age of 25 years.[4]

Once installed in service, women could take advantage of opportunities to learn a trade, to save small amounts of money and to build up useful possessions. Wills and correspondence suggest that some maidservants profited from their experience either by accumulating modest marriage portions or by receiving dowries in their employers' bequests.[5] As part of a trajectory between childhood and adulthood, female domestic service was often regarded as a preparatory stage to the assumption of related responsibilities in marriage, and to the relinquishment of earlier dependent attachments.

Over the last decade, the position of women in the early modern landscape has received increasing attention. Feminist critics and historians have tended to focus upon the opportunities for social and intellectual improvement available to women in the sixteenth and seventeenth centuries. Their scholarship makes much of the fact that women of the upper sort enjoyed a wider education than ever before, and were allowed to cultivate reading and writing skills, sometimes for the first time.[6] Among the middling sort, recent research maintains, women were beginning to play a more important part in the running of their families, to participate in the market economy, to become politically active and to demand a greater independence.[7] There is now a widespread consensus that while these changes were not uniformly in evidence, and did not amount to open challenges to prevailing patriarchal systems, 'the forms of patriarchy', as Jean E. Howard states, 'were certainly in flux'.[8] As some women's roles diversified, it is asserted, so were the ideological mechanisms for situating them confronted with new pressures and contradictions.

However innovative these arguments might appear, questions remain about the selective nature of the evidence. One of the shortcomings of a number of studies, particularly obvious in work devoted to women writers, is the almost exclusive reliance upon an inevitably narrow literary sample.[9] As Margaret W. Ferguson states, generalizing from the 'textual depictions' of the writers' 'experiences' is a 'risky' endeavour, since it cannot be assumed that their activities encompass the entire breadth of contemporary 'ideological stances'.[10] It is because of such critical generalizations that the claims of a recent discussion of women in service are weakened. In 'Servant Girls Claiming Male Dominion', a chapter of her *Oppositional Voices* (1992), Tina Krontiris draws upon poetry, drama and romantic fiction to suggest that the 'profession of lady-in-waiting was being reshaped' in the English Renaissance. She points to the ways in which Margaret Tyler and Isabella Whitney used domestic service in order to gain academic training, and produced texts which interrogated dominant cultural assumptions.[11] Although stimulating, the book rests upon a number of speculative assertions. First, Krontiris provides no firm evidence that Whitney ever worked in service.[12] More serious is her conflation of the 'women writers' who are the object of analysis, and 'other women' who lived 'at that point of English culture'.[13] As writers and, in a more problematic sense, as servants, Tyler and Whitney were exceptional, and a representative deployment of their achievement can at best be only tentative.

With the aim of recovering the maidservant's voice more fully, and then setting it against its literary manifestations, this chapter explores a much wider range of printed and manuscript forms. The first section considers the possibilities for pursuing such a project: it looks at female-authored pamphlets and petitions before arguing that court records offer the most promising access to a woman servant's experience. In that they are mediated through an amanuensis, and do not always survive in their entirety, court records, of course, provide only a local and partial representation of a woman's circumstances.[14] But the traces of women in service who did present themselves, often to protest against magisterial abuse, are still valuable in illuminating the complex relations between gender, service and dependency. I extend the area of enquiry in the second section to discuss writing about women in service in biographies, correspondence and city proclamations. Anxieties about the presence of maidservants within the household and their relationship to patriarchal government are abundantly evident in these materials. In the final three sections of the chapter, I build upon these discussions to assess representations of women in service in drama, popular satires and verse. Across this range of genres, I argue, the maidservant is revealed as the unwitting butt of reductive patriarchal attitudes. At the same time, however, there are glimpses of maidservants protesting against mistreatment, which suggests that the patriarchal mechanism was not always invulnerable to attempts to undermine its influence.

PENNING HER OWN STORY

In the epistle to her 1578 translation of a Spanish romance, Margaret Tyler, who worked as a servant in the households of the Norfolk gentry, defends her right as 'a woman to pen a storie'. Challenging those 'men' who 'claime to be sole possessioners of knowledge', she argues that 'women', too, are entitled to 'discourse in learning' and 'arguments'.[15] If Tyler's address constitutes a clarion call for other women servants to write their histories, her recommendation, it seems, fell upon deaf ears. The woman servant very rarely penned her own story. Among the numerous women's petitions circulating during the civil war, only one can be firmly attributed to women working in service. *The maids petition* (1647), a request for a holiday every second Tuesday in the month, was written by London maidservants to secure more time with their apprentice consorts.[16] As an isolated intervention in a debate about political liberty, the petition represents a small part of larger 'servant' movement in which apprentices agitated for parliamentary and royalist causes.[17]

Other printed productions suggest that the prospect of a maidservant exercising her literacy for her own advantage was greeted with suspicion and levity. Such is the inevitable conclusion to a survey of texts which, upon close inspection, emerge as forgeries. *A letter sent by the maydens of London* is a 1567 pamphlet in which women servants in the city respond to a satire directed against them, take exception to being used as 'slaues [and] bondewomen' by their mistresses, and claim to be hard-working and religious.[18] Almost certainly it was the creation of a man familiar with the domestic environment.[19] In *The ladies remonstrance* (1659), a group of London 'waiting gentlewomen', 'chambermaids' and 'servant maids' arraigns soldiers and their masters for abusing them, so that, as 'the weakest', they are 'thrust to the Wall'.[20] This petition was probably also a spoof or a satire.[21] In these constructions of maidservants' voices, male anxieties about women's resistance to established orthodoxies are a motivating influence. The satires owe their effect to the audience's awareness of their spurious authenticity, and thereby push the idea of a maidservant making herself heard even further into the realms of the unimaginable.

If the maidservant's own voice is difficult to discern on the printed page, then its manifestation must be sought in more

unfamiliar locations. In records of legal business and the workings of the consistory courts can be found details of the conditions of women in service, which offer a richer understanding of
their social experience. In 1623, Katherine Prince, 'servant' to a
Buckinghamshire 'gentleman', made her 'last will and testament'.
It is a representative document, for Prince, in common with other
maidservants of the period, is in debt and has only her 'wearing
Apparell', some pewter kitchen items and a trunk to list in her
inventory. As Prince herself comments, she possesses no more
than 'that small porc[i]on of goodes w[hi]ch god hath giue[n]
me'.[22] From the will there emerges a sense of narrow horizons
and a spartan existence. Women in service, it seems, even in
more prosperous households, lead materially constrictive lives,
and it is only to be expected, therefore, that their voices should
have been correspondingly muted in print.

Confined to a compromising economic situation, and often
working at some geographical remove from their families, women
in service, perhaps not surprisingly, were also vulnerable to abuse.
Cases involving the magisterial abuse of the maidservant were a
recurrent feature of the courts, and they demonstrate the ways
in which her voice simultaneously stands as corroboration of,
and filters through into, the exercise of patriarchal discipline.
Susan Dwyer Amussen has observed that the 'obligation to govern
the household and correct disorder within it gave heads of household considerable power . . . and correction could serve as licence
for senseless ill treatment or sexual exploitation'.[23] Although a
complete record of the case of Mary Baker, a Cambridgeshire
apprentice, is not extant, its broad outlines would seem to bear
out the appositeness of Amussen's statement. Henry Miller, Baker's
husbandman master, was presented to the minister of his parish
on 14 April 1632 to account for her death. The informants, his
neighbours

> tolde . . . of diuers misvsadges he had geuen hir As that he
> made hir carrye her owne dunge out of the house in hir mouth,
> And had drawne hir through a pitt of water in a colde frostie
> morninge w[i]th a bond That he had put a knyfe to hir mouth
> & said he would cutt out hir tonge and that she lyfting vpp
> hir heade, he then cutt parte of hir eyebrowe, all which he
> then acknowledged.[24]

For his part, Miller reduces Baker to a parodic version of the 'silent' and 'obedient' ideal of womanhood extolled in contemporary treatises – the apprentice is silenced in an extreme fashion as her mouth is filled and she is threatened with the removal of her tongue.[25] By contrast, as an apprentice and a young woman, possibly taken on by the parish as a foundling, Baker would have had limited means with which to question her punishment.[26] The dispute has a twofold implication, providing an insight into the worst excesses of gendered assumptions and a powerful impression of a voice struggling to express itself.

What is only implicit in the Cambridgeshire dispute is made explicit in the numerous related cases, which maidservants themselves presented for the attention of contemporary justices. James C. Scott has argued that the petition 'carries a threat', a challenge issued by a subordinate group or individual, and his remark is helpful in illuminating the tensions and conflicts involved in maidservants' efforts to bring their employers to trial.[27] Women in service, for instance, singly or in groups, could file complaints against their masters after having been harassed, made pregnant or turned out of employment.[28] Jane Wright, an Essex maidservant who had borne the child of her master, John Lawrence, appealed to the parish for relief in 1579. Behind Wright's predicament lay an entangled history:

> her Master desiryd her on a certayne night to hold his back w[ch] did ak . . . whervpon the said Wright lyeing downe vppon the bed . . . in her clothes holding his back a good tyme vntill she was a cold was desiryed and entysyd by the said Lawrence & his wyfe . . . to come lye in nakyd bed w[i]th them two at what tyme the said Lawrence had carnall knowledge of her . . . the said dame lyeing in bed w[i]th hym & warranting the said Wright that she should haue no harme and that the other maydes had usyd to do the lyke before.[29]

Although it provides few details as to the mistress's motives, the deposition is most striking for its representation of the domination of one woman by another. Indeed, if the maidservant is to be believed, the mistress's behaviour is part of a long-standing sexual arrangement. It is clear, however, that Wright objects to her own part in the affair, since her reported language centres upon absolving herself from moral complaisance.

On a number of occasions, moreover, an appeal to the parish represented an escape route from more oppressive domestic circumstances. Found pregnant, women in service could be threatened with abortion or subjected to physical attack.[30] Lydia Prynne, a Sussex maidservant, testified in 1655 that her master 'had the carnall knowledge of [her] body', adding, 'I doe acknowledge my selfe to bee with Childe'. The statement doubles as a paternity suit and a graphic record of physical exploitation. In particular, Prynne is concerned to establish that her master 'did twice violentlie put his hand vp into her body (hauing oyled them for that purpose) & said hee would pull away the Childe from her'.[31] It is an indication of the response that Prynne's situation elicited, perhaps, that the secretary alternates between the 'I' and the more common 'she' forms when drawing up the maidservant's statement. In these scribal inconsistencies are the signs of a voice not yet brought into conformity with the conventions of legal discourse.

While the Prynne and Wright cases bristle with elaborate detail, the extent to which the maidservant could be forced into intercourse against her will remains elusive. From related court records, however, it can be established that women servants may often have been raped by their employers or social superiors, even if the number of cases which were never publicized is difficult to determine.[32] An unusually detailed narrative concerns a three-year dispute in Herefordshire, and, once again, it shows women in service claiming a voice, acting as plaintiffs and choosing to litigate. Margery Evans, a 14-year-old servant, maintained that she had been approached on the road in 1631 by Philbert Burghill, a gentleman, who forced her to ride with him to a more isolated spot before raping her with his servant's assistance. Despite the fact that her life was allegedly under threat, Evans publicly accused her attackers, only to find herself imprisoned on what were clearly trumped-up charges. Once released, she appealed for justice to Charles I himself. John Egerton, the first Earl of Bridgewater, was consequently called upon by the Privy Council to set up a special tribunal to investigate the case.[33] These measures notwithstanding, the jury failed to corroborate Evans's allegations. Burghill was finally acquitted on lack of evidence. In the circumstances, this was hardly a surprising decision. An established figure in the community, Burghill exercised a considerable influence, as a note about the affair suggests: he had 'many frends of power both in the English & Welsh' counties.[34] A letter from a local justice to Bridgewater spells out the dilemma in which many of the jurors no doubt found themselves. The acknowledgement that Burghill was of 'evill behavior' quickly gives way to the more substantial recognition that he was also a 'cosin . . . or . . . verie familiar frend' of the chief justice.[35] Without political connections, Evans was to discover that her attempts to vindicate herself would never be accorded a fair hearing.

The Evans affair encapsulates many of the power relationships involved in a discussion of the maidservant's voice. Its beginnings reveal the common view that the female servant could be treated as sexual property. Its conclusion points to the limited legal opportunities available to women in a serving capacity.[36] Although the jury's lengthy proceedings suggest that Evans's situation was taken seriously in some quarters, the case cannot be assumed to be typical. More often, it seems, dissuaded by low numbers of prosecutions and even fewer convictions, women servants hesitated to bring rape charges to court.[37] Richard Napier, the astrologer and physician, worked in London between 1597 and 1634. Of the eight women who came to him to complain about sexual abuse, only one is known to have prosecuted her employer.[38] To accuse a master of rape was to run the risk of losing a position of service, of incurring unwanted expenses and even of provoking a counter-charge of slander.[39] Women servants who wished to pen their own stories faced formidable obstacles. They encountered even greater opposition when they endeavoured to speak and to raise their voices in protest.

VOICES FROM ABOVE

Yet the maidservant's presence was not only confined to statements delivered before the authorities. Over the following pages, I concentrate not so much on recovering voices from below as reading them from above, turning to biographical reflections, bureaucratic legislation and employers' correspondence. These materials describe women in service in the light of contemporary social and moral requirements, and reveal arresting parallels with the preconceptions on display in the courts.

In broadly-based biographical exercises, the woman servant is constructed in terms of an ideal of dutiful behaviour, which contrasts with and also complements patriarchal assumptions about her sexuality. Isabella Whitney composed her *A sweet nosgay, or pleasant posye: contayning a hundred and ten phylosophicall flowers* (1573) to offer instructions to her sisters serving in the capital. 'Good Sisters mine', she writes, 'obserue the rules . . . So shal you wealth posses . . . commende / Your selues to God . . . Then iustly do such deedes, / as are to you assynde'.[40] Her verse takes the form of a programme for ensuring heavenly blessings through a combination of domestic industry and spiritual devotion. In common with moral directions addressed to maidservants in the period, Whitney's collection emphasizes a model of prudent personal management: it is far from an 'oppositional' document.[41] The maidservant's capacity for executing good 'deedes' is more fully elaborated in a later account. Lady Magdalen, Viscountess Montague, served Anne, Countess of Bedford, as a girl. Her experience is related in Richard Smith's biography, published in 1609 in Latin and in 1627 in an English translation:

> She lived three years under the said Countess, whom she so diligently attended, that she did not only perform the office of her gentlewoman, but in the absence of her chambermaid discharged her service also, being ready . . . whensoever the Countess called . . . to rise out of her bed and diligently to attend her. Yea, the right noble virgin being delicately educated did not disdain . . . to perform that base kind of service which curious ears refuse to hear related.[42]

The passage first identifies the place of a 'gentlewoman' and a 'chambermaid' in the household hierarchies. It goes on to blur the distinctions between the two offices as part of its commendatory imperative.[43] At the same time, however, the author suggests that the servant's attitude to the disposal of waste products is the paradoxical guarantee of her obedient efficiency. It is in Lady Magdalen's willingness to function as a factotum that the proof of her 'perfect' service resides.

Catherine Belsey has written: '"Hearth and home", "the bosom of the family": the phrases . . . [isolate] women in a private realm of domesticity which is seen as outside politics and therefore outside the operations of power.'[44] This is one effect of biographical reflections upon the woman servant: 'good' conduct establishes her in a domestic location while also outlawing a more extensive range of behavioural possibilities. The counter-image to these ideals was the woman servant who collapsed distinctions for her own ends, and whose 'deedes' could be construed as socially disruptive. Encomiums centred upon maidservants were perhaps related to more widespread expectations that a period in service would encourage restlessness in women and even create undesirable material prospects. Viewed as particularly troublesome by the authorities were maidservants who confused occupational categories by dressing extravagantly. In 1611 the Common Council in London ruled against those waiting-women and chambermaids who flouted the sumptuary laws by parading in large ruffs, lace trimmings, fine petticoats and fancy aprons and ribbons.[45] For a number of contemporaries, then, domestic service was a profession that could exacerbate women's traditional disorderly tendencies. Adam Martindale, the Lancashire Presbyterian divine, commented in his diary in 1625 that local dress regulations prompted his sister, Jane, to leave home: 'These limitations I suppose she did not very well approve, but having her father's spirit, and her mother's beauty, no persuasion would serve, but up she would [to London] to serve a ladie as she hoped to doe, being ingenious at her needle.'[46] At issue in Martindale's entry is his sister's conception of service as a preferable alternative to a restrictive parental environment. Like her contemporaries in the capital, Jane Martindale looks to the manipulation of woven materials in service as an opportunity to establish independence.

One anxiety underpinning male objections to maidservants' behaviour may well have been that an experience of service could lead to new connections and alliances. In service, women were able to enjoy mutual intimacies that sometimes threatened to collide with the strictures of patriarchal discipline.[47] Comments by mistresses upon their female servants suggest such possibilities. Jane, Countess of Feria, wrote to Sir Thomas Stradling in 1567 about the death of his daughter, Damasyn: 'she loved me as a syster, and served me w[i]th such fidelitye . . . as no woman lyvinge . . . could vau[n]t them selves of soe wise, noble, vertuous, lovynge, carefull, nor able a servant as I.'[48] A servant whose devotion was equal to that of a close relative may also have been privy to her mistress's confidences. Although this is difficult to substantiate, it is implicit in a number of contemporary references. Writing to her husband in 1618, Lady Elizabeth Compton set out her domestic requirements:

Also I would have two Gentlewomen lesse one should be sicke or have some other Lett. Also believe that it is an undecent thing for a Gentlewoman to stand mumping alone when God hath bestow[ed] their Lord & Lady with a great Estate.

Also when I ride a hunting or a hawking, or travel from one House to another; I will have them attending. So for either of those said Women I must & will have for either of them a horse.[49]

Clearly emerging from Compton's letter is her wish for female company. The gentlewoman attendant is seen not only as a sign of the mistress's social standing but also as the practitioner of distinguished conversational abilities. In accompanying her mistress, the servant is obliged to take an active interest in her affairs, to participate in pursuits from which the husband is conspicuously excluded.

Contacts between mistresses and maidservants opened spaces within which familiarities could be exchanged; they also represented a relationship beyond the immediate reach of the master's authority. When masters recommend particular women servants in their correspondence, it is striking that they stress their qualities of sobriety and honesty, as if apprehensive about the dangers of loose speech or private conference.[50] In particular, the potential for the maidservant to influence the mistress was a recurring subject. Sir John Gostwick, a Bedfordshire gentleman, wrote to his son in about 1540: 'lett your wife never have but one woman to wayt uppon her, but in anie wise lett the woman be bothe sad & discrete, or els she may do you & your wyfe much harme & displeasure.'[51] Henry Percy, the Earl of Northumberland, advised his son in 1609: 'Grip into your hands what power soever you will of government, yet will there be certain persons about your wife that you shall never reduce . . . her women . . . will ever talk and ever be unreasonable.'[52] Encapsulated in these comments are magisterial convictions, which express themselves as envy, frustration and a fear of disempowerment.

Between constructions of women in service 'from above', and the attempts made by maidservants themselves to speak, there are revealing points of contact. The inability of the maidservant to pen her own story is caught up in the need to confine her to silence, an imperative that is itself shaped by the proximity of women servants to the mistress and the rhythms of the household. Magisterial abuse, therefore, can be read as an articulation of the fear that women servants constituted a domestic danger: violence answered to specific convictions as well as to more general gendered frustrations.[53] Over the following pages, I discuss representations of women in service in the 'imaginative' literature of the period as seen through the lens of these pervasive patriarchal attitudes.

IMAGINING SERVICE, REPRESENTING PATRIARCHY

Seeking to establish the ways in which women in service were represented in the drama, satires and pamphlets of the English Renaissance, one initially faces several interpretative difficulties. It is not always possible, for instance, to separate out representations of maidservants from constructions of women in general.[54] What is clear is that stereotypical attitudes towards women, when mapped onto women servants, assumed new dimensions and may have had serious material repercussions. Stereotypes of women could take on more dangerous meanings if juxtaposed with the views that circulated about a maidservant's sexuality, while popular expectations about maidservants were sharpened by competing interpretations of women's behaviour. As servants and women, maidservants were twice disadvantaged in contemporary ideologies. Women in service were subject to a double bind, which could lend covert justification to prevailing assumptions while also pushing them in some fresh directions.

Two dominant features stand out from representations of the woman servant, in which questions about social location and sexual determination are crucially linked.[55] First, representations tend to associate the maidservant with a menial social place, as the objections of Lady Coelia in Simon Baylie's play, *The Wizard* (*c.* 1620–40?), demonstrate. She is enraged not so much by her lover's infidelity as his attraction to a woman of lowly status: 'fie Sir, no Sutor of mine shall with my consent fling him self away upon a waiting gentlewoman,' she exclaims.[56] Secondly, the maidservant is imagined in terms of an all-consuming sexuality, whether this takes the form of a desire for marriage or the expression of libidinal requirements. As a by-product of these features, representational distinctions between different forms of female domestic service are flattened or erased. Irrespective of their precise professional capacity, women servants are represented as similarly disempowered and motivated by comparable behaviours. In this way, the woman servant reaffirms patriarchal discipline and functions as a rationale for its continued existence.

Examples of these representational manoeuvres abound in the drama of the period. An oft-repeated situation involves a maidservant who is keen to enter marriage. The older waiting-woman, for whom marriage is a social necessity, was a popular figure, and behind her imagined circumstances lay the material experience of poorer women forced to accept positions of service with more prosperous relatives. In Edward Sharpham's *The Fleire* (1605–6), the elaboration of the character of Fromago, a waiting-gentlewoman, is typical. Taking offence when complimented by Petoune, she remarks: 'and ye come to begin your knauerie on me, ile take you down.'[57] For Fromago, an older, single woman, it is difficult to imagine being found attractive, and her disbelief echoes the association between youth and physical desirability in contemporary sexual discourses. When Petoune proposes marriage, Fromago accordingly adopts a different attitude: 'when shal we be maried? by my troth I ask you, because I haue beene so often deceiued' (IV.i.44–5). While comically modelling Fromago as a disappointed lover, the play simultaneously reflects upon the ways in which marriage functions as a passport to a respectable social identity. Building upon this theme, Beaumont and Fletcher in *The Scornful Lady* (1613–16) explore the predicament of Abigail, a waiting-gentlewoman. 'Alasse poore Gentlewoman, to what a misery hath age brought thee? to what scurvy Fortune?' she laments, as she casts about for a suitor, eventually deciding to compromise and settle upon an elderly curate.[58] As a maidservant without a dowry, Abigail is restricted in her marital opportunities, in contrast to her mistress, the 'scornful lady', whose moneyed privileges allow her to entertain a range of suitors. As Sharpham had done before them, Beaumont and Fletcher point to the links between gendered attitudes, social freedoms and economic resources.

Judging from a broader range of representations, it was not so much the woman servant's desire for marriage as the lengths to which she would go to achieve it that vexed the popular imagination. A recurring scenario involves younger women servants who are prepared to win a husband at any cost. Thus Astutta, the 'servant' to Flavia, the daughter of a senator, in Brome's *The Novella* (1632–3), promises to help her mistress to gain the man she loves only on certain conditions:

> Now Mistris if I chance to set the sadle
> On the right horse; that is, to place your Mayden-head
> Where you would faine bestow it, I trust you will
> Out of your store reward me with a dowry
> Fit to convey me to a *Tradesmans* Bed.[59]

Astutta's ingenuity in assisting her mistress is prompted solely by mercenary motives. Concerned about her possible unmarketability, this well-connected maidservant even contemplates abandoning her lofty ambitions and accepting a tradesman: the rank of the husband is of less importance than the security that a marriage will provide.

More extreme than marital intrigue is the woman servant's participation in domestic crime. Although some women in service chose to marry their masters or relatives, literary representations rarely addressed the prospect. This is not entirely surprising, since a legitimized cross-occupational union introduced a host of tricky domestic and governmental considerations.[60] A small sample of murder pamphlets, however, concerns itself with women servants who, striving to match themselves with their masters, play a key part in bringing about their mistress' deaths. In a publication of 1607, a Lincolnshire tailor plots his wife's downfall. He is aided and abetted by Anne Pottes, a 'seruant' who 'had some little hope to prooue the wife to her Maister, if her mistresse or dame had but once bidden the worlde good night'.[61] But any such hope is dashed when her master, having asphyxiated his wife, marries a local widow. In *The unnaturall father* (1621), John Taylor describes John Rowse, a Surrey fishmonger, and his wife, who, 'wanting a Maidseruant, did entertain . . . *Iane Blundell*, who in short time was better acquainted with her Masters bed then honesty required'. Rowse's wife dies of grief, leaving him and 'his Whore . . . free to vse their . . . vngodly embracements'.[62] Presumably reluctant to exercise his newfound freedom, Rowse marries a third woman before deciding, apparently arbitrarily, to kill his step-children. With both pamphlets, blame among the characters is unevenly distributed, for it is the maidservant who is represented as the focus of criminal responsibility. The narratives offer an explanation for the murders by locating the causes not so much in the husbands' frustrations as the maidservants' aspirations, thereby deflecting attention away from the role taken by a masculine agency. Ultimately, therefore, the moral slant placed upon sexual opportunism has the effect of reinforcing myths about men's weaknesses and women's dissimulations.

With these and other marriage narratives, the maidservant's actions constitute extreme realizations of the dangerous influences that women were stereotypically thought to exercise. Particular preoccupations centre upon the implications of the need to secure a 'good match', and the social losses involved for a master who falls victim to his maidservant's designs. But the representation of the marriage-seeking woman servant differed across generic categories, only reaching its fullest exposition in the prose pamphlet. With its looser literary format and broader field of social circulation, the pamphlet appealed as the most appropriate medium to explore questions about women, service and patriarchal anxiety. The frequency with which the marriage scenario recurs, moreover, points to a more pressing ideological imperative. Because of the long apprenticeships their future husbands served, Vivien Brodsky Elliott argues, some maidservants were obliged to wait until their mid-to late twenties before contracting marriages.[63] In literary representations, accordingly, can be detected an urge to fix a social body that was single and mobile. Viewed as anomalous subjects needing to be placed, women servants, almost of necessity, were imagined in relation to mechanisms that subordinated them to the authority of central social institutions.

A further consideration is the emphasis placed upon marriage as a mode of containment for an otherwise free-floating sexuality. It is certainly the case that contemporary dramatic representations showed the maidservant's marital requirements and her sexual ambitions as close companions. Indeed, the woman servant in pursuit of marriage is invariably discovered as sexually voracious.[64] In Massinger's *The Great Duke of Florence* (1627), Lidia, the daughter of a court tutor, is saluted by Sanazarro, while her 'servant', Petronella, looks on jealously: 'I am her Gentlewoman, wil he not / Kisse me to? This is course ifaith.'[65] She means that a kiss is customary ('course'), but the joke is that she unknowingly simultaneously displays the 'coarseness' of her inclinations in demanding sexual attentions. The anonymous play, *The Wasp* (*c.* 1630–38?), develops the idea: Gilbert greets Luce, the 'woman' of the Countess of Claridon, saying: 'Thou woldst ha bene a good wife fer a bucher, tho lovst flesh so well.'[66] Here in abundance are suggested associations between sex and consumption, and the underlying notion that the woman servant can only be a basic creature of primal physical appetite.

If the woman servant is usually imagined as socially disadvantaged and sexually needy, then it is only a small step to the expectation that her body is readily accessible. Across a range of generic representations can be found situations in which the maidservant serves as the object of fantastic sexual projections. In a satire by William Goddard dated 1615, a gossipy household conversation unfolds:

> If you were wise then you would nere ask why
> My Ladyes womans tayle soe oft doth crie
> Alas her vardingales' a doore soe wide
> As it letts more winde in then t'can abide
> *And thats the cause (Indeed I doe not lie)*
> *Which makes my Ladies womans taile soe crie.*[67]

Upon the suggestion of an open sexuality the humour turns. The association of the tail with the woman's genitalia in the English Renaissance was proverbial, but much of the verse's additional impact derives from the innuendo of 'crie', which can connote both the secretion of fluids and a release of noise. The maidservant is seen to be recovering from a series of sexual encounters while also welcoming further contact: she is simultaneously mocked for an inability to control her bodily functions and reified into a malfunctioning orifice.

SPECTACLES OF ABUSE

To the particular social and sexual inflections placed upon maidservants, contemporary representations suggest, material consequences were attached. The implementation of a dominant ideological perspective was a crucial element in the elaboration of the maidservant as a type easily subjected to abuse. As the ensuing pages suggest, representations of the abused woman servant provide a key with which to unlock contemporary anxieties. In scenes of belittlement or punishment, the effects of a reductive treatment are stressed, and the role of the magisterial class in situations of domestic conflict is brought into focus.

Growing out of popular attitudes is the conviction that the master can use the maidservant as he pleases. So insistent is the drive to draw the maidservant in predominantly sexual terms that her vulnerability to the master's desire assumes all the trappings of a literary convention. At a further remove, as we will see, such representational practices lend paradoxical approval to more extreme positions still, especially those that seek justification in the mentality of rape. Contemporary satires regard the chambermaid as a legitimate target for the master's dalliance, as an early seventeenth-century rhyme about the foibles of the Northamptonshire gentry testifies. 'One beares in his *Pockett Dice'*, it runs, 'the *other* hath an *Iron Vice* / To lock up the *Chamber Mayde*; but turnes his *Wife* to an *other Trade'*.[68] While the chambermaid is retained for purposes of sexual diversion, it is implied, the wife must bear the burden of producing heirs to secure the family line. The inevitable consequence of this abuse of master–maidservant relations, pregnancy, is generally placed in a comic light. *The mous-trap*, a 1606 pamphlet, contains the following verse:

> Madam *Rugosa* knowes not where to finde,
>   one chamber-maid of ten, that likes her mind.
> But still my Lord (on proofe of comely charge)
>   Prefers them to his Seruing-men in mariage.[69]

The 'comely charge' is, of course, the child, presumably the lord's, with which the chambermaid is pregnant. It is this situation that necessitates the hasty marriage contract, and a subsidiary idea is that the chambermaid, because of her condition, is no longer attractive to her master or available for his sexual gratification. The force of the joke depends upon an interplay of several levels of awareness and ignorance, and is sharpened by the minimizing of the master's involvement.

A more probing discussion of the multiple effects of magisterial abuse, which nevertheless hesitates to press the critical dimensions of its material, is offered in Dekker, Ford and Rowley's tragedy, *The Witch of Edmonton* (1621). The play dramatizes the predicament of Winnifride, a 'maid' who is abused first by her master, Sir Arthur Clarington, and then by Frank Thorney, her future husband and a fellow-servant. (While working in service, Winnifride has been in a relationship with Sir Arthur, but she breaks it off to marry Frank on discovering that she is pregnant.) Despite his knowledge of Winnifride's wish to turn 'from a loose whore to a repentant wife', Sir Arthur still demands 'Thy lip, wench', and accuses her of being 'changeable . . . baggage' when she refuses.[70] As the language of Sir Arthur's reproof makes clear, the maidservant is perceived as an assemblage of bodily parts, as an object that is his to exploit. The possibility of Sir Arthur taking Frank's place at the altar never presents itself.

In its later stages, the play explores the options available to the abandoned woman servant forced to find a legitimate social niche. Displaced in the bigamous Frank's affections, Winnifride occupies a number of positions, testing out the roles of boy page and grieving wife who anticipates her husband's execution. But *The Witch of Edmonton* does not permit Winnifride to indict the system that has proved her undoing. While reluctant to grant Frank absolution (V.iii.106–7), she spends the greater part of the play blaming herself for her husband's downfall, and her reflections are broadened out to encompass the failings of women in general. 'I . . . repent I did not bring . . . The dower of a virginity' (I.i.161–2), she states, adding later, 'My fault was lust, my punishment was shame' (V.iii.10). At the close, she is reconstituted as a widow, to be paid a marriage portion which guarantees her eligibility. As a fallen maidservant, Winnifride is a socially undesirable prospect: she must be translated into an ideological opposite to be found acceptable. As part of this process, she is assimilated into the Edmonton yeomanry, and the question of her pregnancy is quietly dropped. Anticipating a 'good report' in her Epilogue (2), she takes comfort in the respectability with which her passivity is rewarded. Ventriloquizing a discourse of personal responsibility wins material compensations, and in the refusal to arraign her abusers lies the assurance of Winnifride's virtuous future.

For a small number of contemporary moralists, the perennial fear was that the fallen or unsuspecting woman servant would drift into beggary, even into prostitution.[71] In a recent study, Paul Griffiths tentatively endorses these views, observing that most 'prostitutes were single young women, and this is . . . conveyed . . . by the high proportion . . . given the age-titles "maid" and "servant" in the courtbooks'.[72] The figure of the professional

prostitute, formerly a maidservant, is, however, conspicuously
absent from the majority of popular literary representations.
Connections between prostitution and service were particularly
sensitive, and touched upon potentially embarrassing questions
about the abnegation of magisterial responsibility. Even the
occasional warning or complaint tended merely to lament the
maidservant-prostitute's situation rather than enquiring into its
causes. Instead, the most common representational scenario describes
the maidservant as a domestic mistress, as a 1613 verse by Henry
Parrot confirms. To a neighbour's innocent question there is an
easy answer:

> How comes it *Mildred* our next neighbours maid,
> That serues for wages scarce foure markes a yeere,
> Should go so rich and gorgiously arai'd,
> As to no little wonder may appeare?
>   Oh, t'is her Maister deales so like a brother,
>   As one good turne deserues to quite another.[73]

At its most immediate level, the verse, rather than showing the
maidservant's dependency on a number of clients, constructs her
as the master's exclusive property. It is a social economy, moreover,
not too far removed from the findings of a number of historians: Miriam Slater, for instance, in her study of the Verneys in
the seventeenth century, argues that women servants willing to
work as mistresses were actively recruited by male members of
the family.[74] More obliquely, the verse, through the coy allusion
to fraternal camaraderie, finds its comic *raison d'être* in a busi-
ness-like transaction of favours. Although the humour is at the
expense of the neighbours rather than the woman servant, the
final pun, 'turne', leaves little doubt as to the sexual services
upon which her continued use of finery depends.

If the professional dimensions of prostitution are remote from
representations of the woman servant's vulnerability to magisterial abuse, less obvious forms of prostitution abound. With the
'bed trick' device, a situation arises in which the mistress chooses
not to have intercourse with her husband or suitor, and persuades
her maidservant to act as her substitute. It is in terms of prostitution that both prose pamphlets and dramas imagine these bodily
exchanges, with the mistress filling the role of the bawd and the
maidservant yielding an easy virtue for material compensation.

The maidservant accepts the charade, only to discover that her subterfuge has disastrous consequences. In *The Cobler of Caunterburie*, a 1590 jest-book, the wife of Mizaldo, a jealous gentleman, is in love with Peter, a local youth. Afraid that her nocturnal rendezvous with him has been discovered, she asks her maidservant to stand in for her in bed:

> vp came *Mizaldo* in a great rage, & straight laying down his partizan fel to beating of his wife [the maidservant], and with a whipcord all so lasht hir bodie, that the blood ran downe the sheetes: and when he had done, in the darke groped, & found a paire of shears & clipt off all the haire of hir head: and that done, opened the dore and went his way.[75]

Between sexual abuse and physical violence, as the passage implies, there are disturbing points of contact. Attracted by the promise of a new gown and petticoat, the maidservant is forced to endure a kind of symbolic defloration, the relish with which Mizaldo cuts her hair providing corroboration of a will to reduce her sexual attractiveness. Throughout the encounter the maidservant remains mute, a grotesque version of willing, wifely complaisance. For the wife and the husband, the maidservant is realized as an unprotesting scapegoat for larger domestic conflicts.

In these most extreme expressions of patriarchal assumptions, several interrelated preoccupations are aired. An abusive treatment ensures the woman servant's submission, and bodily mutilation is the means whereby her voice is stifled. Despite its violent cast, the episode in *The Cobler of Caunterburie* is a distant relation of the more conventional recommendation that women should cultivate silence as their chief moral attribute.[76] It is in such a light that the dramatic representation of the substitution trope can be assessed, and the spectacular deployment of the maidservant's abused body most fully appreciated. In Fletcher's *Women Pleas'd* (1619–23), Isabella, the wife of Lopez, a jealous usurer, arranges a night-time assignation with a gentleman. Fearing that she has been followed, she asks Jaquenett, her 'servant', to take her place on the street corner. Lopez enters and beats the woman he thinks is his wife:

> first ile beat thee,
> Beat thee to pin-dust, thou salt whore, thou varlet,

> Scratch out thine eyes; ile spoile your tempting visage;
> Are ye so patient? ile put my nayles in deeper,
> Is it good whoring?[77]

In a different context, Karen Newman has observed that the spectacle of the fetishized female body in Renaissance drama emphasizes a need to consolidate male mastery, and that women 'were frequently figured synecdochically', as disconnected somatic parts or as 'mouths, gaping and voracious'.[78] *Women Pleas'd* extends this theatrical convention in a scene in which the maid-servant is reduced not so much to fragments as invisibility: as she loses her sight, so will she disappear from public view. The processes whereby the woman servant is disfigured are here elaborated into an attempt to expunge her altogether.

By making a spectacle of the woman servant, these representations establish her as a convenient vehicle for the exorcism of male frustrations. In being scattered or reduced, maidservants are transformed into the material signs of a system that perpetuates itself through various forms of ideological coercion and, at times, physical assault. Because she lacks a voice, the maidservant is constructed as defenceless; and because she is likely to be abused, she can be made to bear the burden of a whole series of displacements and projections. What is missing in these representations is any suggestion that the magisterial class is morally accountable, and a more detailed registration of the social repercussions of a woman servant's unwanted pregnancy, such as infanticide and even suicide.[79] To such eventualities, with all their delicate legal, biological and theological implications, the drama, at least, gave a mute response. Only in the courts were they allowed to make a more forceful intervention. Equally lacking in contemporary representations, to judge from initial impressions at least, is a secure sense either of resistance or a counter-voice. Confined to an objectified status in the popular consciousness, the woman servant, it seems, was considered an unlikely candidate for a bid for personal autonomy.

POWERFUL ILLUSIONS

One of the arguments of this book has been that representations of master–servant relations opened spaces within which subordinate voices could question institutionalized authorities. While this is not the most obvious feature of representations of women in service, it can certainly be suggested that there are moments which afford glimpses of a more interrogative stance. A recurring dramatic scenario discovers mistresses and maidservants exchanging intimacies in such a way as to confront contemporary behavioural strictures, and it is heightened by more occasional images of women servants who do not yield immediately to the pressure of patriarchal influences.

Within the otherwise dominant construction of the woman servant as vulnerable, paradoxically, lies the potential for a dissident perspective. In popular comic collections, for instance, the maidservant is regarded as a threat to the economic privileges upon which male mastery depends, a view which is itself coloured by the critical construction of women in general. Thus William Parkes writes in 1612 of a chambermaid who, rather than accepting a logic of sexual defencelessness, endeavours to make magisterial exploitation her province:

> In another place there is sixe Seruing-men in loue with one Chamber-maid at once, that the seuenth hath beguiled and got with child: yet with the *Curtaine* of seeming honesty most deceitfully drawne, and cunningly handled, will shee make means to deceiue them all.[80]

Whatever bargaining power the chambermaid enjoys admittedly revolves around the question of her sexual availability, a fact which narrows the control she might otherwise be able to exercise. At the same time, however, the situation has a dangerous edge, for male gullibility is satirized and the chambermaid's plan to profit from seven sets of maintenance charges is highlighted. If suitors can be played off against each other, then they can also be rejected altogether, as a scene from Beaumont and Fletcher's *The Faithful Friends* (1613–c. 1621) demonstrates. Flavia, a 'waiting-maid', elects to avoid contact with suitors and, in so doing, makes a virtue of her anomalous singleness:

> by my faith hees a happie man, that once in a moone gets a tuch of my lipps, yet there was a saucie Mercer tother day thrust in vpon mee with his yard in his hand, and ere I was aware made shifte to feele what stuff my petticote was made

> of but I thinke I gaue him a cooling card I taught him what it
> was for a Citizen to meddle with a wayting gentlewoman I
> made him stand at bay like a chased stagge . . .[81]

Part of the speech's effect hinges upon its punning sexual metaphors, the terms 'hand', 'stand', 'stuff', 'thrust' and 'yard' connoting
an attempted penetrative encounter. Because she refuses to countenance the mercer's advances, Flavia can prolong his frustration and consign him to a kind of phallic impotence. Once again,
there is only limited empowerment here, although Flavia is
distinctive in the success with which she asserts a right not to
be treated as sexual merchandise.

More obviously enabling are scenes in the drama in which the
mistress discusses her suitors and lovers with her women servants or companions. Notable in these private conferences is the
maidservant's keenness to attack a system of thought that defines
women only in terms of their 'honourable' credentials. Such is
the persistence with which the criticism is mounted, moreover,
that the maidservant sometimes extends her observations to question the validity of marriage itself. In *Much Ado About Nothing*
(1598), a conversation unfolds between Margaret, a 'gentlewoman',
and Hero, her mistress, about the heaviness of the latter's heart.
A quarrel begins when Margaret dares to counter Hero's rosy
meditations, claiming a position from which to judge and subjecting
the language that maintains social attitudes to a trenchant critique:

> *Margaret.* 'Twill be heavier soon by the weight of a man.
> *Hero.* Fie upon thee, art not ashamed?
> *Margaret.* Of what, lady? Of speaking honourably? Is not marriage
>   honourable in a beggar? Is not your lord honourable without
>   marriage? I think you would have me say, saving your
>   reverence, 'a husband'. And bad thinking do not wrest
>   true speaking, I'll offend nobody. Is there any harm in
>   'the heavier for a husband'? None, I think, and it be the
>   right husband, and the right wife; otherwise 'tis light, and
>   not heavy.[82]

With its *double entendres*, allusions to pregnancy and provision
of rival rhetorical possibilities, Margaret's speech challenges the
conventions that approve sexual dalliance from one point of view
while condemning it from another: only the lord, she suggests,

can remain honourable if he betrays his marital vow of chastity. In this protest against the 'double standard', it is Margaret's practice of a interrogative sophistry that makes the most telling dramatic impact.

Even if already married, it appears, the woman servant is at pains to scrutinize the institutional structures through which a woman's worth is validated. To her mistress's horror at the idea of extra-marital relations, Emilia, the attendant to Desdemona in *Othello* (1601–02), has an expedient response:

> *Desdemona.* Wouldst thou do such a deed for all the world?
> *Emilia.* Why, would not you?
> *Desdemona.* No, by this heavenly light!
> *Emilia.* Nor I neither, by this heavenly light:
>   I might do't as well i'th' dark.
> *Desdemona.* Wouldst thou do such a deed for all the world?
> *Emilia.* The world is a huge thing: it is a great price
>   For a small vice.[83]

Emilia's pragmatic philosophy provides an ironic counterpoint to Desdemona's attachment to contemporary morality. Whereas Desdemona elsewhere in the scene elevates fidelity into an ideal, Emilia makes visible the ways in which women are constructed according to a strict code of virtuous behaviour. Emilia speaks of 'price' and 'vice' (revealing the commercial aspects of sexual transactions, including marriage), and her lines hark back to Iago's materialistic vocabulary, which suggests that the woman servant might insinuate in a comparable fashion to the more obviously treacherous 'ancient'.

From the *Much Ado About Nothing* and *Othello* examples, several conclusions present themselves. A key idea is the woman servant's ability to speak what polite society deems to be unspeakable. The differences in her status and linguistic register mean that this servant has access to an area of information unavailable to her mistress, and is able to pronounce upon moral standards with a degree of impunity.[84] In a category separate from that of the wife (although some of them may have been married), maidservants are permitted to question what the woman's honour signifies in its practical manifestations. Emerging from the maidservant's questions is a more worrying scenario – the prospect of an alternative social formation in which sexual desire can be freely expressed, and the appropriation by women of skills more commonly seen as part of the man's rhetorical armoury. As these possibilities unfold, the ideological occlusions that structure contemporary male–female relations are exposed by a type who might appear ill-equipped to voice a social indictment.

Although scenes of private conference occasionally provide the woman servant with a vocal authority, they are generally subsumed within the surrounding action and do not shift its essential course. A smaller number of plays, however, takes the maidservant's influence to its furthest extreme, expanding her part to encompass a more substantial and transformative inversive scenario. Three plays, *Twelfth Night* (1601), Fletcher's *The Pilgrim* (1621?) and Jonson's *The New Inn* (1629), describe women servants who usurp the positions of the master, the mistress or the steward, thereby achieving an autonomy distinctive in its literary uniqueness. At her early appearances, Maria, the 'waiting-gentlewoman' in *Twelfth Night*, reprimands Sir Toby for his drinking and Feste for his absences.[85] In both cases, she begins to dismantle a carefully gradated system of household allegiances by appropriating some of the mistress's traditional responsibilities. The process is hastened when she assumes Mavolio's role, summoning the steward (III.iv.14–15) and organizing the exorcism of his imaginary demons. Cumulatively, Maria's actions single her out as a particularly dominant presence. It is not coincidental, for instance, that she is addressed as 'Penthesilea', Queen of the Amazons (II.iii.177), and that she is able to subordinate her social superiors, Sir Andrew and Sir Toby, turning upside-down class and gender boundaries. 'Wilt thou set thy foot o' my neck?' (II.v.188), Sir Toby asks, adding, 'Shall I play my freedom at tray-trip, and become thy bond-slave?' (II.v.190–1). Such is the success with which she supervises the steward's downfall that Sir Toby anticipates serving as Maria's feudal underdog. A waiting-gentlewoman waiting to be a lady, Maria eventually marries Sir Toby, but as her jesting abilities substitute for a dowry, the implication is that she will rule as a wife as she did as a servant.

In *Twelfth Night*, therefore, a series of inversive stratagems allows Maria to rise in the Illyrian hierarchy, leaving her dependent status behind in the process. It is a simultaneously fitting and ambiguous end for a work in which a woman servant is applauded for a slow accumulation of power, but a steward is crushed for his more impatient attempts to establish himself. The slightly later play, *The Pilgrim*, widens the social field of the maidservant's inversive behaviour, to the extent that she challenges not so much the mistress as the master, the seat of patriarchal government. Juletta, the 'Maid', torments Alphonso, her master, an angry old gentleman who has made the life of his daughter a misery. Banging on a drum the better to effect her revenge, Juletta describes herself setting out on a 'hunt', suggesting that she is imagined as a combination of an Amazonian warrior and a 'charivari' crowd.[86] Disguised as a page, Juletta goes on to force Alphonso to abandon his horse: the situation represents a parody of magisterial abuse and an evocation of anxieties about the effects of women servants' flouting of contemporary sumptuary regulations. It is only through impersonating a man that Juletta can hope to engineer her master's total capitulation. Writing on the androgyny of the Renaissance stage, Stephen Orgel observes that 'the transvestite actor' is 'a performative construction that both reveals the malleability of the masculine and empowers the feminine, enabling the potential masculinity of women to be realized and acknowledged'.[87] The comment is useful in pinpointing the ways in which Juletta's change of dress generates possibilities unavailable to her as a conventional woman, but it neglects to consider the sexual ramifications of her conduct. For such is the maidservant's experience of different gendered identities that, by the close, a new homoerotic bond has been forged. Choosing to remain a helpmate to her mistress rather than to a spouse, she promises her master: 'My Mistresse is my husband, with her I'le dwell still, And when you play any more prancks you know where to have me' (V.vi.120–1). In these final lines are a number of threatening prospects – a refusal to conform to domestic expectations and the glimmerings of an awakening of same-sex desire.

Perhaps the most far-reaching representation of the inversive scenario occurs in Jonson's *The New Inn*, a play in which a maidservant is given leave to wield authority as part of a legitimized festive occasion. During a day of amorous sports at an inn, Prudence, Lady Frampul's chambermaid, is elected sovereign of the proceedings, an appointment that necessitates a realignment of a much wider spectrum of social relations. In several senses, Prudence assumes a conservative role, correcting participants and dispensing justice: her expert management results in the reunion of the Frampul family and the daughters' planned marriages.[88] The route taken by the play, however, is rarely harmonious. It is never clear, for instance, if Prudence impersonates authority or is overtaken by it. At times, her actions exceed her responsibilities, as when she dictates to her mistress with an alarming imperiousness: 'No disputing / Of my prerogative . . . you know th'authority / Is mine, and I will exercise it swiftly / If you provoke me' (II.vi.104–8). As the ties between Prudence and her mistress disintegrate, so does it become increasingly difficult for the other characters to define her: the chambermaid is addressed variously as 'Fair Lady' (I.vi.28), 'Queen' (I.vi.82), 'mistress steward' (II.iii.16), 'mother' and 'conscience' (II.vi.193–4) and 'stateswoman' (II.vi.252). The concluding reconcilations do little to dilute the servant's predisposition to dominate. Her acceptance of the marriage proposal of a young lord notwithstanding, Prudence retains her air of command, and is described as 'infinite' (V.v.139) or infinitely powerful. 'Me and her mistress', a gentleman remarks, 'she has power to coin / Up into what she will' (V.v.138-9). The final impression is of a system in a state of flux, precipitated by a maidservant's inversive autocracy into a confrontation with uncertain attachments, new identities and freshly created social possibilities.

CONCLUSIONS

Valerie Traub has written that the '*erotic* body' in the English Renaissance 'metaphorically figures precisely the permeability that is constitutive of the early modern subject, its apertures [as] palpably embodying social relations as linguistic and bodily intercourse'.[89] Her observation is helpful in placing in perspective the cultural work performed by sixteenth- and seventeenth-century representations of women, patriarchy and service. Most obviously in the drama, women servants' bodies are either subordinated to magisterial interests or function as reflections of their mistress' chaste reputations. Occupying uncertain positions in the dominant gender ideologies of the period, maidservants could be constructed as sources of sexual power even as they were willed to emulate a virtuous restraint. About the penetration and preservation of this socially stigmatized body gathers a host of contemporary preoccupations.

Beyond these representations, of course, lie patriarchal imperatives. The covert approval granted to an abusive magisterial order

affirms male control, rendering women weak or impotent. Mechanisms for managing women are at work in a plethora of 'comic'
literary devices, which neutralize anxieties by imposing upon
maidservants degradation or dismemberment. Even biographical reflections and moral recommendations, it could be argued,
lend an oblique support to some of these notions. Without
representations of women in service as guardians of virtue,
however occasional, the dramatic spectacle of abusive situations
would make little sense. Each construction involves a network
of related constructions, and depends upon the agency of an
apparent opposite to underscore an ultimately conservative logic.

In view of the prominent place occupied by these attitudes, it
might be assumed that representations appealed primarily to a
male audience. Indeed, some recent studies suggest that the kinds
of satirical verse explored in this chapter formed an important
part of contemporary gentlemen's libraries.[90] That maidservants
themselves could have been consumers appears an unlikely prospect. From the mass of descriptions of women attending the theatres, only three can be firmly tied to women in service. One was
penned by John Earle, who stated in 1628 that the 'waiting-women
Spectators are over-eares in love with' the 'Player', a remark which
significantly associates playgoing with servants of a higher status.[91]
Given lower literacy levels among women, moreover, the possibility that the maidservant might have been tempted to read about
her profession seems even more remote.[92]

But these speculations form only part of a much richer picture.
It needs to be borne in mind that reading skills were often taught
before writing skills (especially for girls), and that women
(although far more rarely than men) also acquired merry tales,
jests, romances, pleasant dialogues, riddles and dramas for their
personal use.[93] In addition, a series of passing remarks recorded
by authors specifies women servants as readers, a common situation imagined being that of the chambermaid and her mistress
enjoying together popular romances.[94] A lord in Shirley's *The
Grateful Servant* (1629) jokes about 'your waiting-gentlewoman,
that is in love with poetry, and will not part with her honour
under a copy of fine verses, or an anagram', and his is not an
isolated statement.[95] Poetic collections, which otherwise denigrate
women and service, similarly include observations about the
reading abilities of 'Maides' and the 'Attendants' of 'faire Ladyes'.[96]
Of course, it is difficult to be categorical, but an anxiety animating

contemporary criticisms might have been the dangers inherent in communities or sororities of women readers, who looked to negative instances of themselves as ironic forms of amusement. To establish in what ways some modes of resistance could be envisaged, we might do well to stress the textual transactions that shaped mistress–maidservant relations. Through the confidences that passed between the mistress and her women servants, a range of information could be transmitted, and a wealth of ideological constructions debated.

What exactly prompted men's anxieties requires further comment. Earlier sections of this chapter suggested that women servants were objects of loathing and longing at one and the same time, since they were linked to verbal outspokenness, social restlessness and attempts to secure a greater economic advantage. It may also have been the case that the spectacle of the boy actor, who played the women servants' roles, provoked a related set of polarized responses with particular social nuances. Most crucial, however, would seem to be the maidservant's location within, and potential to shape the future structure of, the contemporary household. Sometimes sleeping in the same bed as the children of the master and the mistress, women servants lay close to the household's more impressionable members, and were, by extension, privy to its secrets and intimacies.[97] If some women servants served as wet-nurses, as a number of writers claimed, then additional anxieties could be brought into play. Both dependent and depended upon, maidservant-nurses were involved in the well-being of the household at a fundamental level, and it is not to be wondered at that descriptions of their functions should have been so apprehensive. As a 1581 commentator thought, such servants might infect the infant and the family with 'the most pernicious contagion, of foule filthinesse, odious errours, & detestable diseases'.[98] The abused body of the maidservant had the power to jeopardize the master's status and his ability to ensure an inheritance; the nurturing body of the maidservant was feared as a contaminating influence upon the child's emotional and psychological development.

In a wider context, women servants were constructed as sources of anxiety in relation to, and as a material consequence of, broader social transformations. The representation of maidservants who engineer various forms of inversion belonged to a larger debate about the nature of women's traditional roles in a society that was in a process of diversification and change. Maidservants could be deployed to elicit questions about the inferior places that had been assigned to women by a patriarchal order that was itself coming under increasing scrutiny. Positioned on a lower rung of the hierarchy, the woman servant functioned to test beliefs about the close relationship between character and rank: as her sexuality and social location are shown to be mutually constitutive, so does her estate activate with a specific intensity reflections upon moral worth and a woman's ability to manipulate political subjects. It would be tempting to see representations as offering an even more rigorous critique of patriarchal systems, and perhaps there is one still waiting to be uncovered in these traces of subordinated voices that agitate for proper acknowledgement.

NOTES

1. For preliminary studies, see Ilana Krausman Ben-Amos, *Adolescence and Youth in Early Modern England* (New Haven, CT and London, 1994), pp. 133–55; Ilana Krausman Ben-Amos, 'Women Apprentices in the Trades and Crafts of Early Modern Bristol', *Continuity and Change*, 6 (1991), pp. 227–52; Marjorie K. McIntosh, 'Servants and the Household Unit in an Elizabethan English Community', *Journal of Family History*, 9 (1984), pp. 3–23; Michael Roberts, 'Women and Work in Sixteenth-century English Towns', in Penelope J. Corfield and Derek Keene, eds, *Work in Towns 850–1850* (Leicester, London and New York, 1990), pp. 86–102; Michael Roberts, '"Words they are Women, and Deeds they are Men": Images of Work and Gender in Early Modern England', in Lindsey Charles and Lorna Duffin, eds, *Women and Work in Pre-industrial England* (London and Sydney, 1985), pp. 122–80.
2. Warwickshire R. O., CR 1998, Box 60, Folder 1, item 3. See also Essex R. O., D/D By C 29; S.C.L., B.F.M., 2, item 164.
3. Susan Dwyer Amussen, 'The Gendering of Popular Culture in Early Modern England', in Tim Harris, ed., *Popular Culture in England, c. 1500–1850* (Basingstoke and London, 1995), p. 54; Mary E. Finch, *The Wealth of Five Northamptonshire Families 1540–1640*, Northamptonshire Record Society, 19 (1956), pp. 30, 81; F. P. and M. M. Verney, eds, *Memoirs of the Verney Family During the Civil War*, 4 vols (London, 1892–9), vol. IV, p. 175.
4. Vivien Brodsky Elliott, 'Mobility and Marriage in Pre-Industrial England: a Demographic and Social Structural Analysis of Geographic and

Social Mobility and Aspects of Marriage, 1570–1690, with Particular Reference to London and General Reference to Middlesex, Kent, Essex and Hertfordshire', unpublished PhD thesis, University of Cambridge, 1978, pp. 192, 221–2, 324, 334, 336. For literary examples, see Richard Brome, *A Mad Couple Well Match'd* (1637–9), ed. Steen H. Spove (New York and London, 1979), I.i.321–31, 436–7; Richard Niccols, *The furies* (London, 1614; S.T.C. 18521), sig. D1ᵛ; Samuel Rowlands, *Good newes and bad newes* (London, 1622; S.T.C. 21382), sigs C3ᵛ–4ᵛ.

5. Laura Gowing, *Domestic Dangers: Women, Words, and Sex in Early Modern London* (Oxford, 1996), pp. 150–1; R. G. Griffiths, 'Joyce Jeffreys of Ham Castle', *Transactions of the Worcestershire Archaeological Society*, 10 (1933), p. 22; Mary Prior, 'Margerie Bonner: A Waiting Gentlewoman of Seventeenth-Century Wroxton', *Oxfordshire Local History*, 2, Autumn (1984), pp. 4–10.

6. Margaret Patterson Hannay, ed., *Silent But for the Word: Tudor Women as Patrons, Translators, and Writers of Religious Works* (Kent, OH, 1985), passim; Anne M. Haselkorn and Betty S. Travitsky, eds, *The Renaissance Englishwoman in Print: Counterbalancing the Canon* (Amherst, MA, 1991), passim.

7. Bonnie S. Anderson and Judith P. Zinsser, eds, *A History of their Own: Women in Europe from Prehistory to the Present*, 2 vols (Harmondsworth, 1989–90), vol. I.

8. Jean E. Howard, 'Scripts and/versus Playhouses: Ideological Production and the Renaissance Public Stage', in Valerie Wayne, ed., *The Matter of Difference: Materialist Feminist Criticism of Shakespeare* (Ithaca, NY, 1991), p. 236.

9. See Elaine Hobby, *Virtue of Necessity: English Women's Writing, 1649–1688* (London, 1988); Barbara Kiefer Lewalski, *Writing Women in Jacobean England* (Cambridge, MA, 1993).

10. Margaret W. Ferguson, 'Moderation and its Discontents: Recent Work on Renaissance Women (Review Essay)', *Feminist Studies*, 20 (1994), pp. 356, 358.

11. Tina Krontiris, *Oppositional Voices: Women as Writers and Translators of Literature in the English Renaissance* (London and New York, 1992), pp. 14–17, 27–62.

12. The phrases 'apparently' and 'It is quite likely that', deployed in the endnotes, suggest that Krontiris is not entirely certain about the nature of Whitney's 'working' experience. See *Oppositional Voices*, p. 152.

13. Krontiris, *Oppositional Voices*, p. 24. Ferguson voices this objection in her 'Moderation and Its Discontents', p. 356.

14. See Lynda Boose, 'The Priest, the Slanderer, the Historian and the Feminist', *English Literary Renaissance*, 25 (1995), pp. 320–40.

15. Margaret Tyler, 'Epistle to the Reader', in Moira Ferguson, ed., *First Feminists: British Women Writers, 1578–1799* (Bloomington, IN, 1985), p. 56. Tyler is further explored in Louise Schleiner, 'Margaret Tyler, Translator and Waiting Woman', *English Language Notes*, 29, March (1992), pp. 1–8.

16. *The maids petition* (London, 1647; Wing M280), p. 2. For women's petitions in the civil war, see Keith Thomas, 'Women and the Civil War Sects', *Past and Present*, 13, April (1958), pp. 42–62.
17. See *The aprentices advice to the XII. bishops lately accused* (London, 1642; Wing A3583B), pp. 4–5; *The apprentices of Londons petition* (London, 1641; Wing A3586), sig. A3ʳ; *A declaration of the valiant resolution of the famous prentices* (London, 1642; Wing D774), p. 1.
18. *A letter sent by the maydens of London* (London, 1567; S.T.C. 16754.5), sigs. Aiiiʳ, Aiiiiᵛ, Avᵛ.
19. R. J. Fehrenbach, 'A Letter sent by the Maydens of London (1567)', *English Literary Renaissance*, 14 (1984), p. 288.
20. *The ladies remonstrance* (London, [1659]; Wing L160), pp. 2, 5.
21. Patricia Crawford, 'Women's Published Writings 1600–1700', in Mary Prior, ed., *Women in English Society 1500–1800* (London and New York, 1985), p. 263.
22. Buckinghamshire R. O., D/A/Wf/24/256. See also Prior, 'Margerie Bonner', pp. 4–10.
23. Susan Dwyer Amussen, 'Punishment, Discipline, and Power: The Social Meanings of Violence in Early Modern England', *Journal of British Studies*, 34 (1995), p. 17.
24. C.U.L., EDR E44 QS Files 1631–2.
25. See Suzanne W. Hull, *Chaste, Silent and Obedient: English Books for Women 1475–1640* (San Marino, 1982), passim.
26. See Pamela Sharpe, 'Poor children as apprentices in Colyton, 1598–1830', *Continuity and Change*, 6 (1991), pp. 253–70.
27. James C. Scott, *Domination and the Arts of Resistance: Hidden Transcripts* (New Haven, CT and London, 1990), p. 95.
28. Susan Dwyer Amussen, *An Ordered Society: Gender and Class in Early Modern England* (Oxford, 1988), p. 116; Nazife Bashar, 'Women and Crime in England 1558–1700', unpublished PhD thesis, University of Sydney, 1985, p. 168; B.L., Egerton MS. 2713, fo. 300ʳ; C.U.L., EDR D/2/10, fo. 169ʳ; Essex R. O., Q/SBa 2/2; Norfolk R. O., DN / DEP/28, fos 3–11ᵛ, 25–7ᵛ, 89–91ᵛ, 235–42, 244–5ᵛ, 247–51ᵛ, 253–6. Other narratives argued that maidservants falsely brought paternity suits against their masters for material advantage. Perhaps because the actual father was less materially affluent. See Essex R. O., Q/SR 107/44; Somerset R. O., Q/SR 3/88.
29. Essex R. O., D/ACA 8, fo. 244ᵛ. In a similar vein is the case of the maidservant who alleged that intercourse took palce after she had been given aphrodisiacs (Hertfordshire R. O., HAT/SR 28/81).
30. Amussen, *An Ordered*, pp. 113–15; Bashar, 'Women', p. 133; Mark Thornton Burnett, 'Masters and Servants in Moral and Religious Treatises, *c.* 1580–*c.* 1642', in Arthur Marwick, ed., *The Arts, Literature, and Society* (London and New York, 1990), pp. 62–4; Somerset R. O., Q/SR 96/31.
31. West Sussex R. O., Sessions Roll, October 1655, fo. 72ʳ.
32. See Bashar, 'Women', pp. 110–11, 187–8; Bodl. Lib., Ashmole MS. 410, fo. 117ʳ; Ann Kussmaul, *Servants in Husbandry in Early Modern England* (Cambridge, 1981), p. 47. For some qualifications, see Richard

Adair, *Courtship, Illegitimacy and Marriage in Early Modern England* (Manchester and New York, 1996), pp. 83–8.

33. H.L., EL 7381, 7382, 7384, 7385, 7403. The case is also discussed in Suzanne Gossett, '"Best Men are Molded out of Faults": Marrying the Rapist in Jacobean Drama', *English Literary Renaissance*, 14 (1984), p. 313; Leah Sinanoglou Marcus, 'The Milieu of Milton's *Comus*: Judicial Reform at Ludlow and The Problem of Sexual Assault', *Criticism*, 25 (1983), pp. 293–327.

34. H.L., EL 7399.

35. H.L., EL 7394.

36. One can only speculate about the very different direction the case might have taken were Evans to have fallen pregnant. As conception was invariably read as consent, however, it is unlikely that a pregnancy would have worked in the servant's favour. See Amussen, 'Punishment', p. 50; Nazife Bashar, 'Rape in England between 1550 and 1700', in The London Feminist History Group, ed., *The Sexual Dynamics of History: Men's Power, Women's Resistance* (London, 1983), p. 36; Miranda Chaytor, 'Household and Kinship: Ryton in the late 16th and early 17th Centuries', *History Workshop*, 10, Autumn (1980), p. 48.

37. See Bashar, 'Rape in England', pp. 33–4; Gossett, '"Best Men are Molded"', pp. 311–12.

38. Michael Macdonald, *Mystical Bedlam: Madness, Anxiety, and Healing in Seventeenth-Century England* (Cambridge, 1981), p. 88. See also Miranda Chaytor, 'Husband(ry): Narratives of Rape in the Seventeenth Century', *Gender and History*, 7 (1995), p. 385.

39. Chaytor, 'Husband(ry)', p. 381; Gowing, *Domestic Dangers*, pp. 75–6.

40. Isabella Whitney, *A sweet nosgay, or pleasant posye: contayning a hundred and ten phylosophicall flowers* (London, 1573; S.T.C. 25440), sigs Cvii^v–viii^r. For a contrary interpretation to that offered here, see Ann Rosalind Jones, *The Currency of Eros: Women's Love Lyric in Europe, 1540–1620* (Bloomington and Indianapolis, 1990), pp. 36–78.

41. See Sir Geoffrey Fenton, *Golden epistles* (London, 1582; S.T.C. 10794), pp. 223–5; Robert Herrick, *Hesperides* (published 1648), in *The Poetical Works*, ed. L. C. Martin (Oxford, 1956), pp. 151, 262; Gervase Markham, *Hobsons horse-load of letters* (London, 1617; S.T.C. 17360a), sigs O1^v–2^r.

42. Richard Smith, *The Life of Lady Magdalen Viscountess Montague (1538–1608)*, ed. A. C. Southern (London, 1954), p. 11.

43. The passage also depends upon its readers' knowledge of the elevated positions occupied by waiting-gentlewomen in contemporary noble households. Such servants were given their own table for meals or even ate with the lord's entourage. See W.A., Sir William Russell's Papers, item 6; Staffordshire R. O., D(W)1734/3/3/282, fos 4^{r-v}; Wiltshire R. O., 865/389, p. 10.

44. Catherine Belsey, 'Disrupting Sexual Difference: Meaning and Gender in the Comedies', in John Drakakis, ed., *Alternative Shakespeares* (London and New York, 1985), p. 177.

45. C.L.R.O., P.D. 10. 211. See comments in Edmund Cobbes, *Mundanum speculum, or, the worldlings looking glasse* (London, 1630; S.T.C. 5453), p. 194; I. H., *This worlds folly* (London, 1615; S.T.C. 12570), sig. A3ᵛ; Barnaby Rich, *The honestie of this age* (London, 1614; S.T.C. 20986), sig. G3ʳ.
46. Richard Parkinson, ed., *The Life of Adam Martindale*, Chetham Society, 1st ser., 4 (1845), pp. 7–8.
47. See the suggestive comments in Bernard Capp, 'Separate Domains? Women and Authority in Early Modern England', in Paul Griffiths, Adam Fox and Steve Hindle, eds, *The Experience of Authority in Early Modern England* (Basingstoke and London, 1996), pp. 117–45.
48. John Montgomery Traherne, ed., *Stradling Correspondence: A Series of Letters Written in the Reign of Queen Elizabeth* (London, 1840), p. 343. See also Claire Cross, 'Northern Women in the Early Modern Period: The Female Testators of Hull and Leeds 1520–1650', *Yorkshire Archaeological Journal*, 59 (1987), pp. 84, 86; Griffiths, 'Joyce Jeffreys', p. 21.
49. B.L., Additional MS. 4176, fos 163ʳ⁻ᵛ.
50. Bodl. Lib., MS. Eng. hist. c. 476, fo. 19ʳ; L.P.L., MS. 3197, fo. 83ʳ, MS. 3198, fo. 183ʳ. The sentiments were also echoed by mistresses. See Bristol R. O., AC/C60/14.
51. A. G. Dickens, 'Estate and Household Management in Bedfordshire, c. 1540', *Bedfordshire Historical Record Society*, 36 (1956), p. 42.
52. G. B. Harrison, ed., *Advice to His Son by Henry Percy, Ninth Earl of Northumberland (1609)* (London, 1930), p. 99.
53. See also Frances E. Dolan, *Dangerous Familiars: Representations of Domestic Crime in England, 1550–1700* (Ithaca, NY and London, 1994), pp. 66–7.
54. For recent studies of literary representations, see Pamela Joseph Benson, *The Invention of Renaissance Woman: The Challenge of Female Independence in the Literature and Thought of Italy and England* (University Park, PN, 1992); Katherine Usher Henderson and Barbara F. McManus, eds, *Half Humankind: Contexts and Texts of the Controversy about Women in England, 1540–1640* (Urbana and Chicago, 1985); Linda Woodbridge, *Women and the English Renaissance: Literature and the Nature of Womankind, 1540–1620* (Brighton, 1984).
55. For some preliminary remarks, see Mark Thornton Burnett, 'Popular Culture in the English Renaissance', in William Zunder and Suzanne Trill, eds, *Writing and the English Renaissance* (London and New York, 1996), pp. 108–15.
56. Simon Baylie, *The Wizard*, ed. Henry De Vocht (Louvain, 1930), V.vii.2629–30.
57. Edward Sharpham, *The Works*, ed. Christopher Gordon Petter (New York and London, 1986), IV.i.37–8.
58. Francis Beaumont and John Fletcher, *The Dramatic Works*, ed. Fredson Bowers, 10 vols (Cambridge, 1966–96), vol. II, IV.i.1–2.
59. Richard Brome, *The Dramatic Works*, ed. John Pearson, 3 vols (London, 1873), vol. I, I.ii.p. 117.
60. For maidservant marriages, see Elliott, 'Mobility and Marriage', pp.

117, 333; L.P.L., MS. 3205, fo. 16ʳ; McIntosh, 'Servants', p. 21. For isolated literary representations, see Thomas Randolph, *The Jealous Lovers* (1632), in *The Poetical and Dramatic Works*, ed. W. Carew Hazlitt, 2 vols (London, 1875), vol. I, V.viii.pp. 168–9; Sir John Harington, *The Letters and Epigrams* (1590s), ed. Norman Egbert McClure (Philadelphia, 1930), p. 249.

61. Thomas Cash, *Two horrible and inhumane murders done in L<in>colneshire, by two husbands upon their wives* (London, 1607; S.T.C. 4768), sig. A3ʳ. For a stimulating discussion of these materials, see Dolan, *Dangerous Familiars*, pp. 25, 151.

62. John Taylor, *The unnaturall father* (London, 1621; S.T.C. 23808a), sig. A3ᵛ.

63. Elliott, 'Mobility and Marriage', pp. 334, 336.

64. For an exception to the rule, see Henry Glapthorne, *Albertus Wallenstein* (1634–9), in *The Plays and Poems*, [ed. R. H. Shepherd], 2 vols (London, 1874), vol. II, I.iii.p. 24, III.iii.pp. 50, 53, a play in which a 'gentlewoman' servant's chaste morality is the prompt for socially inversive actions and eventual familial disintegration. Interestingly, the maidservant who seeks an advantageous match in the drama is exonerated when it is revealed that she is a noblewoman in disguise. See Philip Massinger, *The Guardian* (1633), in *The Plays and Poems*, ed. Philip Edwards and Colin Gibson, 5 vols (Oxford, 1976), vol. IV, IV.ii.107–13, V.iv.232–48.

65. Massinger, *Plays and Poems*, ed. Edwards and Gibson, vol. III, II.iii. 47–8.

66. *The Wasp*, ed. J. W. Lever, Malone Society (Oxford, 1974 [1976]), III.ii.1138.

67. William Goddard, *A neaste of waspes latelie found out in the Law-Countreys* (London, 1615; S.T.C. 11929), sig. Giiᵛ.

68. B.L., Additional MS. 5832, fo. 204ᵛ. See also Henry Parrot, *The mastive, or young-whelpe of the olde-dogge* (London, 1615; S.T.C. 19333), sig. F3ʳ.

69. Henry Parrot, *The mous-trap* (London, 1606; S.T.C. 19334), sig. B3ʳ. See also George Chapman, *An Humorous Day's Mirth* (1597), in *The Comedies*, ed. Allan Holaday (Urbana, Chicago and London, 1970), V.ii.248–9; Francis Lenton, *Characterismi; or, Lentons leasures* (London, 1631; S.T.C. 15463), sigs B12ʳ⁻ᵛ; Sir Nicholas Le Strange, *'Mery Passages and Jeasts': A Manuscript Jestbook* (1630s–1640s), ed. H. F. Lippincott (Salzburg, 1974), pp. 103–4.

70. Thomas Dekker, John Ford and William Rowley, *The Witch of Edmonton*, ed. Simon Trussler and Jacqui Russell (London, 1983), I.i.157, 192, 219.

71. Edward Hake, *Newes out of Powles churchyarde* (London, 1579; S.T.C. 12606), sigs Fviiiᵛ–Giʳ; Humphrey Mill, *A nights search* (London, 1640; S.T.C. 17921), pp. 244–6; H[enry] P[eachum], *The art of living in London* (London, 1642; Wing P942), sigs A4ʳ⁻ᵛ.

72. Paul Griffiths, 'The Structure of Prostitution in Elizabethan London', *Continuity and Change*, 8 (1993), p. 49.

73. Henry Parrot, *Laquei ridiculosi: or springes for woodcocks* (London, 1613;

S.T.C. 19332), sig. D7ᵛ.
74. Miriam Slater, *Family Life in the Seventeenth Century: The Verneys of Claydon House* (London, 1984), p. 72.
75. *'The Cobler of Caunterburie' and 'Tarltons Newes out of Purgatorie'*, ed. Geoffrey Creigh and Jane Belfield (Leiden, 1987), p. 72.
76. For literary injunctions enjoining women servants to silence, see Thomas Churchyard, *The firste parte of Churchyardes chippes* (London, 1575; S.T.C. 5232), sig. Ciiiiᵛ; Robert Hill, *Christs prayer expounded, a christian directed, and a communicant prepared* (London, 1610; S.T.C. 13473), p. 181.
77. Beaumont and Fletcher, *Works*, ed. Bowers, vol. V, III.iv.98–102.
78. Karen Newman, *Fashioning Femininity and English Renaissance Drama* (Chicago and London, 1991), p. 10.
79. For unique literary examples, see Richard Cooke, *A White Sheete* (1629), in Lena Cowen Orlin, ed., *Elizabethan Households: An Anthology* (Seattle and London, 1995), pp. 60–1; 'No Natural Mother' (1634), in Hyder E. Rollins, ed., *A Pepysian Garland: Black-Letter Broadside Ballads of the Years 1595–1639* (Cambridge, 1922), pp. 425–30; John Ricketts, *Byrsa Basilica* (*c.* 1633), ed. R. H. Bowers (Louvain, 1939), V.xi.p. 168. On infanticide and suicide, see Burnett, 'Masters and Servants in Moral and Religious Treatises', p. 64; Dolan, *Dangerous Familiars*, p. 144; S. J. Stevenson, 'Social and Economic Contributions to the Pattern of "Suicide" in South-east England, 1530–1590', *Continuity and Change*, 2 (1987), pp. 227, 248–9.
80. William Parkes, *The curtaine-drawer of the world* (London, 1612; S.T.C. 19298), p. 12.
81. [Francis Beaumont and John Fletcher], *The Faithful Friends*, ed. G. M. Pinciss and G. R. Proudfoot, Malone Society (Oxford, 1970 [1975]), II.ii.1006–16.
82. *Much Ado About Nothing*, ed. A. R. Humphreys (London and New York, 1984), III.iv.25–35.
83. *Othello*, ed. E. A. J. Honigmann (London and New York, 1997), IV.iii. 63–8.
84. One extension of this scenario is the maidservant who actively participates in the mistress's corruption and subsequent downfall. For a pertinent discussion, see Jan C. Stirm, 'Representing Women's Relationships: Intersections of Class, Race and Generation in English Drama, 1580–1642', unpublished PhD thesis, University of California, Los Angeles, 1995, pp. 148–212.
85. *Twelfth Night*, ed. J. M. Lothian and T. W. Craik (London and New York, 1984), I.iii.4–6, I.v.16–18.
86. Beaumont and Fletcher, *Works*, ed. Bowers, vol. VI, III.v.4.
87. Stephen Orgel, *Impersonations: The Performance of Gender in Shakespeare's England* (Cambridge, 1996), p. 106.
88. Ben Jonson, *The New Inn*, ed. Michael Hattaway (Manchester, 1984), II.vi.78–80, III.ii.273–4.
89. Valerie Traub, *Desire and Anxiety: Circulations of Sexuality in Shakespearean Drama* (London and New York, 1992), p. 15.
90. See T. A. Birrell, 'Reading as Pastime: The Place of Light Literature

in some Gentlemen's Libraries of the 17th Century', in Robin Myers and Michael Harris, eds, *Property of a Gentleman: The Formation, Organisation and Dispersal of the Private Library 1620–1920* (Winchester, 1991), p. 120.

91. John Earle, *Microcosmography*, ed. Alfred S. West (Cambridge, 1951), p. 82. See also Ben Jonson, *Epicoene* (1609), ed. L. A. Beaurline (London, 1966), Prologue, 23; R. M., *Micrologia* (London, 1629; S.T.C. 17146), sig. B3ᵛ.

92. 'Close to 90% of the women in seventeenth-century England could not even write their names', David Cressy observes, adding, 'In all sources and in all areas and periods, the literacy of women lagged behind that of men.' See his *Literacy and the Social Order: Reading and writing in Tudor and Stuart England* (Cambridge, 1980), pp. 41, 128.

93. Paul Morgan, 'Frances Wolfreston and "Hor Bouks": A Seventeenth-Century Woman Book-Collector', *The Library*, 11 (1989), pp. 211–19.

94. Edmund Gayton, *Pleasant notes upon Don Quixot* (London, 1654; Wing G415), p. 17; Sir Thomas Overbury, *The Overburian Characters*, ed. W. J. Paylor (Oxford, 1936), p. 43; Anthony Stafford, *The guide of honour* (London, 1634; S.T.C. 23124), sig. A6ᵛ.

95. James Shirley, *The Dramatic Works*, ed. William Gifford and Alexander Dyce, 6 vols (London, 1833), vol. II, III.iv.p. 59.

96. Parrot, *The mastive*, sig. I1ʳ; Henry Peacham, *Thalias banquet* (London, 1620; S.T.C. 19515), sigs A3ᵛ–4ʳ.

97. Arthur Collins, ed., *Letters and Memorials of State*, 2 vols (London, 1746), vol. II, p. 43; Paul Griffiths, *Youth and Authority: Formative Experiences in England 1560–1640* (Oxford, 1996), pp. 270–1.

98. Bartholomaeus Battus, *The christian mans closet*, tr. W. Lowth (London, 1581; S.T.C. 1591), fo. 54ʳ. For the association of servants and disease, see Bristol R. O., AC/C61/15; Thomas Salter, *The Mirrhor of Modestie* (1579?), ed. Janis Butler Holm (New York and London, 1987), pp. 83–5; W.Y.A.S., Leeds, TN/C, II, item 184.

5

The Noble Household

The staff of the great noble households of sixteenth- and seventeenth-century England were organized according to a strictly hierarchical scheme.[1] Occupying the lower positions were the 'yeomen' servants such as grooms, stable-hands, waiters, footmen and musicians. At the upper levels could be found the 'gentlemen' servants responsible for household government: the steward, chamberlain, comptroller, receiver, secretary and gentleman usher all fell into this category. Collectively, these senior servants made up the lord's 'chief officers'.[2]

While yeomen servants make infrequent appearances in the literary materials of the period, chief officers feature prominently. Indeed, their portrayal forms part of a long-standing tradition. Dishonest, unscrupulous and ambitious stewards, for instance, are staple ingredients of romances, religious treatises and the theatrical repertoire from the medieval period onwards.[3] Concentrating on dramatic representations, this chapter discusses the particular inflections placed upon the steward and, to a lesser extent, the gentleman usher in the English Renaissance. It suggests that popular attitudes towards stewards and gentlemen ushers, although partly indebted to a history of literary stereotypes, can be more profitably understood as expressions of aristocratic anxieties about the future of the noble household at a critical stage in its development.

Throughout the chapter, I argue that dramatic representations and magisterial constructions of chief officers' conduct interweave in a mutually constitutive fashion. The first section considers correspondence and household ordinances as key elements in the discursive elaboration of the steward's domestic morality. What emerges from these materials is a powerful dramatic impression of a steward who simultaneously subscribes to and exceeds the responsibilities imposed upon him by his overlords. In the second section, I build upon these findings, suggesting that the steward and the gentleman usher also appear in the drama as the possessors of a host of secret vices. The regularity with which these servants abnegate their role, and the rapidity with which their ambitions are quashed, point to a larger preoccupation with the possibility that the chief officer could endanger aristocratic power structures. A comparable anxiety animates the expectation that the steward and the gentleman usher are 'upstart' types in an unstable social environment, an area of concern which the third and fourth sections address. As the position of the nobility came under threat in the period, and as the composition of the servant body changed and diversified, the dramatic realization of a chief officer who has lost his social bearings took on an urgent contemporary importance.

FUNCTIONS OF OFFICIALDOM

Frequently scholars with expertise in classical learning or languages, stewards and gentlemen ushers brought a range of skills to bear on the execution of their duties.[4] From a survey of the records of sixteenth- and seventeenth-century noble households, moreover, it is clear that educational advantages were integral to a chief officer's elevated position and to his ability to supervise the domestic order. As the officer entrusted with the greatest responsibility among the servants, the steward could lay claim to the highest authority. He was obliged to keep a watchful eye on the personnel of the establishment, devising regulations for the kitchen staff, drawing up lists of household employees and appointing bailiffs. More specifically, his office necessitated checking the contents of the wine-cellar, buying provisions, paying wages and keeping the accounts as a bursar or treasurer.[5] In smaller households, the steward may also have exercised manorial as well as domestic responsibilities: because of his visibility in a number of capacities, he was perhaps the most easily identifiable of a lord's chief officers in the popular consciousness.

'In its upper echelons', Felicity Heal has written, 'the aristocratic household existed to articulate and enhance the reputation of its head: senior servants personated and expressed his qualities.'[6] In this regard, of greater significance than his practical functions was the steward's symbolic versatility. Placed in a category above that of the other servants, and imagined as a reflection of the master's personal worth, the steward was encouraged to see himself as a guardian of the household's morality. It was upon the steward's cultivation of a virtuous working environment, employers maintained, that the stability of the domestic unit depended. Prominent in fathers' addresses to their sons are recommendations to choose chief officers noted for their discretion and sobriety.[7] In household ordinances, similarly, ideals of scrupulous rectitude are promulgated. As Lionel Cranfield, the Earl of Middlesex, stated, writing to his steward in 1622: 'Your carriage and conversation (in ye eies of my houshold) must bee guided, and ruled with a setled grauitie, not shewinge any example of lightnes, or rashnes in your actions: least ye noatinge thereof in you, might worke imitation and contempt, and scorne in others.'[8] Central to Cranfield's advice is the belief that the steward's failure to respect proprieties could have dangerous repercussions. Behind the injunction lies the figure of a model steward, whose practical efficiency goes hand-in-hand with an exemplary deportment.

To pinpoint areas of overlap between household regulations and material practice is hazardous; nevertheless, a number of references suggests that some masters and mistresses found in day-to-day economic transactions justification for instituting their domestic idealism. They felt sufficiently confident to complain to their stewards about difficult servants who troubled the establishment.[9] In addition, they sometimes extended the relationship to make assurances of friendship, addressing their stewards by their Christian names, relaying to them court news, granting gifts and complaining of illness, poor business and marital problems.[10] On occasions, the employer was even capable of acknowledging the considerable power enjoyed by the steward, and the dependency of the family upon his allegiance.[11] Awaiting execution in the Tower in 1572, the fourth Duke of Norfolk sent a bible to his steward, William Dyx, penning in the fly-leaf: 'Farewell good dyx, your servys hathe bene so faythefull unto me as I ame sorye that I cane not make profe off my good wyll to recompence ytt.'[12] In 1610, Lady Elizabeth Berkeley wrote to her steward, Smyth, 'of your loue and zeale . . . I doubt not, soe by your continuall and effectuall indeuors, I haue had longe since sufficient triall . . . I pray you . . . continue in . . . [the] good offices to us, which you haue always ben readie to performe'.[13] As the language of these protestations suggests, the steward was viewed

as part of a network of exchanges in which patronage and grati-
tude could be traded for personal loyalty. The logical development of a steward valued for his moral integrity was one willing
to devote himself to his adopted family with all the trappings of
self-sacrifice.

By the same token, it was not unusual for stewards to reproduce in their own correspondence the values visited upon them
by their superiors. At least on paper, the codes of reciprocity
that cemented the power of the noble household reappear in many
chief officers' discursive reflections upon their services. When
stewards write to their employers or neighbours, they draw
attention to their determination to instil a sense of virtue in the
other servants, and to treat each member of the household with
a judicious impartiality.[14] Taking a greater pride in the trust
reposed in them, stewards could also accept the charge of instructing their mistress' children in 'good . . . learneing' and an honourable 'life'.[15] Indeed, where the family's children were concerned,
the steward and the mistress seem to have shared a particularly
close relationship. William Whitehall, the steward of the
Newdigates of Warwickshire, was disturbed in 1617 and wrote:
'M[aste]r Io[hn] is not well w[hi]ch doth wond[e]rfull trouble &
greave my La[dy]. I pray god restore him, and spare him to her
or els yt will breake her hartt.'[16] From these fragments of domestic
intimacy, it can be established that, at least in some cases, stewards not only constructed themselves according to prevailing moral
imperatives; they simultaneously reinvented those requirements
in extensions to their central responsibilities.

For the steward, then, an involvement in the family's affairs
was an index of the esteemed place he occupied in the household hierarchy. With the gentleman usher, a rather less expan-
sive range of functions came into play. Whereas the entire
establishment fell to the steward's care, the gentleman usher's
area of influence was generally limited to the master's chamber
and to the hall. A marshall who ensured that the seating arrangements were observed, the gentleman usher was still, however,
in the words of an early sixteenth-century household book, one
of the 'greatist' of a lord's officers.[17] He commanded the yeomen
servants, sewers, carvers and cupbearers on ceremonial occasions,
saw the fires lit, prepared accommodation for guests, entertained
strangers and could be called upon to distribute provisions. When
his master and mistress were present, he was expected to be in

constant attendance.[18] In the absence of the steward, the gentleman usher was often entitled to fill his position and to assume additional powers; like the steward, he was an officer vital to the successful operations of domestic government.[19]

What emerges from these various inscriptions of the workings of the noble household is a rich impression of the partnership shared between authority and discipline. For in addition to setting an example to the rest of the servants, both the steward and the gentleman usher were instructed to reprimand actions inimical to wider domestic harmonies. In 1634, the Duke of Buckingham formulated his conception of the gentleman usher as follows: 'Hee is . . . to haue especiall care there be noe disorder by swearing, ribald speeches, offensiue languages or quarelling at any tyme; and to doe all thinges both comely and decently as well for his owne Creditt as for my honor and service.'[20] Rather more explicit in its definition of infractions was the recommendation of John, the Earl of Bridgewater, in 1652. He required his steward to 'suffer noe ordinarie and common Swearer drunckhard, professed whore-master, anie Popishe factious, or other negligent, disorderlie, or irreligious person whatsoever to bee, & reside within [the] Howse'.[21] It was as the lord's eyes and ears, and as the defender of his good name, that the gentleman usher and the steward could be most highly prized. So much authority was granted to chief officers that it is sometimes difficult to ascertain from the available evidence where their own responsibilities ended and those belonging to their masters and mistresses began.

The popular image of stewards and gentlemen ushers on the contemporary stage grew out of, and was mediated through, such aristocratic constructions of chief officers' behaviour. Indeed, the drama often pushed to an extreme the implications of the recommendations elaborated in household ordinances. In *Twelfth Night* (1601), Malvolio goes to great lengths to put into practice the disciplinary aspects of his office, railing against the excesses of Sir Toby and his confederates with all the attention to detail of his rule-book counterparts:

My masters, are you mad? . . . Have you no wit, manners, nor honesty, but to gabble like tinkers at this time of night? Do ye make an ale-house of my lady's house, that ye squeak out your coziers' catches? . . . Is there no respect of place, persons, nor time in you? . . . My lady bade me tell you, that . . . she's nothing

allied to your disorders. If . . . it would please you to take leave
of her, she is very willing to bid you farewell.[22]

Galling for Malvolio is the way in which the household is transformed into a haunt of vagabonds and a place of scurrilous entertainment, thus undermining its status and endangering the
reciprocal exchanges so crucial to the maintenance of the nobility's pre-eminence. A disorderly household, as Malvolio implies,
reflects poorly upon the mistress's reputation. Not only are symbolic dimensions affected: the household is also materially
disrupted, riven by confusions over rituals and boundaries, and
plagued by servants and knights whose combined actions make
a mockery of carefully gradated domestic hierarchies.

If Malvolio expresses his proximity to contemporary constructions of the steward through noisy protest, then Antonio, the
steward in Webster's *The Duchess of Malfi* (1612–14), registers his
via quieter and subtler forms of rhetorical propriety. Antonio's
connection with household ordinances is of an altogether more
broadly allusive variety. Delio's description of Antonio as 'formal . . .
in . . . habit' in the first scene establishes at once a sense of the
steward's gravity and punctiliousness.[23] In the opening stages of
the play, Antonio's adherence to conventions is stressed. He falls
back on *sententiae* in admonishing Bosola (I.i.74–82), seems to
be recalling the similes of character books in his descriptions of the
Cardinal (I.i.156–67) and, when praising the Duchess (I.i.187–205),
is stilted and imitative. Even when pressed to register a
personal opinion, Antonio resorts to classical instances: 'as out
of the Grecian horse issued many famous princes,' he remarks,
'so, out of brave horsemanship, arise the first sparks of growing
resolution' (I.i.143– 5). Not surprisingly, his wordy mannerisms
are the object of comment, as when Delio rebukes: 'Fie Antonio, /
You play the wire-drawer with [your] commendations' (I.i.205–6).
In Antonio, the civility expected of the steward is widened to
encompass a range of formulaic responses, to the extent that it
seems as if he has little sense of an autonomous identity.

DERELICTING DUTIES

The *Twelfth Night* and *The Duchess of Malfi* examples, however,
are not merely replications of contemporary household requirements.

It is also suggested that Antonio and Malvolio exceed as well as observe the duties accompanying their offices. In *The Duchess of Malfi*, Delio's function is to puncture Antonio's stuffy view of himself. In *Twelfth Night*, Malvolio's predilection for pomposity raises questions about the nature of his authority. It is never clearly established that Olivia seeks her cousin's departure, which suggests that Malvolio is prepared to read his mistress's silence on the subject according to personal priorities, to put in the place of what she does not say his own moral outrage. By concealing the exact source of Malvolio's indignation, even though his actions answer to the demands of his job description, *Twelfth Night* hints at the potential for an abuse of the domestic power network.

Caught in something of a double bind, Malvolio and Antonio are not untypical. Across the whole range of dramatic representations, stewards and gentlemen ushers are simultaneously discovered as exaggerated offshoots of their idealized equivalents and as figures who fail to meet their essential obligations. A common preoccupation is that the steward upholds high principles in public, but is incapable of maintaining them in private. With an increasing attention to the socially divisive implications of their actions, chief officers are realized as drunken, fraudulent, lascivious and ambitious. Not so much a stereotype as a summation of aristocratic anxieties, this version of the chief officer engages nervous attitudes towards the household economy, an uneasiness about the need to invest power in a servant and a conviction that intemperance would gain sway over prudent domestic management. The dominant dramatic scenario, aligned with a parodic reading of the rule-book, shows up cracks in the popular image of the chief officer and the larger instabilities which affected the cultural location of the noble household itself.

In particular, the lure of the bottle is represented as a powerful counter-force to the need to remain abstemious. In Beaumont and Fletcher's *The Scornful Lady* (1613–16), Savill, the steward, is attacked by his master, the Elder Loveless, for being a 'Drunkard' and for having wasted 'three hundred pounds in drinke'.[24] As the monetary reference makes clear, the worrying underside to Savill's behaviour is his neglect of a thrifty attitude towards the household's finances. That the steward's secret drinking is a species of embezzlement is confirmed in Henry Glapthorne's *The Lady Mother* (1633–5). The play centres upon Lovell, the steward, whose greatest vice is retiring to the cellar to indulge his passion for his mistress's sack. Addressing a bottle, Lovell declares:

> I create thee my companion, & thou Cup shalt be my freind, why so now goe to & goe to, lets haue a health to o^r M^{rs} & first to myne, sweet companion fill to my kind friend, by thy leaue freind Ile begin to my Companion, [a] health to my Mrs Soe, now my – hands in Companion fill, and heres a health to my freinds M^{rs} very good, & now I will conclude ... .[25]

Here the danger is that Lovell has created for himself an alternative community to the domestic order, one in which levelling impulses place mistresses and servants on an equal footing. More disturbing, perhaps, is that Lovell's companion, his bottle, becomes inseparable in his mind from his mistress, suggesting a failure to discriminate between the agent of his intoxication and the source of his infatuation. The final impression is of a household in which hierarchical niceties have ceded place to a carnival of muddled identifications.

Because the steward was responsible for the provisions of the household, he enjoyed a freedom of access which, in the aristocratic mind, at least, could easily be abused. To dramatic representations of the steward's abnegation of his responsibilities can be added masters' reflections upon the drinking habits of officers in their service. In 1631, the Earl of Strafford wrote to Richard Marris, his steward, about his worsening drinking problem: 'if you haue not as much respect and creditt w[i]th me as any seruant ought to expect of his Maister itt is your owne fault ... if you still be inthrauled w[i]th that vngouerned appetite I must truly tell you I shall lessen in my esteeme of and my affection towards you extreamly.'[26] Of interest in the complaint is the suggestion of personal betrayal, an attenuated development of the contemporary assumption that the steward's behaviour was a guide to the lord's honourable credentials. But a drunken chief officer, as dramatic representations demonstrate, could also spell economic disaster, a possibility never far from employers' imaginations. In 1634, William Arundell, a Wiltshire gentleman, left John Sherlocke, his butler, in charge of 'Sixteene or Seaventeene hogsheads of ... good beere, and ... a Tiere of Clarett' in the winecellar. When he returned home to discover the contents had been consumed, the butler was blamed.[27] As the details of Arundell's statement suggest, the disappearance of so many items from the cellar's inventory is a costly loss to contemplate. If the steward's exemplary abstemiousness was integral to his symbolic function, it was also implicated in important material considerations.

The economic significance of the steward's behaviour, however, was not only addressed metaphorically. A number of dramas takes the wasteful steward figure one stage further and represents his actions in terms of specific financial dealings. Given the steward's official duties, it is not coincidental that his use of money should emerge as so recurrent a subject of enquiry. At first sight, the steward appears as a morally impeccable accountant. As some stewards were entrusted with substantial sums, and even loaned money to their employers at times of adversity, so do the dramatic representations initially reveal the chief officer to possess considerable financial acumen.[28] In *Timon of Athens* (1604–8), a play which describes the repercussions of indiscriminate expenditure, Flavius, the steward, is the only character who spends constructively. Timon, his profligate master, is forced to break up his house, and Flavius comforts the other servants:

> Good fellows all,
> The latest of my wealth I'll share amongst you.
> Wherever we shall meet, for Timon's sake
> Let's yet be fellows. Let's shake our heads, and say,
> As 'twere a knell unto our master's fortunes,
> 'We have seen better days'. Let each take some;
> [*Giving them money.*
> Nay, put out all your hands. Not one word more;
> Thus part we rich in sorrow, parting poor.[29]

In this scene, the steward distributes money in a demonstration of the sound principles that underpin his domestic government. The effect is to bind the servants in an equitable fellowship, a sharp contrast with the material acquisitiveness subscribed to by Titus's parasitical entourage. When they hesitate to accept Flavius's gifts, moreover, the servants display a magnanimity of spirit that recalls the qualities for which their master was originally venerated. Through Flavius, the slow decline of Titus's magisterial reputation is highlighted.

Notwithstanding Flavius's exemplary stewardship, the majority of dramatic representations concentrates on chief officers whose attitude towards money appears in far less favourable light. It is the potential for the steward to misuse his financial responsibilities that seems to exercise the greatest fascination. In the seduction scene of *The Duchess of Malfi*, Antonio and his mistress move from a discussion of accumulating, saving and hoarding to an acknowledgement of the economy of sexual desire: the Duchess refers to her 'large expense' (I.i.365) and characterizes her steward as an 'upright treasurer' (I.i.372). Expressing their feelings for each other, mistress and servant continue to exploit financial terms. The Duchess sees herself as a 'wealthy mine' (I.i.429), and Antonio will not 'come' to her 'in debt' (I.i.462), suggesting that the economic requirements of the steward's office dictate the form of all other relations. Yet Antonio is only intermittently an 'upright treasurer'. At the start of the scene, his description of the Duchess is rife with connotations of monetary value (I.i.187–9), and it opens up questions about why precisely the steward is so keen to remain in her employment. It is Antonio's supposed false dealing with money, furthermore, to which the Duchess refers when she wishes to have him banished. '[Y]ou have yielded me / A million of loss', she states, 'I am like to inherit / The people's curses for your stewardship' (III.ii.183–5). Although the claims are a part of a ruse to protect Antonio, the expectation that they will be accepted points to a wider contemporary belief that stewards were morally corruptible. The 'false' steward was a figure of general currency and proverbial familiarity.[30]

Certainly it was the possibility that the steward could abuse his financial responsibilities that vexed masters and mistresses most deeply. There are even records of stewards who actively sought their employers' economic downfall. Christopher Danby, a steward to a wealthy Yorkshire family, plotted between 1592 and 1609 a 'wicked and lewde practize and conspiracie' to defraud his master of thousands of pounds and to poison and murder his wife.[31] But the greater part of employers, it would seem, were worried less by the likelihood of actual embezzlement than by the need to delegate the supervision of their incomes. Private accounts were kept, possibly in an attempt more closely to regulate disbursements, and reminders were sent to chief officers, threats and blandishments.[32] '[Your] recepts . . . must be beter loked to . . . I do not se that we receue the halfe we had wont to doe,' wrote the Countess of Shrewsbury to her steward in 1612.[33] Sir Arthur Ingram, a Yorkshire knight, replied indignantly to Mattison, his steward, in about 1622: 'I haue re[ceiued] you[r] letter and w[i]th all a nott of chardges the w[hi]ch semes so strange to me as I know nott whatt to say to itt.'[34] While there are no direct accusations in the statements above, an aristocratic dissatisfaction with the situation is clearly implicit. Scratch the surface of the letters, and a steward who diverts funds for illicit ends will quickly emerge.

It was to such broad discursive anxieties that dramatic constructions of stewards' financial mismanagement were directed. What is found in the drama, moreover, is an imaginative development of the 'false' steward figure projected in aristocratic accounts and correspondence. For the dominant scenario discovers stewards who are bent upon diverting funds for their own use. In Anthony Munday's *The Downfall of Robert, Earl of Huntingdon* (1597–8), Warman, the steward, is described by the prologue as an 'ill fac't miser, brib'd in either hand . . . Who *Iudas* like betraies his liberall Lord'.[35] The means whereby Warman has 'Wasted' his master's 'treasure' and 'increast' his own 'store' (Sc. ii, 352) are perceived, typically, in terms of personal treachery. A comparable but more carefully elaborated example is provided in Jonson's *The Case is Altered* (*c*. 1597–8), in which Jaques, the steward, steals his master's treasure. Turning his back on society, Jaques withdraws into obscurity and solitude, finally burying his riches:

> I'll hide and cover it with this horse-dung:
> Who will suppose that such a precious nest
> Is crowned with such a dunghill excrement?
> In, my dear life; sleep sweetly, my dear child.
> Scarce lawfully begotten, but yet gotten,
> And that's enough. Rot all hands that come near thee,
> Except mine own. Burn out all eyes that see thee,
> Except mine own. All thoughts of thee be poison
> To their enamoured hearts, except mine own.[36]

In this play, the secretive tendencies of the steward are granted their most searching exposition. Particularly striking about Jaques's behaviour is the way in which he substitutes money for the family he should ideally serve, treating his 'precious nest' with the fussiness of an over-protective parent. The domination of the steward by his wealth constitutes a timely reminder of his refusal to acknowledge his master's authority. There is still, however, in the accumulating rhetoric of the passage, a hint of the steward's accounting skills, even if the obligation to spend has been overtaken by a species of excremental retentiveness.

Together these representations suggest that the steward formed an important part of a dialogue about the material foundations on which the greatness of aristocratic families was founded. They suggest, too, that the steward is at his most attractive as a dramatic subject, and paradoxically at his most powerful, when he is able to operate in a private capacity and to rearrange the economic systems in which he is implicated. Economic concerns, in fact, reverberate throughout representations of chief officers' derelictions of their duties, never more so than in scenes in which they fall prey to the violence of their sexual instincts. Hand-in-hand with his wasteful attitude towards money in the popular mind went the chief officer's profligate sexuality. This was, of course, a particularly dangerous vice in a domestic economy in which both the steward and the gentleman usher were viewed as moral yardsticks. Contemporary letter-books and pamphlets describe gentlemen ushers who use gold or finery to capture the affections of the female members of the household: their humour trades upon the servants' manipulation of a sober deportment and a smart appearance to secure personal advantage.[37] In Middleton's *A Mad World, My Masters* (1605–6), Follywit, a young gentleman disguised as a courtesan, is pursued by Gunwater, the steward to Sir Bounteous Progress. Such is the force of Gunwater's passion that he fails to see through Follywit's charade:

> Come, lady, you know where you are now? . . . There stands a casket. I would my yearly revenue were but worth the wealth that's lock'd in't, lady; yet I have fifty pound a year, wench . . . you might admit a choice gentleman into your service . . . I have the command of all the house; I can tell you, nothing comes into th' kitchen but comes through my hands.[38]

Underpinning this passage is the implication that Gunwater will steal from his master's coffers to gain sexual favours, prostituting his economic powers and his moral responsibilities simultaneously. Nor will this be the first time, the play suggests, that the steward has exploited his authority for dubious purposes.

Beyond the failure to order their emotions lies an anxiety about stewards' corruptive influences. When Mallfort, the steward in

The Lovers' Progress, composed by Fletcher in about 1623 and revised by Massinger in 1634, falls in love with a scheming maidservant, he becomes so obsessed that he neglects his financial obligation to 'cast accompt', and is treated as an object of general mockery.[39] The recommendations of household ordinances are parodically recast in Mallfort's abandonment of chaste respectability and in the imitative possibilities that the spectacle of his unseemly behaviour produces. '[A]ll the house', Clarinda, the maidservant, tells him, 'takes notice / Of your ridiculous fopperie' (II.i.p. 94).

A more unsettling realization of a chief officer's sexual actions is developed in plays in which a gentleman usher endeavours to establish a personal relationship with a social superior. In Chapman's *The Gentleman Usher* (1602–3), the ultimate foolishness of Bassiolo, the usher of the title, is to push the intimacy that could obtain between chief officers and their employers into prohibited areas. Bassiolo seeks to promote an unseemly camaraderie between himself and a gentleman. His opportunity comes when Vincentio employs Bassiolo as a go-between. The facility with which Bassiolo agrees to Vincentio's demands, coupled with his gullibility, illuminates an incipient restlessness, which the dramatic action implicitly castigates. It also demonstrates an underlying homoerotic attraction. Indeed, the play as a whole, as Mario DiGangi has persuasively argued, attests to 'the difficulty of dismantling or controlling the disorderly significations of male homoerotic relations'.[40] These concerns are abundantly in evidence when Bassiolo offers to lie down on the ground with Vincentio, his 'friend', and the barriers between them dissolve in an image of the collapse of all social distinctions.[41] They are no less sharply illustrated in the scene in which Bassiolo addresses Vincentio as 'sweete *Vince*' (III.ii.133), the abbreviation of the gentleman's name offering powerful corroboration of the familiarity Bassiolo so desperately requires. The implications of same-sex relations are finally clarified when Bassiolo likens his relationship with Vincentio to that between a 'man and wife' (III.ii.135). It is an index of Bassiolo's transgression that he blurs not only master-servant hierarchies but also the heterosexual norms that legitimized the marital institution.

Although *The Gentleman Usher* is continually punctuated with passionate declarations, the shock waves of the usher's conduct do not substantially alter the course of the play's direction. In

other dramas of the period, however, there is a fuller consideration of an officer's sexual and social compulsions. When the steward concentrated his sexual ambitions on his mistress, the most
dangerous aspects of an abuse of authority could be revealed. A
motivating energy in Malvolio's behaviour in *Twelfth Night* (1601)
is his recollection of an earlier precedent. What excites him is
not so much Olivia's letter as the fact that 'The Lady of the Strachy'
married her 'yeoman of the wardrobe' (II.v.39–40). It is only by
recalling the yeoman servant's good fortune that the steward can
convince himself that Olivia 'uses me with a more exalted respect
than any one else that follows her' (II.v.26–8). The 'Strachy'
allusion has not been traced, which may suggest that liaisons
between noble household servants and their mistresses were
regarded in typological terms in the period. Interestingly, while
Malvolio's grand schemes are crushed, other 'problematic' relationships are allowed to continue. *Twelfth Night* is profoundly
inconsistent – apprehensive about class transgressions, but rela-
tively accepting of gender confusions.[42] Despite lacking obvious
social qualifications, Viola/Cesario and Sebastian face limited
opposition when they decide to contract marriages, even though
their unions leave crucial questions unanswered: Orsino is drawn
to the idea of fraternization with a eunuch, while Olivia is stimulated by Viola/Cesario's embracing of 'boy and man' (I.v.161)
and by the ambiguous sexual territory which she/he inhabits.
Amidst a frenzy of communal couplings, Malvolio's marital fantasy
goes unconsummated, leading to the suspicion that the mobility
he represents belongs to a more unsettling order of ambition
than the allure of the transvestite.

Pierre Bourdieu has commented that 'a transgression of the
principle of male pre-eminence – of which the limiting case was
the marriage of a man-servant to his female employer – incurred
great disapproval'.[43] His formulation is of particular relevance
to *Twelfth Night*, and to the inglorious defeat of Malvolio's mat-
rimonial aspirations. But *mésalliance* activated economic and
political anxieties as well as patriarchal objections. To countenance
a servant-mistress relationship was to run the risk of granting
an inferior economic ascendancy, as a number of contemporary
disputes demonstrate.[44] It was also to bestow upon servants a
measure of political autonomy. Formerly one of the gentlemen
ushers of Protector Somerset, Francis Newdigate married the
Duchess dowager, Anne, the daughter of Sir Edward Stanhope,

and was elected as a Wiltshire MP in 1559 and 1563, probably through his mistress's influence.[45] Once again, such easy ascents into the oligarchy may not have found favour with an establishment used to maintaining power through more traditional inheritance networks.

In contemporary terms, a chief officer's desire for his mistress posed the greatest threat to status alignments and social boundaries. To the advantageous marriages that senior servants were able to secure a significant class dimension was attached. After the death of her husband, Henry Grey, the Duke of Suffolk, Frances, the Duchess dowager, married in 1557 Adrian Stokes, her Master of the Horse, a man some 15 years her junior. Princess Elizabeth was rumoured to have condemned the match and to have exclaimed: 'Has the woman so far forgotten herself as to marry a common groom?'[46] In Elizabeth's horrified reaction is a self-conscious manipulation of the conventional perception that cross-class unions flouted existing hierarchical distinctions. When not addressed to their mistresses, this critical rhetoric was directed at servants themselves. For instance, in 1553, after some years of widowhood, Catherine Willoughby, the Duchess of Suffolk and Frances's stepmother, chose for her second husband Richard Bertie, her gentleman usher but also her companion and adviser. Although classically educated and from a respectable family, Bertie found it difficult to achieve social acceptance.[47] Unsuccessful in his 1570 application for the Willoughby title, Bertie was provoked to send a stormy letter to Sir William Cecil in which he protested that 'the arms I give I received from my father, and they are the same which are mentioned in the scroll that he shewed to the heralds'.[48] One can only be speculative, but it may have been that Bertie's origins as a servant disqualified him in Cecil's mind from advancing to higher honours.[49] For a chief officer to marry his mistress was already an anomaly; for him to gain a title as a result was an even more troubling situation to contemplate.

It is perhaps not coincidental, therefore, that *Twelfth Night* reserves its sharpest comments for the ways in which Malvolio's marital ambitions introduce delicate class considerations. The play takes some of its force from contemporary anxieties about the implications of chief officers and mistresses crossing an unspoken sexual divide. When Malvolio muses upon the life-changes in front of him, he notably imagines scoring victories over Sir Toby, whose title arguably places him above the steward on the social scale: 'I will be proud, I will read politic authors, I will baffle Sir Toby, I will wash off gross acquaintance' (II.v.161–3). Throughout, it is Malvolio's constant reluctance to acknowledge class divisions that provokes the fiercest complaint, a professional failing that vexes Sir Toby more than any other: 'Art any more than a steward?' (II.iii.113–14), the disgruntled knight demands. Malvolio may respect his essential household duties, but he is unwilling to distinguish between their finer social gradations. By the close, the last traces of an official role have been taken over by the steward's confidence in his own magnificence. Furthermore, as his self-absorption worsens, so do the efforts to enrage him increase. Fabian delights in addressing Malvolio as 'man' rather than 'sir' (III.iv.88–9), a particularly injurious epithet for a steward who prides himself on his elevated status. For the steward, there is no greater effrontery than being dictated to by those he hopes to dominate. As he states in his letter, it is humiliating to be forced to take second place to the '*rule*' of his mistress's '*drunken cousin*' (V.i.303). Class tensions continue to surface in the final stages, and they gain an additional force from the exposure of Malvolio's secret vice to the uncomfortable glare of public ridicule.

If Malvolio's chief derelictions take the form of an abuse of servant–mistress relations, however, the example the steward represents is not entirely typical. An exception to the rule that a steward can only be unsuccessful in his marital ambitions is Antonio in *The Duchess of Malfi* (1612–14). In becoming the Duchess's husband, Antonio is able to enjoy social freedoms denied to Malvolio and to shed some of the markers of his dependent attachment. Whereas Malvolio is transformed and falls victim to fantastic delusions, moreover, Antonio is permitted to grow in integrity and self-assurance. He greets Delio, recently returned to court: 'Our noble friend, my most beloved Delio!' (III.i.1). Expansiveness and openness distinguish the steward, earlier dry and diffident. As suited to the role of husband as that of dutiful servant, the exchange suggests, Antonio finds in his marriage and the children that accompany it a new vitality. In response to Antonio's queries, Delio is polite, even deferential: 'I did sir; and how fares your noble duchess?' (III.i.4). By calling his friend 'sir', Delio treats Antonio with a fresh admiration and respect. Registered in the possessive 'your' is an acknowledgement of the steward's increased status, of his now considerable political influence.

Antonio, then, stands as the most intriguing version of a steward who is seen to fall short of a household ideal. It may be that his ambivalent role in the seduction scene minimizes the gravity of his actions – the steward only begins to woo when he realizes that his attentions will be welcomed. Alternatively, the secrecy that surrounds the marriage means that the broader, public aspects of the match do not develop into a more urgent dramatic debate. Finally, it is clear that, while Antonio benefits from his marriage, he retains many of his original stewardly qualities. Unlike Malvolio, Antonio never loses his dignity: the steward is unique in being able to move out of his class while still preserving the authority so crucial to the exercise of his professional capacities.

OFFICES ECLIPSED

Up to this point I have argued that the realization of an erring chief officer is intimately related to a matrix of aristocratic priorities, which involved economic anxieties and localized domestic conflicts. But this dominant treatment, I suggest, has its genesis in a wider context and constitutes an ideological response to larger social pressures, including contemporary changes to the composition of the servant body, new attitudes towards officers' roles and the declining importance of the noble household in the popular consciousness.

On many occasions in the drama, the derelictions of stewards and gentlemen ushers have a common denominator. Accompanying representations of stewards and gentlemen ushers whose secret vices belie their public exterior is the conviction that domestic offices have been filled by unsuitably qualified candidates. That is, officers are imagined as 'upstarts' – types who have risen suddenly or illegitimately from lowly conditions to elevated positions. Strikingly, it is precisely at the moment when the officer abuses his responsibilities that his social origins are brought into play. Given particular attention is the fear that officers are no longer the possessors of 'gentle attributes', a key factor in their inability properly to administrate.[50]

On an initial inspection, it seems to be gentlemen ushers who bear the brunt of this 'upstart' accusation. In *The Gentleman Usher* (1602–3), Vincentio, to win Bassiolo's confidence, claims that officers can advance through merit not lineage. The language

Vincentio deploys – 'extraordinarie spirits . . . wil not stand . . .
On birth and riches . . . be [they] poore / Or basely borne' (III.ii.
58–60, 62–3) – suggests that he has Bassiolo in mind, and that
the gentleman usher's unorthodoxies are bound up with the
possibility of his not being a gentleman at all. What is only implicit
in *The Gentleman Usher* is made explicit in Jonson's *A Tale of a
Tub* (early 1630s), in which a gentleman usher is reminded of
his obscure beginnings when he cheekily refuses to obey Lady
Tub, his mistress. She explodes:

> when I heard his name first, Martin Polecat,
> A stinking name, and not to be pronounced
> Without a reverence, in any lady's presence;
> My very heart e'en earned, seeing the fellow
> Young, pretty and handsome; being then I say,
> A basket-carrier, and a man condemned
> To the saltpetre works; made it my suit
> To Master Peter Tub, that I might change it;
> And call him as I do now, by Pol-Martin,
> To have it sound like a gentleman in an office,
> And make him mine own foreman, daily waiter . . .[51]

At issue in the speech are the ways in which language shapes
identity, and this is registered in Lady Tub's belief that invert-
ing her usher's name will conceal the animal associations of his
proletarian origins. But the change of name is not matched by
an equivalent transformation in Pol-Martin's character, and it is
soon apparent that the usher can only be an imitation of a 'gentle'
original, a simulacrum for his mistress's social and sexual fantasies.

If, in representations of gentlemen ushers, a status indictment
is hinted at, in plays featuring stewards a more forcible con-
demnation of chief officers' 'upstart' characteristics is advanced.
Indeed, it is with a peculiar critical intensity that the genealogies
of stewards are investigated. *King Lear* (1604–5) dramatizes Kent's
attack on Oswald, Goneril's steward, who shows his disdain for
authority from an early stage. Impersonating a major-domo, Kent
parodically announces the steward's arrival, only to turn his titles
to scurrilous invective:

> A knave, a rascal, an eater of broken meats; a base, proud,
> shallow, beggarly, three-suited, hundred-pound, filthy worsted-

stocking knave; a lily-livered, action-taking, whoreson, glass-gazing, super-serviceable, finical rogue; one-trunk-inheriting slave; one that wouldst be a bawd in way of good service, and art nothing but the composition of a knave, beggar, coward, pandar, and the son and heir of a mongrel bitch.[52]

A general preoccupation with blood dominates in the speech: honour and nobility conventionally defined the 'gentle' servant, but Oswald is unable to display either quality, fails to respond to Kent's drawing of his sword and flees as soon as the possibility of conflict presents itself.[53] More specifically, the reference to inheritance ('one-trunk . . . slave') pinpoints a concern about how the aristocratic system can reproduce itself when it is challenged by 'mongrel' hybrids, while the image of the steward as a conduit for sexual exchange ('a bawd') refracts further anxieties about the corruption of a pure stream of lineage. To Kent, at least, it is as if the traditional order of chief officers is perilously close to extinction.

Although Oswald's position and behaviour infuriate Kent, they do not appear to trouble the other characters, suggesting that *King Lear* represents only a localized intervention in a discussion about officers' social status. Later dramas, however, broaden the debate and contemplate the connections between the acquisition of high rank and upward mobility. *The Duchess of Malfi* (1612–14) represents an extended examination of the laws of preferment, the nature of gentility and the situation of the aristocratic system, and it is through Antonio and Bosola that these concerns are ventilated. Despite his opening reflections upon the virtues of well-managed households (I.i.4–22), Antonio is by no means an ideal steward figure. Images of 'poison' (I.i.14) and '*diseases*' (I.i.15) in his address hint at adulteration, while the reference to 'flatt'ring sycophants' (I.i.8), who aspire to 'instruct' their 'princes' (I.i.20), implies that the steward, too, can be seen as an instrument of infiltration, even as a locus for presumptuous tendencies. As the rest of the play reveals, these suggestions are explicitly articulated in the accusations of Antonio's detractors, although the 'truth' of their content is never clearly established. Instead, Antonio's presumed audacity in marrying the Duchess is translated into an indicator of his inferiority. According to Ferdinand, Antonio is 'A slave, that only smell'd of ink and counters, / And ne'er in's life look'd like a gentleman, / But in the audit-time' (III.iii.72–4), an identification taken up by Bosola, who describes the steward as a 'base, low fellow' (III.v.117). The rhetorical parallelism of the statements confirms that the steward-'upstart' type, like the 'false' steward, was of general currency. It also demonstrates that the prospect of an 'upstart' exercising key responsibilities provoked anxious reactions. As Frank Whigham argues, the play dwells repeatedly upon the predicament of the 'threatened aristocrat, frightened by the contamination of his supposedly ascriptive social rank, and obsessively preoccupied with its defence'.[54] In this respect, Antonio is a particularly unsettling figure, since he is able to ascend the hierarchy without having to divulge the details of his origins or the extent of his social credentials.

While Antonio occupies a charged place at the start of *The Duchess of Malfi*, he participates less actively in ensuing scenes, and it is Bosola who comes to the fore in the final stages. Notwithstanding Antonio's dwindling role, the two servants are frequently linked, the effect of which is to suggest that the antagonisms aroused by the steward's change in fortune are not restricted in their significance. At once it appears as if Bosola is Antonio's ideological opposite. He is likened to one of the poisonous flatterers that Antonio criticizes (I.i.52, 77), and his unscrupulous methods of advancement set off the dutiful vigilance that seals the steward's success. But Bosola is simultaneously Antonio's substitute. The statement that his corruption 'Grew out of horsedung' (I.i.287) brings to mind Antonio's uncertain background, and the similarity between them is enhanced when he is taken into the Duchess's confidence. 'Am I not thy duchess?' (IV.ii.134), she asks Bosola, as if she were addressing her steward, and actually seems to confuse him for her husband as she dies (IV.ii.350). A sense of Antonio and Bosola's interlocking destinies is conveyed in her mistake, and even the last words of the servants invite comparison: they centre upon flight, exile and restless movement. Embodied in these areas of overlap is the broader point that Antonio's promotion inaugurates what becomes a cyclical process: 'upstart' servants ignoring the handicap of their descent and inveigling themselves into aristocratic power structures. The steward's experience is elaborated into the sign of a deeper social and epistemological malaise.

It is part of the contemporary valency of these dramatic representations that they participate in larger discussions about the relationship between gentility and service in a shifting social landscape. The lines of demarcation between employment in a noble household and the achievement of eminence were keenly scrutinized in the period, and in a variety of cultural venues. Of course, it was not necessarily common for chief officers to enter the gentry or the aristocracy, and the promotion to a title was more likely to have been the result of a slow accumulation of fortunes over several generations. Most often, officers had to be content only with a modest improvement in their circumstances, such as that experienced by Timothy Pusey, the steward to Bess of Hardwick, whose appointment as a Nottinghamshire sheriff enabled him to arrange advantageous marriages for his daughters.[55] Patronized by wealthy masters, however, a smaller number of officers rose to prominence with spectacular rapidity and a seeming ease. John Thynne, the son of a humble Shropshire farmer, became steward to Edward Seymour, later Protector Somerset, in 1536. With his master's assistance, he bought up land, obtained a post in the city, was knighted in 1547 and married in 1548 the daughter and heiress of Sir Richard Gresham, a former mayor of London. His crowning achievement was the construction of Longleat, his country house, a project still continuing at his death in 1580. Like his dramatic counterparts, Thynne was considered as something of a *parvenu*, as a sixteenth-century Wiltshire satire pillorying his grand architectural ambitions attests.[56]

Nor was the unpopularity generated by such success stories merely a local phenomenon. In 1598, when it was proposed that Sir Gilly Meyrick, the steward of the Earl of Essex, should fill the vacant office of the deputy lieutenantship of the county of Radnor, the Earl of Pembroke felt obliged to protest. His complaint follows a familiar course:

> I know that [he] . . . is a knight; I hear that he is rich; I mislike not his credit, and envy not his wealth; but I also know that he is [a] . . . household servant, not residing in Radnorshire . . . nor of any kin there, only brought thither by marriage with his wife, and she no inheritrix neither.[57]

Clearly emerging from the letter is an attempt to define 'gentility' in conventional terms: the details of Meyrick's knighthood, reputation and economic resources are all instrumental to Pembroke's purpose. But there is also evident a resistance to the steward's mobility, since his riches are comparatively new and his honours only recently acquired. As in the dramatic representations, Meyrick's *arriviste* status is the prompt for reflections upon the measure of power to which chief officers were entitled. The anxieties circulating in the drama crystallized a debate of greater scope and potentially crucial social consequence.

If Thynne and Meyrick stand out as exceptional, moreover, this may only be an illusory impression. For a range of materials suggests that the non-gentle officer in pursuit of honours was rapidly establishing himself as a familiar cultural property. In the same year as Pembroke voiced his objections to Meyrick's dubious qualifications, I. M. published *A health to the gentlemanly profession of seruing-men*, a treatise with a direct bearing on the social 'upstarts' that the drama anatomizes. Mainly concentrating on the larger noble households, I. M. argues that the established order of 'gentle' servants is dying out, neglected by prodigal or illiberal lords and shunted into obscurity by the demands of an 'aspyring' and 'presumptuous' new class. Now the sons of yeomen, not gentlemen, infected by the 'ambicious desire of dignitie', enter service.[58] Older attitudes have suffered, as 'seruice' is regarded as a 'very seruile seruitude', and beyond the ideological shift lies the growing influence of the cash-nexus. No longer are servants rewarded with land or payments in kind; instead, they agitate for and receive wages.[59] Although composed at the end of the Elizabethan period, *A health to the gentlemanly profession of seruing-men* has all the hallmarks of a classic Marxist manifesto.

I. M.'s treatise offers a helpful point of entry into the unpredictable terrain of gentility and aristocratic service in England in the sixteenth and seventeenth centuries. Of course, not all of its statements can be accepted at face value. There are isolated indications, for instance, that land continued to be leased to senior servants, and that the profession may not have been anathema to younger sons from gentle families.[60] Nevertheless, the implications of I. M.'s discussion are difficult to ignore, especially as the author's sentiments chime with a louder chorus of contemporary complaint. In 1602, William Basse, a retainer to Lord Wenman, wrote in a rhyming lament that 'Serving-men' of 'gentle blood' are 'slightly reckon'd' by their 'hard commanders'. The good name of aristocratic service, Basse observes, is increasingly under threat from the members of the 'meaner sort' who strive to join his 'brotherhood'.[61] The compiler of a book of household ordinances, possibly Richard Brathwait, agreed, remarking in 1605 that younger and 'ignorant' gentlemen ushers, not 'long trained and experienced in that kinde of service', were becoming a typical commodity. This was one manifestation, according to Brathwait, of the common belief that 'disgrace' accompanied the 'gentleman of good ... discent' who elected 'to serve an Earle as an Officer in his house'.[62] For Brathwait, as for a host of other commentators, the offices that had underpinned the greatness of the noble household were, by the beginning of the seventeenth century, mere shadows of an earlier glory.

From these descriptions several conclusions emerge. If the 'gentle' servant is on the decline, the 'upstart' servant is in the ascendant. Employment in a noble household is derided or looked at expediently, by the general populace, by masters and even by 'gentle' servants themselves. Although the accounts differ in points of detail, they unite in their shared conviction that aristocratic service is adapting to ensure its continued survival. They also acquire richer resonances in the light of recent historical work. For a number of studies has demonstrated that a gradual shrinkage in the size of the noble household was indeed accompanied by a rise in cash payments to a smaller domestic staff. At the same time, gentlemen seem to have been drawn with a decreasing frequency to the promise of a career with a local magnate. In the household lists of Lord Howard of Naworth from the 1610s to the 1640s, there appear no names of gentlemen from the northern counties.[63] The protests of Basse, Brathwait and I. M., and images of 'upstart' officers in the drama, therefore, take on additional meanings as meditations upon the material forces that were pushing contemporary establishments towards more streamlined versions of their feudal predecessors.

Beyond these developments lay a further series of shifts in aristocratic mentality and ideological investment. Placing children in a great establishment for a period of instruction was not as fashionable as it had been in the later medieval period, and in the sixteenth and seventeenth centuries younger sons from gentle families would have more probably followed a course of classical education at the Inns of Court or the universities. Ambitions were moving away from a private sphere to relocate themselves at court, a growing centre for professional employment.[64] To facilitate this process, aristocratic families began to spend

greater amounts of time in London, having reduced the personnel of their country residences and economized upon the hospitable practices that defined the rural life. By the end of the
seventeenth century, the elaborate rankings of chief officers had
invariably been replaced by an urban skeleton staff, consisting
of a housekeeper and a single footman who could boast only
bourgeois origins.[65] The offices of the noble household had been
engulfed by a permanent eclipse.

Earlier parts of this chapter argued for the acute sensitivity of
the drama to these developments. More absorbing, perhaps, are
the ways in which the drama draws attention to the effects of
social displacement on chief officers, and to the processes whereby
noble households chose to adapt and diversify. An increasingly
popular figure is that of the chief officer who is no more than a
comic remnant of a previous incarnation. In Brome's *The Northern Lasse* (1629), it is implied that Howdye, the gentleman usher
to a widow, has been transplanted from a larger household in
the country to a smaller one in the metropolis. It is a move that
leads to a corresponding diminution and even debasement of
his essential duties. As Howdye explains, he is now expected

> To be able to relate how this Ladies tooth does; and tother
> Ladies toe. How this Maides Milk does: and how tothers Doctor
> lik'd her last water: how this Ladies husband; and how tother
> Ladies dogge slept last night: how this childe, that Monkey,
> this Nurse, that Parrat, and a thousand such. Then his
> neatnesse . . . about the person of his Lady . . . to conuey a pin
> into her ruffe neatly, or adde a help to her head dressing, as
> well as *Iohn among the Maydes*.[66]

The speech provides a nuanced sense of the transformations that
have overtaken the usher's role. In a newly shrunken setting,
Howyde has no influence in the hall, for there is no hall to
supervise, and can wield little authority over the other servants,
for there are no servants employed to be disciplined. The only
accounting to be done is in cataloguing the ailments of his
mistress's acquaintances, and in comparing the quality of the
milk of the wet-nurses. This change in the usher's social function is read as a loss of male mastery, particularly since his
responsibilities are exercised not in the master's chamber but in
the mistress's boudoire.

As the same time as they detail the fate of chief officers uprooted from their customary locations, dramatic representations also concern themselves with the measures that aristocratic employers were introducing in order to embrace a city lifestyle. A recurring preoccupation is the effect on stewards of the master or the mistress's absenteeism. 'Sir, your fathers old friends hold it the sounder course for your body and estate, to stay at home, and marry, and propagate, and governe' (I.i.15–17) states Savill, the steward in *The Scornful Lady* (1613–16), endorsing a paradigm of the country as a place of health and fertility, and remonstrating with his master, the Elder Loveless, over his decision to go up to town to be at court. Since Savill subsequently falls from grace, an accusing finger is pointed at the Elder Loveless for his failure to respect crucial magisterial obligations. The steward's speech looks forward to a proclamation issued in 1632, which urged aristocratic families in London to return to the country to honour their dispensation of a traditional hospitality.[67] On Caroline audiences, therefore, the topicality of a steward's melancholy reminiscences in Shirley's *The Lady of Pleasure* (1635) would not have been lost:

> The case is altered since we lived i'th' country:
> We do not invite the poor o'th' parish
> To dinner, keep a table for the tenants,
> Our kitchen does not smell of beef, the cellar
> Defies the price of malt and hops, the footmen
> And coachdrivers may be drunk like gentlemen
> With wine, nor will three fiddlers upon holidays
> With aid of bagpipes (that called in the country
> To dance and plough the hall up with their hobnails)
> Now make my lady merry.[68]

The emphasis of the passage falls upon the disappearance of the steward's managerial responsibilities. Because the mistress refuses to pay court to her tenants, the steward is robbed of the opportunity to organize. Because decreasing sums of money are discharged on foodstuffs, there is little for the steward to account. Typically, the mistress's parsimony is conceived of in terms of social displacement: it is difficult to distinguish between the gentlemen servants and the yeomen servants, and the footmen and coachdrivers consume wine like any aristocrat. This is the price to pay, the steward suggests, for abandoning pastoral pleasures for city leisure.

The effects of social dislocation are more obviously apparent, however, in the ways in which chief officers wrestle with ideological crises, and are led to interrogate the constitution of their own identities. Either because they are 'upstarts' or because they are affected by new economic pressures, chief officers in the drama worry about how to achieve self-definition in environments otherwise lacking in traditional values. In a world in which aristocratic employment is subject to derision, and in which forms of recompense for services rendered are under debate, the question of how stewards and gentlemen ushers are to conduct themselves assumes a vital relevance. On many occasions, chief officers' efforts to master linguistic conventions suggest the plight of a displaced class, which is cut off from or not yet accommodated to the dominant culture. The unbending Malvolio in *Twelfth Night* (1601) has characteristic particularities, but, like Antonio, he is also made up of the language of his social superiors. Maria describes him as 'an affectioned ass, that cons state without book, and utters it by great swarths' (II.iii.147–9) and scorns his self-conscious mimicry. Frequently the steward merely replicates Olivia's commands (I.v.140–7), transmitting her messages and sentiments (II.ii.1–15 and II.iii.95–101), and even his anticipation of his mistress's love is an ecstasy of recollections and reported statements (II.v.166–70). It is entirely appropriate that, prevented from being able to express himself as an authentic subject, Malvolio should be trapped by an anagrammatic puzzle that spells his downfall. At the end, he can do no more than quote fragments of a letter incomprehensible to a general audience, although he is finally given a pen and paper to write in his own words. *Twelfth Night* stands finally as a disquisition upon a servant who is learning how best to communicate.

If part of the impact of *Twelfth Night* resides in the manipulation of signs, comedy in *The Gentleman Usher* (1602–4) arises from Bassiolo's more showy appropriation of the rhetoric of his betters. Magpie-like, the gentleman usher picks up bits of courtly vocabulary, as when he says of Vincentio, 'what a phrase / He used at parting! . . . I'll ha't yfaith' (II.i.121–3). He also prides himself on the fact that his letter contains 'more choice words . . . Than in any three of *Guevaras* golden epistles' (IV.ii.14–15), although his delight is tempered by Margaret, who maintains that the document can have no claims to originality. It is a patchwork, Margaret recognizes, of 'Some words, pickt out of Proclamations, / Or great mens Speeches; or well-selling Pamphlets' (III.ii.394–5), and such is her embarrassment that she attempts to school the usher in proper epistolary techniques. For Bassiolo, internalizing household ordinances alone is not a viable option. Ill-at-ease in his office, the usher feels it necessary to refer to alternative constructions of courteous behaviour to manage the transition from one mode of service to another. In want of a classical education, this chief officer finds himself in a rhetorical quagmire, disoriented by the lessening of his responsibilities and divided in his loyalties. No longer a reflection of his lord's reputation, Bassiolo is but a pale imitation of aristocratic ascendancy.

POLITIC LAUGHTER

I have been arguing, then, that dramatic representations of flawed chief officers spoke to a range of contemporary aristocratic preoccupations. The most frequently articulated anxiety is that stewards and gentlemen ushers will overstep the boundaries they themselves were enjoined to maintain, thereby damaging the household's symbolic role and precipitating it into practical confusion. Given such an unwelcome prospect, it is only to be expected that representations should equally invest in efforts to limit the extent of disorder, to incorporate senior servants within the system that their actions endanger. Quite often, the drama views a chief officer's behaviour from a comic perspective, using laughter to release stereotypical expectations and reinscribe forgotten moral standards. No less frequently, it shows the officer forgiven by an indulgent employer. Out of officers' derelictions and displacements evolves the need to restore them to domestic grace.

To a life of economic and sexual dissipation, dramatic representations of stewards suggest, there is an ignominious conclusion. Senior servants who stray from the path of domestic virtue are stripped of the badges of their profession and made to endure forms of symbolic deprivation and social humiliation. Following an unsuccessful attempt to seduce Follywit, Gunwater, the steward in Middleton's *A Mad World, My Masters* (1605–6), discovers that his master's casket has been opened and that its contents, including his 'chain' (IV.iii.82) of office, have disappeared. As the steward rushes about the stage in a desperate search for the precious commodity, it is implied that this is the ironic reward for his moral bankruptcy. When his master, the Elder Loveless, returns home in Beaumont and Fletcher's *The Scornful Lady* (1613–16), Savill, the steward, is swiftly reprimanded. Not only are his keys removed, signs of the steward's seniority, but he is ordered to labour as a groom in one of the neighbouring stables. The indignity is apposite in several respects. First, Savill is expelled from the household, the sphere of his control. Secondly, he is demoted from the rank of a gentleman servant to that of a yeoman servant, a move which robs him of a claim to gentility as well as domestic comfort. Unsurprisingly, Savill responds to the sentence with a suitably melodramatic lament: 'I will runne mad first, and if that get not pitty, / Ile drowne my selfe, to a most dismall ditty' (III.ii.224–5).

The effect of these reductive strategies is, at first sight, to reaffirm assumptions about the property and privileges of the ruling élite. Through comically punitive scenes, domestic stability is reinstated, and distinctions between the servant classes and their more powerful overlords are given a new lease of vitality. More generally, the circumstances in which the steward is placed function to confirm him as a potentially ridiculous type. Mallfort, the steward in *The Lovers' Progress* (1623/1634), is forced to go down on his knees to kiss the feet of Clarinda, the maidservant: his actions constitute a grotesque inversion of household hierarchies. Later in the play, he dresses in armour for his 'Mistresses pleasure' (IV.i.p. 126), becoming a parody of a Spenserian adventurer. Even on occasions when it is not obvious that a steward has failed to execute his duties, a tendency to realize him in relation to comic priorities is apparent. Humour at the chief officer's expense is the overriding imperative. In Brome's *A Mad Couple Well Match'd* (1637–9), Saveall, the steward, denounces Carelesse, his master's nephew. Owing to a confusion, Saveall unknowingly reads to Mistress Anne Crostill, a prim widow, a letter addressed to a prostitute. He explodes: 'You have employed mee basely, made mee your / Carrier of scandall, and scurrility to the hands / Of noblenesse and vertue.'[69] The encounter is diverting in that it shows the role of a household officer blurring into that of a common intermediary. Most distressing for Saveall, but amusing for the audience, is that his exemplary stewardship has been put to the service of bawdy procurement.

On occasions when a comic treatment of the steward would be dramatically incongruous, offers of forgiveness are elaborated as antidotes to the escalation of further disorders. In scenes of attempted reconciliation, the steward, rather than being rejected from the establishment, is tempted with the opportunity of returning to its fold. 'My maister I abus'd in his distresse: / In mine, my kinsman leaues me confortlesse' (Sc. xiv, 2291–2) regrets Warman, the banished steward in Munday's *The Downfall of Robert, Earl of Huntingdon* (1597–8), but, by the final stages, his penitent reflections have won him back magisterial favour. During the course of the play, Warman was drawn to exercise a tyrannical power over the landless poor, to the extent that he is finally obliged to experience with a particular intensity the social implications of his rescue from obloquy.

But, as dramatic representations expose the traditional order's failure to accommodate new social forces, so do they suggest that the moral displacements of chief officers may never be rectified. In the final stages of a number of plays, there are residual energies that exceed the drive towards closure. For example, despite the Duke's desire for Malvolio to be entreated 'to a peace' (V.i.379) in *Twelfth Night* (1601), the steward is conspicuously absent from the climactic celebrations. He leaves the stage vowing to 'be reveng'd on the whole pack of you' (V.i.377), thereby drawing attention to the provisional nature of the reunions and the arbitrariness with which new relations are contracted. One is forcibly reminded that Malvolio is only ever brought to account in a parody of justice overseen by the household's fool, and these discrepancies are further reinforced by the inconsistency with which other socially disruptive actions are countenanced. Part of the play's disjunctive effect is that Maria, who has imitated her mistress's script, escapes punishment, whereas Malvolio is briefly gaoled for an arguably less serious misdemeanour. At the end of *Twelfth Night*, the occlusions and differences that support the domestic order are brought dramatically into focus.

In some ways, Malvolio's experience prepares the way for the greater confusions that afflict Bassiolo in the culminating scenes of *The Gentleman Usher* (1602–4). By the close, it is apparent that Bassiolo has been gulled so successfully that he is even prepared to make public his homoerotic leanings; as he states before an uncomprehending court: 'Here in thy bosome I will lie sweete *Vince*, / And die if thou die; I protest by heauen' (V.iv.172–3).

The drive to reintegrate an errant chief officer, then, meets, in this play, at least, with only partial success. It sparks off, in addition, reflections upon the intersections between political power, erotic persuasion and domestic instability. Bassiolo may be prevented from realizing his ambitions, but the ways in which his schemes are checked reveal a worrying edge to bonds of dependency and divisions beneath the surface of the household's service ideals.

CONCLUSIONS

Throughout this chapter my concern has been to assess dramatic representations of household officers in terms of their social embeddedness. As part of this procedure, I have described the points of contact between popular attitudes towards stewards and gentlemen ushers and a wider cultural network. For aristocratic families, a belief in the dissembling character of their chief representatives, coupled with a need to depend upon them, placed master–servant relations under considerable strain and lent support to engrained assumptions. Complaints about chief officers' intrigues, petty jealousies, thefts and extortions are a recurring feature of employers' papers and memoirs, and, in their volume and frequency, furnished a rich seam for dramatists to mine.[70]

Popular expectations were also a barometer of broader movements in the social formation, and were reinvented as traditional centres of power shifted to new locations. Changes in the dispensation of wealth and the hiring practices of the aristocracy are the necessities out of which emerged the view that service was becoming progressively less privileged and exclusive. As some families elected to modify the nature and purposes of their expenditure, so did ideas about aristocratic service appear less well-defined and inflexible. The origins of chief officers began to diversify, a phenomenon accompanied by an interest in the drama in the steward or gentleman usher who attempts to overcome the handicap of his 'low estate' through political preferment. Such was the perceived threat of the 'upstart' officer, moreover, that myths about the 'false steward' were reactivated: a development specific to the English Renaissance found a suitable representational niche in an older literary stereotype.

Laughter, in the hands of playwrights, gained popularity as a powerful means of exorcizing the worries that inevitably attended new social and economic configurations. Fears were fought with ridicule, and in the drama the discontented and ambitious were prevented from bringing their plans to fulfilment. John Manningham singled out in 1602 the 'good practise' in *Twelfth Night* 'to make the steward beleeve his Lady widdowe was in Love with him', and indicates that he found entertainment in the spectacle.[71] As the Manningham example suggests, the satirical treatment of chief officers seems to have appealed most to the aristocratic members of contemporary audiences. The revised version of *The Lovers' Progress*, for instance, was staged in the early 1630s at the second Blackfriars theatre, which attracted gentle spectators who enjoyed witty and intellectual performances. Although the repertory of the Salisbury Court (where was first produced *The Lady Mother* of 1633–5) sometimes mocked the lesser gentry, landlords from the country were also known to have frequented the playhouse.[72] In the comic perspectives afforded by these 'private' productions, there was implicit a variety of affirmatory aristocratic messages.

If comic devices served the purpose of closing off challenges to the traditional order, however, then they also worked to illuminate the predicaments that affected stewards and gentlemen ushers themselves. For part of the complex effect of contemporary dramatic representations is that they mock chief officers and explore the uncertainties of their profession in equal measure. Because officers simultaneously strive for coherent values and neglect important ethical standards, they become the agents and the casualties of social process, the opponents and the defenders of aristocratic positions. Their actions bring to mind the difficulties of a beleaguered class, which is still in the throes of establishing for itself a stable ideological place. Even as they were seeking to impose limits on chief officers' powers, dramatic representations were creating opportunities for the questions of a displaced social grouping to find release.

The dramatic image of the noble household, therefore, was multivalent in its implications. It conformed to the belief systems of the ruling élite and engaged matters of urgent debate. A type such as Malvolio, to cite only one example, is a paradoxical combination of frigidity and sensuality, both a fool and a representative of authority who subscribes to and at the same time defies traditional modes of conduct. The steward joins other chief officers who, in failing to imitate their masters or in falling from positions of power, are used to show a lightly veiled questioning of aristocratic prerogatives. As a whole, the situations of these officers stimulate speculation about a social order dependent upon exchanges between men, and about the continuing viability of a domestic system which inculcates principles of abstemious moral government. The theatre finally discharged a range of functions, both permitting a critical undercurrent to express itself and providing a forum within which contemporary anxieties were granted their most forceful and enduring statement.

NOTES

1. Felicity Heal, 'Reciprocity and Exchange in the Late Medieval Household', in Barbara A. Hanawalt and David Wallace, eds, *Bodies and Disciplines: Intersections of Literature and History in Fifteenth-Century England* (Minneapolis and London, 1996), pp. 179–80.
2. See Simon Adams, ed., *Household Accounts and Disbursement Books of Robert Dudley, Earl of Leicester*, Camden Society, 5th ser., 6 (1995), p. 29; [Richard Brathwait], *Some Rules and Orders for the Government of the House of an Earle* (1605), in *Miscellanea Antiqua Anglicana* (London, 1821), pp. 3–50; Suffolk R. O., Bury St Edmunds, E2/42/1.
3. Mark Thornton Burnett, 'Ophelia's "false steward" Contextualized', *The Review of English Studies*, 46 (1995), pp. 48–56; Peter R. Moore, 'Ophelia's False Steward', *Notes and Queries*, 41 (1994), pp. 488–9.
4. For details of their scholarship and skills, see B.L., Additional MS. 33508, fos 3^r, 23^r, 57^r, 78^r, Egerton MS. 2646, fos 44^r–5^v; George Cavendish, *The Life and Death of Cardinal Wolsey* (1556–8), in Richard S. Sylvester and Davis P. Harding, eds, *Two Early Tudor Lives* (New Haven, CT and London, 1962); M. E. James, 'The Concept of Order and the Northern Rising of 1569', *Past and Present*, 60, August (1973), p. 57; L.P.L., MS. 697, fo. 115^r, MS. 3198, fos 93^r, 144^r, MS. 3206, fo. 1001^r; W.Y.A.S., Leeds, TN/C, II, item 161.
5. D. R. Hainsworth, *Stewards, Lords and People: The Estate Steward and his World in later Stuart England* (Cambridge, 1992), pp. 6–22, 42–7; H.L., Ellesmere MS. 1180, unfoliated; Lancashire R. O., DDF 2422; Suffolk R. O., Bury St Edmunds, E2/42/1, fo. 4^r.
6. Heal, 'Reciprocity and Exchange', p. 180.
7. Lincolnshire R. O., 2 Ancaster 14/17; Sir Walter Mildmay, *A Memorial for a Son, from his Father, 1570* (Hazelgrove, 1893), p. 2.
8. L.P.L., MS. 3361, fo. 8^r. See also L.P.L., MS. 684/7, fo. 243^r, MS. 884, item 27.

9. G.C.L., Smyth of Nibley Papers, II, item 78; S.C.L., W.W.M., Strafford Papers 21a, item 64.

10. B.L., Additional MS. 33588, fo. 52^r, Egerton MS. 2646, fos 45^r–6^v; G.C.L., Smyth of Nibley Papers, II, items 55, 74; L.P.L., MS. 704, fo. 185^r, MS. 3198, fos 97^r, 141^r, 210^r, 231^r; S.C.L., W.W.M., Strafford Papers 21a, item 57; F. P. and M. M. Verney, eds, *Memoirs of the Verney Family During the Civil War*, 4 vols (London, 1892–9), vol. III, p. 95. See also B.L., Additional MS. 33588, fo. 54^r; S.C.L., W.W.M., Strafford Papers 21a, item 33; W.Y.A.S., Leeds, TN/C, II, item 371; W.A., second Earl's papers, item 41.

11. Chief officers may also have been encouraged to use their local influence to assist their masters in bids for political preferment. See Carol Rawcliffe and Susan Flower, 'English Noblemen and Their Advisers: Consultation and Collaboration in the Later Middle Ages', *Journal of British Studies*, 25 (1986), pp. 157–77; Henry Slingsby, *The Diary*, ed. Daniel Parsons (London, 1836), p. 50.

12. A.C. MS., the fourth Duke of Norfolk's New Testament, fly-leaf. Cf. A.C. MS. T4, T5. The family seems to have been particularly well served by their stewards. In the Fitzalan Chapel at Arundel there is a memorial to Robert Spyller (*c.* 1560–1633/4), the steward to Anne, Countess of Arundel, and to her son, the fourteenth 'Collector' Earl of Arundel. Spyller's is the only non-family memorial. See *The Fitzalan Chapel Guide* (Shoreham-by-Sea, n.d.), p. 1.

13. B.L., Additional MS. 33588, fo. 54^r. For other examples of masters and mistresses who thanked their servants (and whose kindnesses were acknowledged), see B.L., Egerton MS. 2645, fo. 108^r; L.H., Dudley Papers, IV, fo. 13^r; Slingsby, *Diary*, ed. Parsons, p. 51; W.A., second Earl's papers, item 31.

Corroboration of the dedicated service of chief officers can be found in their extended periods of employment (up to 30 years, in some cases) and in the ways in which they passed on their responsibilities to their relatives. Details of father and son (or nephew) teams of officers appear in Barry Coward, *The Stanleys Lords Stanley and the Earls of Derby 1385–1672: The Origins, Wealth and Power of a Landowning Family*, Chetham Society, 3rd ser., 30 (1983), p. 86; Edwin F. Gay, 'The Temples of Stowe and Their Debts: Sir Thomas Temple and Sir Peter Temple, 1603–1653', *Huntington Library Quarterly*, 2 (1939), pp. 408–11; G.C.L., Smyth of Nibley Papers, II, items 90–116; L.P.L., MS. 3206, fos 113^r, 119^r; Verney, eds, *Memoirs*, vol. III, p. 95; W.Y.A.S., Leeds, TN/C, II, item 133, TN/C, IV, item 106, TN/EA/13/36, TN/YO/C/II/4. For periods of employment, see B.L., Additional MS. 34172, fo. 1^r; Essex R. O., D/DBa A1, D/DBa A3; Kent A. O., U1475 A6/12–15, U1475 A9/1–7; Staffordshire R. O., D(W)1734/3/3/300, D(W)1734/3/4/94.

14. John Samuel Fletcher, ed., *The Correspondence of Nathan Walworth and Peter Seddon*, Chetham Society, 1st ser., 109 (1880), pp. 27–8; Gay, 'The Temples', p. 433; Menna Prestwich, *Cranfield: Politics and Profits under the Early Stuarts* (Oxford, 1966), pp. 407–9, 525–6; P[eter] S[amwaies], *The wise and faithful steward* (London, 1657; Wing S546A), pp. 16, 19, 28.

15. Warwickshire R. O., CR136C1915.
16. Warwickshire R. O., CR136B521. Cf. Clwyd R. O., D/G/3275. These intimacies may even have been based upon 'blood' connections, since some chief officers were related to their employers. See Mary E. Finch, *The Wealth of Five Northamptonshire Families 1540–1640*, Northamptonshire Record Society, 19 (1956), p. 81; John Harland, ed., *The House and Farm Accounts of the Shuttleworths*, Chetham Society, 1st ser., 46 (1858), pp. 1014–15; Northamptonshire R. O., Fitzwilliam Misc. Vol. 19; Gladys Scott Thomson, *Life in a Noble Household 1641–1700* (London, 1950), p. 44.
17. Bodl. Lib., MS. Eng. hist. b. 208, fo. 68^v.
18. Bodl. Lib., MS. Eng. hist. b. 208, fos 70^r, 76^r, 78^v; B.L., Additional MS. 33588, fos 45^r–6^v; Alice T. Friedman, *House and Household in Elizabethan England: Wollaton Hall and the Willoughby Family* (Chicago and London, 1989), pp. 42, 185–7; Kent A. O., U1475 E35.
19. Wiltshire R. O., 865/389, pp. 3, 8. Contemporary seating arrangements also give an indication of the gentleman usher's elevated status. See V. Sackville-West, *Knole and the Sackvilles*, 4th edn (London, 1958), pp. 85–8; W.A., Sir William Russell's Papers, item 6.
20. Wiltshire R. O., 865/389, pp. 8, 15. See also [Brathwait], *Some Rules and Orders*, p. 10; L.P.L., MS. 1072, fo. 5^r; Suffolk R. O., Bury St Edmunds, E2/42/1, fo. 11^r.
21. Buckinghamshire R. O., D/X 1/44, fo. 3^r.
22. *Twelfth Night*, ed. J. M. Lothian and T. W. Craik (London and New York, 1984), II.iii.87–93, 95–8, 100–1.
23. John Webster, *The Duchess of Malfi*, ed. John Russell Brown (Manchester, 1984), I.i.3.
24. Francis Beaumont and John Fletcher, *The Dramatic Works*, ed. Fredson Bowers, 10 vols (Cambridge, 1966–96), vol. II, III.ii.197, 207–8.
25. Henry Glapthorne, *The Lady Mother*, ed. Arthur Brown, Malone Society (Oxford, 1958 [1959]), II.i.588–94.
26. S.C.L., W.W.M., Strafford Papers 21a, item 67.
27. B.L., Harleian MS. 6715, fos 103^{r-v}.
28. Gay, 'The Temples of Stowe', p. 434; G.C.L., Smyth of Nibley Papers, II, items 60, 61; L.P.L., MS. 709, fo. 29^r; S.C.L., W.W.M., Strafford Papers 21a, item 60; Narasingha P. Sil, '"Jentell Mr. Heneage": A Forgotten Tudor Servant', *Notes and Queries*, 31 (1984), p. 170; W.Y.A.S., Leeds, TN/C, I, item 281, TN/C, II, item 306; W.A., second Earl's Papers, item 33.
29. *Timon of Athens*, ed. H. J. Oliver (London, 1979), IV.ii.22–9.
30. See Burnett, 'Ophelia's "false steward" Contextualized', pp. 48–56.
31. P.R.O., STAC 8/120/2. Cf. Hainsworth, *Stewards*, p. 34; L.H., Seymour MSS, Box II, fo. 133^r; Northamptonshire R. O., Fitzwilliam Misc. Vol. 30.
32. B.L., Additional MS. 19208, fos 41^r–58^r, Stowe MS. 774; Kate Mertes, *The English Noble Household 1250–1600: Good Governance and Politic Rule* (Oxford, 1988), p. 25; Warwickshire R. O., CR136B616, CR136B621, CR136B623, CR136B627. Employers also signed, checked and audited the accounts themselves: see Kent A. O., U1475 A4/6, U1475

042; Northamptonshire R. O., Fitzwilliam Misc. Vol. 225.

33. L.P.L., MS. 709, fo. 60ʳ. It is also worth noting in this connection the comment recorded by Lady Mary Grey in about 1573. In a letter to her brother-in-law, she stated: 'I . . . wold willingly mett withe sum trusty servant whom I myght geve credett vnto to do my bussenes truly and faythefull[y] butt I fynd itt very hard to com by many or allmost any'. See L.H., Seymour Papers, V, fo. 180ʳ.

34. W.Y.A.S., Leeds, TN/C, XXII, item 41. Cf. S.C.L., W.W.M., Strafford Papers 21b, item 133.

35. Henry Chettle and Anthony Munday, *The Huntingdon Plays: A Critical Edition of 'The Downfall' and 'The Death of Robert, Earl of Huntingdon'*, ed. John Carney Meagher (New York and London, 1980), Sc. i, 90, 92.

36. Ben Jonson, *The Complete Plays*, ed. G. A. Wilkes, 4 vols (Oxford, 1981–2), vol. I, III.v.13–21.

37. Richard Brathwait, *Ar't asleepe husband?* (London, 1640; S.T.C. 3555), pp. 161–6; A. R. Braunmuller, ed., *A Seventeenth-Century Letter-Book* (Newark, 1983), p. 391; James Cleland, *The institution of a young noble man* (London, 1607; S.T.C. 5393), pp. 138–9; Francis Lenton, *Characterismi; or, Lentons leasures* (London, 1631; S.T.C. 15463), sigs F9ʳ⁻ᵛ.

38. Thomas Middleton, *A Mad World, My Masters*, ed. Standish Henning (London, 1965), IV.iii.1, 5–7, 12–13, 15–16. Cf. Jonson, *The Case*, in *Plays*, ed. Wilkes, vol. I, II.vi.8–17.

39. Francis Beaumont and John Fletcher, *The Works*, ed. Arnold Glover and A. R. Waller, 10 vols (Cambridge, 1905–12), vol. V, I.i.p. 76.

40. Mario DiGangi, 'Asses and Wits: The Homoerotics of Mastery in Satiric Comedy', *English Literary Renaissance*, 25 (1995), p. 207. For a comparable discussion of the homoerotic dimensions of service in *Twelfth Night*, see Lisa Jardine, *Reading Shakespeare Historically* (London and New York, 1996), pp. 65–77.

41. George Chapman, *The Comedies*, ed. Allan Holaday (Urbana, Chicago and London, 1970), III.ii.162.

42. For a related discussion, see Dympna Callaghan, '"And all is semblative a woman's part": Body Politics and *Twelfth Night*', *Textual Practice*, 7 (1993), p. 434.

43. Pierre Bourdieu, *The Logic of Practice*, tr. Richard Nice (Stanford, CA, 1990), pp. 157–8.

44. Thomas Swyft, the servant of Sir William Cornwallis, 'to seek . . . higher and greater advancementes by sinister and vnlawfull meanes' in 1594, tricked his master's daughter into signing what she thought was a bill of debt (in fact, a marriage contract). The scheme was discovered and Swyft punished and dismissed. See P.R.O., STAC 7/1/6.

45. John Gough Nichols, 'The Origin and Early History of the Family of Newdegate', *Surrey Archaeological Collections*, 6 (1874), p. 237; *Return of the Name of every Member of the Lower House of Parliament of England, Scotland, and Ireland, with Name of Constituency represented, and Date of Return, from 1213 to 1874*, Parliamentary Papers, 62, 2 pts (London, 1878), part 1, pp. 402, 406.

46. George Edward Cokayne, ed., *The Complete Peerage*, 13 vols (London, 1910–40), vol. IV, p. 421; Evelyn Read, *Catherine, Duchess of Suffolk: A Portrait* (London, 1962), p. 140.
47. Read, *Catherine*, pp. 48, 90–2.
48. H.M.C., *Hatfield House*, 24 vols (London, 1883–1976), vol. I, p. 483.
49. For a bill passed by the House of Commons in 1572 ruling that no household servants should become justices or high constables, see T. E. Hartley, ed., *Proceedings in the Parliaments of Elizabeth I*, 3 vols (Leicester, 1981–95), vol. I, pp. 395, 397, 401.
50. See *Arden of Faversham*, ed. M. L. Wine (London, 1973), I, 25–30; Chettle and Munday, 'The Downfall', Sc. ii, 348–51; Glapthorne, *The Lady Mother*, I.i.46–50, 52–6, 58–68.
51. Jonson, *Plays*, ed. Wilkes, vol. I, I.vi.23–33.
52. *King Lear*, ed. Kenneth Muir (London, 1975), II.ii.13–21.
53. As Richard Strier observes, Kent is 'incensed that [Oswald] . . . should *look like* a gentleman and a true courtier (sword bearing was a class privilege)'. See his *Resistant Structures: Particularity, Radicalism, and Renaissance Texts* (Berkeley, Los Angeles and London, 1995), p. 187.
54. Frank Whigham, *Seizures of the Will in Early Modern English Drama* (Cambridge, 1996), p. 191.
55. Chatsworth House, Hardwick MS. 7; H. Hampton Copnall, ed., *Nottinghamshire County Records* (Nottingham, 1915), p. 14; *H.M.C., Cowper*, 3 vols (London, 1888–9), vol. II, p. 13; Robert Thoroton, *The antiquities of Nottinghamshire* (London, 1677; Wing T1063), pp. 5, 62, 251. See also Adams, ed., *Household Accounts*, pp. 29, 463–4.
56. David Burnett, *Longleat: The Story of an English Country House* (London, 1978), pp. 15–22; L.H., Thynne Papers, XLIX, fos 284^r–7^r; Alison D. Wall, ed., *Two Elizabethan Women: Correspondence of Joan and Maria Thynne, 1575–1611*, Wiltshire Record Society, 38 (1983), pp. xvii–xviii.
57. H.M.C., *Hatfield*, vol. VIII, p. 233.
58. I. M., *A health to the gentlemanly profession of seruing-men* (London, 1598; S.T.C. 17140), sigs E3^v, E4^v.
59. I. M., *A health*, sigs G2^v, I2^r.
60. On leases of land, see G. Eland, ed., *Shardeloes Papers* (London, 1947), p. 55; Hampshire R. O., 31M57/525; L.H., Seymour MSS, Box XVII, No. 77; Verney, eds, *Memoirs*, vol. III, p. 97. On younger sons entering aristocratic service, see J. P. Cooper, *Land, Men and Beliefs: Studies in Early-Modern History* (London, 1983), p. 93; H.M.C., *Various*, 8 vols (London, 1901–14), vol. II, p. 204; Loseley House, Papers of Sir Christopher and Sir William More, IX, No. 135; F. H. Mares, ed., *The Memoirs of Robert Carey* (Oxford, 1972), p. 48.
61. William Basse, *Sword and Buckler* (1602), in *The Poetical Works*, ed. R. Warwick Bond (London, 1893), pp. 5, 11–12, 19–20.
62. [Brathwait], *Some Rules and Orders*, pp. 10, 15–16.
63. Coward, *The Stanleys*, p. 89; Felicity Heal, *Hospitality in Early Modern England* (Oxford, 1990), pp. 164–6.
64. Heal, *Hospitality*, pp. 165–6; Heal, 'Reciprocity and Exchange', pp. 194–5; Mertes, *The English Noble Household*, pp. 190–1.

65. See Richard Curteys, *The care of a christian conscience* (London, 1600; S.T.C. 6134), sigs F6ᵛ–7ʳ; F. J. Fisher, 'The Development of London as a Centre of Conspicuous Consumption in the Sixteenth and Seventeenth Centuries', *Transactions of the Royal Historical Society*, 4th ser., 30 (1948), pp. 37–50; Henry Peacham, *Coach and Sedan* (London, 1636; S.T.C. 19501), sig. D1ᵛ; John Taylor, *The water-cormorant his complaint* (London, 1622; S.T.C. 23813), sig. C2ᵛ.

66. Richard Brome, *The Northern Lasse*, ed. Harvey Fried (New York and London, 1980), IV.i.127–35.

67. Heal, *Hospitality*, pp. 117–18, 120.

68. James Shirley, *The Lady of Pleasure*, ed. Ronald Huebert (Manchester, 1986), II.i.121–30.

69. Richard Brome, *A Mad Couple Well Match'd*, ed. Steen H. Spove (New York and London, 1979), III.i.95–7.

70. See Friedman, *House and Household*, pp. 44, 59–63; H.H., Cecil Papers, IX, fo. 31ʳ; L.P.L., MS. 708, fo. 149ʳ, MS. 3199, fo. 221ʳ; L.H., Seymour Papers, VII, fo. 23ʳ; S.C.L., B.F.M., 2, item 77; Elizabeth Venables, 'Some Account of General Robert Venables', in *Chetham Miscellanies*, Chetham Society, 1st ser., 83 (1871), p. 19; W.Y.A.S., Leeds, TN/C, II, item 95. For less specialized complaints, see F. R. Raines, ed., *The Stanley Papers*, Chetham Society, 1st ser., 70 (1867), p. 36 (the relevant remarks are from the account of the Isle of Man); Sir Christopher Wandesforde, *A Book of Instructions* (1636) (Cambridge, 1777), p. 80.

71. Robert Parker Sorlien, ed., *The Diary of John Manningham of the Middle Temple, 1602–1603* (Hanover, 1976), p. 48.

72. Andrew Gurr, *Playgoing in Shakespeare's London* (Cambridge, 1987), pp. 76–8, 177–82.

Bibliography

PRIMARY SOURCES: MANUSCRIPT

Arundel Castle

The fourth Duke of Norfolk's New Testament, flyleaf. MS.
  letter from the Duke to William Dyx, 1572.
T4 and T5. The will of Thomas, the fourth Duke of Norfolk, 1571.

Bethlem Royal Hospital

Bridewell court books.

Bodleian Library

Ashmole MSS.
MS. Aubrey 1, 2. John Aubrey, *The Naturall Historie of Wiltshire, 1685.*
MS. Eng. hist. b. 208. An early sixteenth-century Northumberland household book.
MS. Eng. hist. B. 216, c. 474–484. Herrick family papers.

Bristol Record Office

AC/C60/14. Letter of Florence Smyth, 1630s.
AC/C61/15. Letter from John Poulett to Tom Smyth, late sixteenth- to early seventeenth-century.

British Library

Additional MS. 4176. Historical letters written in the reigns of James I and Charles I.
Additional MS. 5832. Cole's manuscripts: miscellaneous collections in prose and verse.
Additional MS. 18913. The Laws, Customs and Ordinances of the Fellowship of the Merchant Adventurers, 1608.
Additional MS. 19208, fos 41ʳ–58ʳ. Accounts of Sir Robert Kempe, 1584–96.
Additional MS. 27999–28005. Original correspondence of the Oxenden family, 1589–1710.
Additional MS. 33508. Letters to and accounts of Anthony Garnett, steward to Anthony Browne, the first Viscount Montague of Cowdray, 1568–70.
Additional MS. 33588. Papers and correspondence of the Berkeley family.

Additional MS. 33852, I. Account book of the Company of Bakers at York, 1543–80.
Egerton MS. 784. Diary of William Whiteway of Dorchester, 1618–34.
Egerton MSS 2645–6. Papers of the Barrington family.
Egerton MS. 2713. Correspondence and papers of the Gawdy family, 1509–1751.
Harleian MS. 2143, fo. 57ᵛ. Abstract of a trial in Star Chamber, 1595.
Harleian MS. 6715. Examinations, Informations and Affidavits taken before Francis Ashley, Justice of the Peace for the County of Dorset, 1614–35.
Lansdowne MSS.
Stowe MS. 774. Accounts of Roger North, the second Baron North, 1575–89.

Buckinghamshire Record Office

D/A/Wf/24/256. Will of Katherine Prince, 1623.
D/X 1/44. The household regulations of John, the first Earl of Bridgewater, 1652.

Cambridge University Library

EDR D/2/10. Diocese of Ely Office Act Book, 1576–80.
EDR E44 QS Files 1631–2. Diocese of Ely quarter sessions files.

Chatsworth House

Hardwick MS. 7. Accounts of Timothy Pusey, 1591–7.

Clothworkers' Company

Court Book 1558–81.
Court Book 1581–1605.
Court Book 1605–23.
Court Book 1623–36.

Clwyd Record Office

D/G/3275. Letter of Samuel Woode to Rowland Jewkes, 1639.

Corporation of London Records Office

Journals of the Common Council.
MC6/1–554. Mayor's Court Interrogatories, 1628, 1641–1710.
P.D.10.211. Act of Common Council, 1611.
Remembrancia.
Repertories of the Court of Aldermen.

Essex Record Office

D/ACA 8. Archdeaconry of Colchester Act Book, 1578–80.
D/DBa A1. Accounts of John Kendall, 1623–33.
D/DBa A3. Accounts of John Hawkins signed by John Kendall, 1646–51.
D/D By C 29. Letter of Nora Grey, 1609.
Q/SBa 2. Sessions bundles, 1621–58.
Q/SR. Quarter sessions rolls.

Gloucestershire County Library

Smyth of Nibley Papers.

Goldsmiths' Company

Court Book K, 1, 1557–66.
Court Book O, 3, 1604–11.

Greater London Record Office

MJ/GDR. Gaol Delivery Rolls.
MJ/SBB. Sessions of the peace and oyer and terminer books.
MJ/SR. Sessions of the peace and oyer and terminer rolls.

Guildhall Library

MS. 4329/4. Court minutes of the Carpenters' Company, 1618–35.
MS. 4647. Weavers' Company Ordinance and Record Book, 1577–1641.
MS. 4655/1. Court minutes of the Weavers' Company, 1610–42.
MS. 4655/2. Weavers' Company court minute books, 1653–4.
MS. 5570/1. Fishmongers' Court Ledger 1, 1592–1610.
MS. 8200/1. Court minutes of the Apothecaries' Company, 1617–51.

Hampshire Record Office

31M57/525. Lease of land from William, Lord Sandys, to Robert Bethell, his servant, 1590.

Hatfield House

Cecil papers.

Hertfordshire Record Office

HAT/SR. Quarter sessions rolls.

Huntington Library, California

Ellesmere MS. 1180. Orders for the conduct of the household of Sir Thomas Egerton, *c.* 1603.
Ellesmere MSS 7381–7403. Papers of John, the first Earl of Bridgewater, 1632–4.

Kent Archives Office

U269 098/1. Letter of Anne Cranfield, Countess of Middlesex, *c.* 1667.
U1475 A4/6. Accounts of John Leke, 1578–9.
U1475 A6/12–15. Accounts of John Passwater, 1572–6.
U1475 A9/1–7. Accounts of John Passwater, 1552–70.
U1475 E35. Orders appointed by Robert Sidney, the second Earl of Leicester, to be observed in his house, 1625–6.
U1475 042. Accounts of Hercules Rainsford, 1577–8.

Lambeth Palace Library

MS. 684/7. A book of orders for officers and servants in the household of the Archbishop of York, 1628.
MS. 884. Orders and statutes to be observed in the house of Thomas Cranmer, Archbishop of Canterbury, to which are added orders of a later date, 1561–6.
MSS 604–709, 3192–3206. The Shrewsbury and Talbot papers.
MS. 1072. Regulations of the officers of the Archbishop of Canterbury, belonging to his palace at Lambeth, early seventeenth century.
MS. 3361. 'A Booke . . . [of] sondry ordres, and deuties, to be understood [in the] . . . houshold' of Lionel Cranfield, Earl of Middlesex, 1622.

Lancashire Record Office

DDF 2422. Regulations of the household of Edward, the third Earl of Derby, 1569.

Lincolnshire Archives Office

2 Ancaster 14/17. Advice from John Guevara to Robert Bertie, the thirteenth Lord Willoughby d'Eresby, 1601.

Longleat House

Dudley Papers, IV, fo. 13^r. Letter of Lord Robert Dudley to Anthony Foster, *c.* 1564.
Seymour MSS and Papers.
Thynne Papers, XLIX, fos 284^r–7^r. A satirical verse about Sir John Thynne by William Darrell, 1575.

Loseley House

Papers of Sir Christopher and Sir William More, IX, No. 135. Letter from Edward Lyvesey to Sir William More, late sixteenth or early seventeenth century.

Norfolk Record Office

DN/DEP/28. Deposition book of the Norwich diocese, 1596.

Northamptonshire Record Office

Fitzwilliam Misc. Vols.

North Yorkshire County Record Office

QSM 2/10, MIC 97. Quarter sessions minute and order book, 1655–69.

Public Record Office

C2. Court of Chancery, Proceedings.
PC. Registers of the Privy Council.
PROB 11/19/27. Will of John Winchcombe, 1520.
Req. 2. Court of Requests, Proceedings.
SP. State Papers.
STAC. Star Chamber, Proceedings.

Sheffield City Library

Bacon Frank Muniments.
Wentworth Woodhouse Muniments, Strafford Papers.

Somerset Record Office

Q/SR. Quarter sessions rolls.

Staffordshire Record Office

D(W)1734/3/3/282. List of provisions for dinner and supper of the Paget family, 1573.
D(W)1734/3/3/300. Account of land of Thomas Willoughby, 1554–5.
D(W)1734/3/4/94. An account of the legal charges of Richard Cupper, 1575.

Suffolk Record Office, Bury St Edmund's Branch

E2/42/1. 'A Breuiate towching the order and gouernmente of A Noblemans house', c. 1605.

Tyne and Wear Joint Archives Service, Newcastle

GU/Ma/4. Merchant Adventurers' Charter and Act Book.

Warwickshire Record Office

CR136B521. Letter from William Whitehall to Thomas Rode, 1617.
CR136B616, CR136B621, CR136B623, CR136B627. Accounts of John
   Newdigate, 1630–7.
CR136C1915. Will of Lady Anne Newdigate, 1610.
CR1998, Box 60, Folder 1, item 3. Letter from Agnes Throckmorton,
   1611.

West Sussex Record Office

Sessions Roll, October 1655.

West Yorkshire Archive Service, Leeds

TN/C. Correspondence of the Ingram family.
TN/EA/13/36. Accounts of John Mattison the younger, 1645–52.
TN/YO/C/II/4. Letter from Richard Baldwin to John Mattison the
   younger, 1652.

Wiltshire Record Office

865/389. 'A Book of Rules laid down by the Duke of Buckingham for
   the Ordering of his Household', 1634.

Woburn Abbey

The papers of Francis, the second Earl of Bedford, 26–41.
Sir William Russell's papers, item 6. A late sixteenth- or early seventeenth-century list of servants at dinner.

PRIMARY SOURCES: PRINTED

The actors' remonstrance, or complaint, London, 1643; Wing A453.
Adams, Simon, ed., *Household Accounts and Disbursement Books of Robert
   Dudley, Earl of Leicester*, Camden Society, 5th ser., 6 (1995).
The apprentices advice to the XII. bishops lately accused, London, 1642; Wing
   A3583B.
The apprentices of Londons petition, London, 1641; S.T.C. A3586.
Arber, Edward, ed., *A Transcript of the Registers of the Company of Sta-
   tioners of London, 1554–1640*, 5 vols, London, 1875–94.
Arden of Faversham, ed. M. L. Wine, London, 1973.
Arthington, Henry, *Prouision for the poore, now in penurie*, London, 1597;
   S.T.C. 798.

Barlow, John, *An exposition of the second epistle to Timothy, the first chapter*, London, 1625; S.T.C. 1434.

Basse, William, *The Poetical Works*, ed. R. Warwick Bond, London, 1893.

Battus, Bartholomaeus, *The christian mans closet*, tr. William Lowth, London, 1581; S.T.C. 1591.

Baylie, Simon, *The Wizard*, ed. Henry De Vocht, Louvain, 1930.

Beaumont, Francis and John Fletcher, *The Dramatic Works*, ed. Fredson Bowers, 10 vols, Cambridge, 1966–96.

[Beaumont, Francis, and John Fletcher], *The Faithful Friends*, ed. G. M. Pinciss and G. R. Proudfoot, Malone Society, Oxford, 1970 (1975).

Beaumont, Francis, *The Knight of the Burning Pestle*, ed. Sheldon P. Zitner, Manchester, 1984.

Beaumont, Francis and John Fletcher, *The Works*, ed. Arnold Glover and A.R. Waller, 10 vols, Cambridge, 1905–12.

Birch, Thomas, ed., *The Court and Times of James I*, 2 vols, London, 1848.

Blackstone, Sir William, *Commentaries on the Laws of England*, 4th edn, 4 vols, Dublin, 1771.

Blundeville, Thomas, *A newe booke containing the arte of ryding*, London, 1561?; S.T.C. 3158.

Bolton, Edmund, *The cities advocate, in this case of honor and armes; whether apprentiship extinguisheth gentry?*, London, 1629; S.T.C. 3219.

Bond, Ronald B., ed., *'Certain Sermons or Homilies' (1547) and 'A Homily against Disobedience and Wilful Rebellion' (1570): A Critical Edition*, Toronto, Buffalo and London, 1987.

Bownd, Nicholas, *The doctrine of the sabbath*, London, 1595; S.T.C. 3436.

Bradford, John, *The copye of a letter*, Wesel? 1556?; S.T.C. 3504.5.

Brathwait, Richard, *Ar't asleepe husband?*, London, 1640; S.T.C. 3555.

[Brathwait, Richard], *Some Rules and Orders for the Government of the House of an Earle* (1605), in *Miscellanea Antiqua Anglicana*, London, 1821.

Braunmuller, A. R., ed., *A Seventeenth-Century Letter Book*, Newark, 1983.

Brome, Richard, *The Dramatic Works*, ed. John Pearson, 3 vols, London, 1873.

—— *The English Moore; or The Mock-Mariage*, ed. Sara Jayne Steen, Columbia, 1983.

—— *A Mad Couple Well Match'd*, ed. Steen H. Spove, New York and London, 1979.

—— *The Northern Lasse*, ed. Harvey Fried, New York and London, 1980.

Calisto and Melebea (printed *c.* 1525), in Richard Axton, ed., *Three Rastell Plays*, Cambridge, 1979.

Cash, Thomas, *Two horrible and inhumane murders done in L<in>colneshire, by two husbands upon their wives*, London, 1607; S.T.C. 4768.

Cavendish, George, *The Life and Death of Cardinal Wolsey*, in Richard S. Sylvester and Davis P. Harding, eds, *Two Early Tudor Lives*, New Haven and London, 1962.

C(hamberlain), R., *Jocabella, or a cabinet of conceits*, London, 1640; S.T.C. 4943.

Chambers, E. K., ed., *The Elizabethan Stage*, 4 vols, Oxford, 1923.

Chapman, George, *The Comedies*, ed. Allan Holaday, Urbana, Chicago and London, 1970.

Chappell, William and J. Woodfall Ebsworth, eds, *The Roxburghe Ballads*, 9 vols, London, 1871–97.

Chettle, Henry and Anthony Munday, *The Huntingdon Plays: A Critical Edition of 'The Downfall' and 'The Death of Robert, Earl of Huntingdon'*, ed. John Carney Meagher, New York and London, 1980.

Chettle, Henry, *Kind-harts dreame*, London, 1593?; S.T.C. 5123.

—— *Piers Plainness: Seven Years' Prenticeship* (1595), in James Winny, ed., *The Descent of Euphues: Three Elizabethan Romance Stories*, Cambridge, 1957.

Churchyard, Thomas, *The firste parte of Churchyardes chippes*, London, 1575; S.T.C. 5232.

Cleland, James, *The institution of a young noble man*, London, 1607; S.T.C. 5393.

Climsell, Richard, *A pleasant new dialogue: or, the discourse between the serving-man and the husband-man*, London, c. 1640; S.T.C. 5427.

Cobbes, Edmund, *Mundanum speculum, or, the worldlings looking glasse*, London, 1630; S.T.C. 5453.

'The Cobler of Caunterburie' and 'Tarltons Newes out of Purgatorie', ed. Geoffrey Creigh and Jane Belfield, Leiden, 1987.

Cokayne, Aston, *The Obstinate Lady*, ed. Catherine M. Shaw, New York and London, 1986.

Cokayne, George Edward, ed., *The Complete Peerage*, 13 vols, London, 1910–40.

Coke, Sir Edward, *The second part of the Institutes*, London, 1671; Wing C4952.

Collier, J. Payne, ed., *Trevelyan Papers, Part II*, Camden Society, 1st ser., 84 (1863).

Collins, Arthur, ed., *Letters and Memorials of State*, 2 vols, London, 1746.

Cooke, J., *Greene's Tu Quoque*, ed. Alan J. Berman, New York and London, 1984.

Cooke, Richard, *A White Sheete* (1629), in Lena Cowen Orlin, ed., *Elizabethan Households: An Anthology*, Seattle and London, 1995.

Coote, Edmund, *The English schoole-maister*, London, 1627; S.T.C. 5713.

Copley, Anthony, *Wits fittes and fancies*, London, 1595; S.T.C. 5738.

Copnall, H. Hampton, ed., *Nottinghamshire County Records*, Nottingham, 1915.

Cowley, Abraham, *The English Writings*, ed. A. R. Waller, 2 vols, Cambridge, 1905–6.

Craven, Wesley Frank and Walter B. Hayward, eds, *The Journal of Richard Norwood*, New York, 1945.

Crosse, Henry, *Vertues common-wealth*, London, 1603; S.T.C. 6070.

Cupids schoole: wherein, yongmen and maids may learne divers sorts of complements, London, 1632; S.T.C. 6123.

Curteys, Richard, *The care of a christian conscience*, London, 1600; S.T.C. 6134.

Cyuile and Vncyuile Life (1579), in W. C. Hazlitt, ed., *Inedited Tracts*, London, 1868.

Daines, Simon, *Orthoepia Anglicana: or, the first principall part of the English grammar*, London, 1640; S.T.C. 6190.

Darell, Walter, *A short discourse of the life of seruing-men*, London, 1578; S.T.C. 6274.

Davies, John, *Wits Bedlam*, London, 1617; S.T.C. 6343.

Day, Angel, *The English secretorie*, London, 1586; S.T.C. 6401.

A declaration of the valiant resolution of the famous prentices, London, 1642; Wing D774.

Dekker, Thomas, *The Dramatic Works*, ed. Fredson Bowers, 4 vols, Cambridge, 1953–61.

—— *Foure Birds of Noahs Arke*, ed. F. P. Wilson, Oxford, 1924.

—— *The Shoemaker's Holiday*, ed. Anthony Parr, London and New York, 1990.

Dekker, Thomas, John Ford and William Rowley, *The Witch of Edmonton*, ed. Simon Trussler and Jacqui Russell, London, 1983.

Deloney, Thomas, *The Novels*, ed. Merritt E. Lawlis, Bloomington, IN, 1961.

[Denny, Sir William], *Pelecanicidium: or the Christian adviser against self-murder*, London, 1653; Wing D1051.

D'Ewes, Sir Simonds, *A compleat journal of the votes*, London, 1693; Wing D1247.

Doddridge, Sir John, *Honors pedigree*, London, 1652; Wing D1793.

Earle, John, *Microcosmography*, ed. Alfred S. West, Cambridge, 1951.

Eland, G., ed., *Shardeloes Papers*, London, 1947.

Elton, Edward, *An exposition of the epistle to the Colossians*, London, 1615; S.T.C. 7612.

Elton, G. R., ed., *The Tudor Constitution: Documents and Commentary*, 2nd edn, Cambridge, 1982.

Everinden, Humphrey, *A brothers gift: containing an hundred precepts, instructing to a godly life*, London, 1623; S.T.C. 10601.

Fehrenbach, R. J. and E. S. Leedham-Green, eds, *Private Libraries in Renaissance England*, 4 vols, Binghamton, 1992–5.

Felltham, Owen, *Resolves, Divine, Moral, Political* (c. 1620), Oxford, 1840.

Fenton, Sir Geoffrey, *Golden epistles*, London, 1582; S.T.C. 10794.

Ferne, Sir John, *The blazon of gentrie*, London, 1586; S.T.C. 10824.

Fitzgeffrey, Henry, *Satyres: and satyricall epigram's*, London, 1617; S.T.C. 10945.

Fletcher, John Samuel, ed., *The Correspondence of Nathan Walworth and Peter Seddon*, Chetham Society, 1st ser., 109 (1880).

Gad, Ben-Arod, *The wandering-jew, telling fortunes to English-men*, London, 1640; S.T.C. 11512.

Gascoigne, George, *The Complete Works*, ed. John W. Cunliffe, 2 vols, Cambridge, 1907–10.

Gayton, Edmund, *Pleasant notes upon Don Quixot*, London, 1654; Wing G415.

Giustinian, Sebastian, *Four Years at the Court of Henry VIII*, tr. Rawdon Brown, 2 vols, London, 1854.

Glapthorne, Henry, *The Lady Mother*, ed. Arthur Brown, Malone Society, Oxford, 1958 (1959).

—— *The Plays and Poems*, [ed. R. H. Shepherd], 2 vols, London, 1874.
Goddard, William, *A neaste of waspes latelie found out in the Law-Countreys*, London, 1615; S.T.C. 11929.
—— *A satirycall dialogue or a sharplye-invective conference*, London, 1616?; S.T.C. 11930.
Gosson, Stephen, *The ephemerides of Phialo, deuided into three bookes*, London, 1579; S.T.C. 12093.
Gouge, William, *Gods three arrowes: plague, famine, sword*, London, 1631; S.T.C. 12116.
—— *Of domesticall duties*, London, 1622; S.T.C. 12119.
Guazzo, Stefano, *The ciuile conuersation*, tr. B. Young, London, 1586; S.T.C. 12423.
H., I., *This worlds folly*, London, 1615; S.T.C. 12570.
Hake, Edward, *Newes out of Powles churchyarde*, London, 1579; S.T.C. 12606.
Harington, Sir John, *The Letters and Epigrams*, ed. Norman Egbert McClure, Philadelphia, 1930.
Harland, John, ed., *The House and Farm Accounts of the Shuttleworths*, Chetham Society, 1st ser., 46 (1858).
Harrison, G. B., ed., *Advice to His Son by Henry Percy, Ninth Earl of Northumberland (1609)*, London, 1930.
Harrison, William, *The Description of England*, ed. Georges Edelen, Ithaca, NY, 1968.
Hartley, T. E., ed., *Proceedings in the Parliaments of Elizabeth I*, 3 vols, Leicester, 1981–95.
Henderson, Katherine Usher and Barbara F. McManus, eds, *Half Humankind: Contexts and Texts of the Controversy about Women in England, 1540–1640*, Urbana and Chicago, 1985.
Herrick, Robert, *The Poetical Works*, ed. L. C. Martin, Oxford, 1956.
Heywood, Thomas, *The Dramatic Works*, ed. R. H. Shepherd, 6 vols, London, 1874.
—— *The Four Prentices of London*, ed. Mary Ann Weber Gasior, New York and London, 1980.
Heywood, Thomas and Richard Brome, *The Late Lancashire Witches*, ed. Laird H. Barber, New York and London, 1979.
Hieronymus, *von Braunschweig*, *The noble experyence of the vertuous handywarke of surgeri*, London, 1525; S.T.C. 13434.
Hill, Robert, *Christs prayer expounded, a christian directed, and a communicant prepared*, London, 1610; S.T.C. 13473.
Historical Manuscripts Commission, Cowper, 3 vols, London, 1888–9.
Historical Manuscripts Commission, Hatfield House, 24 vols, London, 1883–1976.
Historical Manuscripts Commission, Various, 8 vols, London, 1901–14.
Howell, James, *Epistolae Ho-Elianae*, London, 1650; Wing H3072.
Hughes, Paul L. and James F. Larkin, eds, *Tudor Royal Proclamations*, 3 vols, New Haven, CT and London, 1964–9.
I., T., *A world of wonders. A masse of murthers. A couie of cosonages*, London, 1595; S.T.C. 14068.5.
The institucion of a gentleman, London, 1568; S.T.C. 14105.

Jackson, Abraham, *The pious prentice, or, the prentices piety*, London, 1640; S.T.C. 14295.

Johnson, Richard, *The nine worthies of London*, London, 1592; S.T.C. 14686.

Jonson, Ben, *The Complete Plays*, ed. G. A. Wilkes, 4 vols, Oxford, 1981–2.

—— *Epicoene*, ed. L. A. Beaurline, London, 1966.

—— *The New Inn*, ed. Michael Hattaway, Manchester, 1984.

Jordan, Thomas, *The walks of Islington and Hogsdon*, London, 1657; Wing J1071.

The ladies remonstrance, London, [1659]; Wing L160.

Lambe, John, *A briefe description of the notorious life of J. Lambe*, London, 1628; S.T.C. 15177.

Langham, Robert, *A Letter*, ed. R. J. P. Kuin, Leiden, 1983.

Leland, John, *The Itinerary of John Leland in or about the Years 1535–1543*, ed. Lucy Toumlin Smith, 5 vols, London, 1907–10.

Lenton, Francis, *Characterismi; or, Lentons leasures*, London, 1631; S.T.C. 15463.

Le Strange, Sir Nicholas, *'Mery Passages and Jeasts': A Manuscript Jestbook*, ed. H. F. Lippincott, Salzburg, 1974.

A letter sent by the maydens of London, London, 1567; S.T.C. 16754.5.

Lilly, William, *A History of his Life and Times, from the Year 1602 to 1681*, 2nd edn, London, 1826.

Ling, Nicholas, *Politeuphuia wits common wealth*, London, 1597; S.T.C. 15685.

Locke, John, *Two Treatises of Government*, ed. W. S. Carpenter, London, 1990.

Lyly, John, *'Campaspe'/'Sappho and Phao'*, ed. G. K. Hunter and David Bevington, Manchester and New York, 1991.

M., I., *A health to the gentlemanly profession of seruing-men*, London, 1598; S.T.C. 17140.

M., R., *Micrologia*. London, 1629; S.T.C. 17146.

[Machin, Lewis], *Every Woman in Her Humour*, ed. Archie Mervin Tyson, New York and London, 1980.

Mackay, Charles, ed., *A Collection of Songs and Ballads Relative to the London Prentices and Trades*, Percy Society, 1 (1841).

Mactatio Abel (c. 1400–c. 1450), in A. C. Cawley, ed., *The Wakefield Pageants in the Towneley Cycle*, Manchester, 1958.

The maids petition, London, 1647; Wing M280.

Mares, F. H., ed., *The Memoirs of Robert Carey*, Oxford, 1972.

Markham, Gervase, *Hobsons horse-load of letters*, London, 1617; S.T.C. 17360a.

Massinger, Philip, *The Plays and Poems*, ed. Philip Edwards and Colin Gibson, 5 vols, Oxford, 1976.

Mery Tales and Quick Answers (1567), in W. Carew Hazlitt, ed., *Shakespeare Jest-Books*, 2 vols, London, 1864, vol. I.

Middleton, Thomas, *A Mad World, My Masters*, ed. Standish Henning, London, 1965.

—— *The Phoenix*, ed. John Bradbury Brooks, New York and London, 1980.

Middleton, Thomas and William Rowley, *The Changeling*, ed. Joost Daalder, London and New York, 1990.

Mildmay, Sir Walter, *A Memorial for a Son, from his Father, 1570,* Hazelgrove, 1893.

Mill, Humphrey, *A nights search,* London, 1640; S.T.C. 17921.

Morrice, Thomas, *An apology for schoole-masters,* London, 1619; S.T.C. 18170.

Munday, Anthony and others, *Sir Thomas More,* ed. Vittorio Gabrieli and Giorgio Melchiori, Manchester and New York, 1990.

N., D., *Londons looking-glasse. Or the copy of a letter, written by an English travayler, to the apprentices of London,* London, 1621; S.T.C. 18327.

Niccols, Richard, *The furies,* London, 1614; S.T.C. 18521.

Nixon, Anthony, *A straunge foot-post, with a packet full of strange petitions,* London, 1613; S.T.C. 18591.

Nourse, Timothy, *Campania foelix,* London, 1700; Wing N1416.

The Ordinances of the Clothworkers' Company, London, 1881.

Overbury, Sir Thomas, *The Overburian Characters,* ed. W. J. Paylor, Oxford, 1936.

P., B., *The prentises practise in godlinesse, and his true freedome,* London, 1608; S.T.C. 19057.

Parkes, William, *The curtaine-drawer of the world,* London, 1612; S.T.C. 19298.

Parkinson, Richard, ed., *The Life of Adam Martindale,* Chetham Society, 1st ser., 4 (1845).

Parrot, Henry, *Laquei ridiculosi: or springes for woodcocks,* London, 1613; S.T.C. 19332.

—— *The mastive, or young-whelpe of the olde-dogge,* London, 1615; S.T.C. 19333.

—— *The mous-trap,* London, 1606; S.T.C. 19334.

Pasquils Jestes (1609), in Lena Cowen Orlin, ed., *Elizabethan Households: An Anthology,* Seattle and London, 1995.

Peacham, Henry, *Coach and Sedan,* London, 1636; S.T.C. 19501.

—— *Thalias banquet,* London, 1620, S.T.C. 19515.

P[eachum], H[enry], *The art of living in London,* London, 1642; Wing P942.

The petition of the weamen of Middlesex, London, 1641; Wing P1838.

Pick, Samuel, *Festum voluptatis, or the banquet of pleasure,* London, 1639; S.T.C. 19897.

The Pride of Life (c. 1350), in Peter Happé, ed., *Tudor Interludes,* Harmondsworth, 1972.

Prothero, G. W., ed., *Select Statutes,* 4th edn, Oxford, 1913.

R., W., *The most horrible and tragicall murther of John lord Bourgh,* London, 1591; S.T.C. 20593.

Raine, James, ed., *Yorkshire Diaries and Autobiographies in the Seventeenth and Eighteenth Centuries,* Surtees Society, 77 (1886).

Raines, F. R., ed., *The Stanley Papers,* Chetham Society, 1st ser., 70 (1867).

Randolph, Thomas, *The Poetical and Dramatic Works,* ed. W. Carew Hazlitt, 2 vols, London, 1875.

The Rare Triumphs of Love and Fortune, ed. John Isaac Owen, New York and London, 1979.

Return of the Name of every Member of the Lower House of Parliament of England, Scotland, and Ireland, with Name of Constituency represented, and Date of Return, from 1213 to 1874, Parliamentary Papers, 62, 2 pts, London, 1878.

Rich, Barnaby, *Faultes faults, and nothing else but faultes*, London, 1606; S.T.C. 20983.

——*The honestie of this age*, London, 1614; S.T.C. 20986.

Ricketts, John, *Byrsa Basilica*, ed. R. H. Bowers, Louvain, 1939.

Roberts, Henry, *Haigh for Devonshire*, London, 1600; S.T.C. 21081.

——*Lancaster his allarums*, London, 1595; S.T.C. 21083.

Rogers, Thomas, *Leicester's Ghost*, ed. Franklin B. Williams, Jr, London, 1972.

Rollins, Hyder E., ed., *An Analytical Index to the Ballad-Entries (1557–1709) in the Registers of the Company of the Stationers of London*, Chapel Hill, NC, 1924.

——*A Pepysian Garland: Black-Letter Broadside Ballads of the Years 1595–1639*, Cambridge, 1922.

Rowlands, Samuel, *Good newes and bad newes*, London, 1622; S.T.C. 21382.

[Rowlands, Samuel], *Greenes ghost haunting conie-catchers*, London, 1602; S.T.C. 12243.

Salter, Thomas, *The Mirrhor of Modestie*, ed. Janis Butler Holm, New York and London, 1987.

S[amwaies], P[eter], *The wise and faithful steward*, London, 1657; Wing S546A.

Shakespeare, William, *As You Like It*, ed. Agnes Latham, London, 1991.

——*King Henry VI, Part II*, ed. Andrew S. Cairncross, London, 1988.

——*King Lear*, ed. Kenneth Muir, London, 1975.

——*Much Ado About Nothing*, ed. A. R. Humphreys, London and New York, 1984.

——*Othello*, ed. E.A.J. Honigmann, London and New York, 1997.

——*Timon of Athens*, ed. H.J. Oliver, London, 1979.

——*Twelfth Night*, ed. J. M. Lothian and T. W. Craik, London and New York, 1984.

Sharpham, Edward, *The Works*, ed. Christopher Gordon Petter, New York and London, 1986.

Shirley, James, *The Dramatic Works*, ed. William Gifford and Alexander Dyce, 6 vols, London, 1833.

——*The Lady of Pleasure*, ed. Ronald Huebert, Manchester, 1986.

Slingsby, Sir Henry, *The Diary*, ed. Daniel Parsons, London, 1836.

Smith, Richard, *The Life of Lady Magdalen Viscountess Montague (1538–1608)*, ed. A. C. Southern, London, 1954.

Smith, Sir Thomas, *De Republica Anglorum*, ed. Mary Dewar, Cambridge, 1982.

Sorlien, Robert Parker, ed., *The Diary of John Manningham of the Middle Temple, 1602–1603*, Hanover, NH, 1976.

Sorocold, Thomas, *Supplications of saints*, London, 1612; S.T.C. 22932.

Sparke, Michael, *The crums of comfort with godly prayers*. London, 1628; S.T.C. 23016.

Stafford, Anthony, *The guide of honour*, London, 1634; S.T.C. 23124.

Stow, John, *The abridgement or summarie of the English chronicle*, London, 1607; S.T.C. 23330.

——*A Survey of the Cities of London and Westminster*, ed. John Strype, 2 vols, London, 1720.

——*A Survey of London*, ed. Charles Lethbridge Kingsford, 2 vols, Oxford, 1908.

Strype, John, *Annals of the Reformation*, 4 vols, Oxford, 1824.

A students lamentation that hath sometime been in London an apprentice for the rebellious tumults lately in the citie hapning, London, 1595; S.T.C. 23401.5.

Tawney, R. H. and Eileen Power, eds, *Tudor Economic Documents*, 3 vols, London, 1924.

Taylor, John, *The unnaturall father*, London, 1621; S.T.C. 23808a.

——*The water-cormorant his complaint*, London, 1622; S.T.C. 23813.

Thoroton, Robert, *The antiquities of Nottinghamshire*, London, 1677; Wing T1063.

Traherne, John Montgomery, ed., *Stradling Correspondence: A Series of Letters Written in the Reign of Queen Elizabeth*, London, 1840.

Tuvil, Daniel, S^t. *Pauls threefold cord*, London, 1635; S.T.C. 24396.5.

Tyler, Margaret, 'Epistle to the Reader', in Moira Ferguson, ed., *First Feminists: British Women Writers, 1578–1799*, Bloomington, IN, 1985.

Vallans, William, *The honourable prentice: or, this taylor is a man*, London, 1615; S.T.C. 24588.

Venables, Elizabeth, 'Some Account of General Robert Venables', *Chetham Miscellanies*, Chetham Society, 1st ser., 83 (1871).

Verney, F. P. and M. M., eds, *Memoirs of the Verney Family During the Civil War*, 4 vols, London, 1892–9.

Wall, Alison D., ed., *Two Elizabethan Women: Correspondence of Joan and Maria Thynne, 1575–1611*, Wiltshire Record Society, 38 (1983).

Wandesforde, Sir Christopher, *A Book of Instructions*, Cambridge, 1777.

The Wasp, ed. J. W. Lever, Malone Society, Oxford, 1974 (1976).

Webster, John, *The Duchess of Malfi*, ed. John Russell Brown, Manchester, 1984.

West, Richard, *The court of conscience or Dick Whippers sessions*, London, 1607; S.T.C. 25263.

Whitney, Isabella, *A sweet nosgay, or pleasant posye: contayning a hundred and ten phylosophicall flowers*, London, 1573; S.T.C. 25440.

Whythorne, Thomas, *The Autobiography*, ed. James M. Osborn, London, New York and Toronto, 1962.

Wickins, Nathaniel, *Woodstreet-compters-plea, for its prisoner*, Amsterdam, 1638; S.T.C. 25587.

Wilkins, George, *The Miseries of Enforced Marriage*, ed. Glenn H. Blayney, Malone Society, Oxford, 1963 (1964).

Wotton, Sir Henry, *Letters of Sir Henry Wotton to Sir Edmund Bacon*, London, 1661; Wing W3644.

Yates, James, *The castell of courtesie, whereunto is adioyned the holde of humilitie: with the chariot of chastitie*, London, 1582; S.T.C. 26079.

SECONDARY SOURCES: PRINTED

Adair, Richard, *Courtship, Illegitimacy and Marriage in Early Modern England*, Manchester and New York, 1996.

Amussen, Susan Dwyer, 'The Gendering of Popular Culture in Early Modern England', in Tim Harris, ed., *Popular Culture in England, c. 1500–1850*, Basingstoke and London, 1995, pp. 48–68.

——*An Ordered Society: Gender and Class in Early Modern England*, Oxford, 1988.

——'Punishment, Discipline, and Power: The Social Meanings of Violence in Early Modern England', *Journal of British Studies*, 34 (1995), pp. 1–34.

Anderson, Bonnie S. and Judith P. Zinsser, eds, *A History of their Own: Women in Europe from Prehistory to the Present*, 2 vols, Harmondsworth, 1989–90.

Anderson, Linda, 'Shakespeare's Servants', *The Shakespeare Yearbook*, 2, Spring (1991), pp. 149–61.

Archer, Ian W., *The Pursuit of Stability: Social Relations in Elizabethan London*, Cambridge, 1991.

Babcock-Adams, Barbara, '"A Tolerated Margin of Mess": The Trickster and His Tales Reconsidered', *Journal of the Folklore Institute*, 11 (1975), pp. 147–86.

Bakhtin, Mikhail M., *Rabelais and His World*, tr. Hélène Iswolsky, Cambridge, MA, 1968.

Bashar, Nazife, 'Rape in England between 1500 and 1700', in The London Feminist History Group, ed., *The Sexual Dynamics of History: Men's Power, Women's Resistance*, London, 1983, pp. 28–42.

——'Women and Crime in England 1558–1700', unpublished PhD thesis, University of Sydney, 1985.

Beier, A. L., *Masterless Men: The Vagrancy Problem in England 1560–1640*, London and New York, 1985.

Bellamy, John, *The Tudor Law of Treason: An Introduction*, London, 1979.

Belsey, Catherine, 'Disrupting Sexual Difference: Meaning and Gender in the Comedies', in John Drakakis, ed., *Alternative Shakespeares*, London and New York, 1985, pp. 166–90.

Ben-Amos, Ilana Krausman, *Adolescence and Youth in Early Modern England*, New Haven, CT and London, 1994.

——'Women Apprentices in the Trades and Crafts of Early Modern Bristol', *Continuity and Change*, 6 (1991), pp. 227–52.

Benson, Pamela Joseph, *The Invention of Renaissance Woman: The Challenge of Female Independence in the Literature and Thought of Italy and England*, University Park, PN, 1992.

Bernthal, Craig A., 'Treason in the Family: The Trial of Thumpe v. Horner', *Shakespeare Quarterly*, 42 (1991), pp. 44–54.

Bevington, David, 'Theatre as Holiday', in David L. Smith, Richard Strier and David Bevington, eds, *The Theatrical City: Culture, Theatre and Politics in London, 1576–1649*, Cambridge, 1995, pp. 101–16.

Bindoff, S. T., *The House of Commons 1509–1558*, 3 vols, London, 1982.

Birrell, T. A., 'Reading as Pastime: The Place of Light Literature in some

Gentlemen's Libraries of the 17th Century', in Robin Myers and Michael Harris, eds, *Property of a Gentleman: The Formation, Organisation and Dispersal of the Private Library 1620–1920*, Winchester, 1991, pp. 113–31.

Blagden, Cyprian, 'The Stationers' Company in the Civil War Period', *The Library*, 13 (1958), pp. 1–17.

Boose, Lynda, 'The Priest, the Slanderer, the Historian and the Feminist', *English Literary Renaissance*, 25 (1995), pp. 320–40.

Bourdieu, Pierre, *The Logic of Practice*, tr. Richard Nice, Stanford, CA, 1990.

Bowden, Peter, *The Wool Trade in Tudor and Stuart England*, London, 1962.

Bristol, Michael D., *Carnival and Theater: Plebeian Culture and the Structure of Authority in Renaissance England*, New York and London, 1985.

Brooks, Christopher, 'Apprenticeship, Social Mobility and the Middling Sort, 1550–1800', in Jonathan Barry and Christopher Brooks, eds, *The Middling Sort of People: Culture, Society and Politics in England, 1550–1800*, Basingstoke and London, 1994, pp. 52–83.

Burke, Peter, *Popular Culture in Early Modern Europe*, London, 1978.

Burnett, David, *Longleat: The Story of an English Country House*, London, 1978.

Burnett, Mark Thornton, '"Fill gut and pinch belly": Writing Famine in the English Renaissance', *Explorations in Renaissance Culture*, 21 (1995), pp. 21–44.

——'"For they are actions that a man might play": Hamlet as Trickster', in Peter J. Smith and Nigel Wood, eds, *'Hamlet': Theory in Practice*, Buckingham and Philadelphia, 1996, pp. 24–54.

——'Henry Chettle's *Piers Plainness: Seven Years' Prenticeship*: Contexts and Consumers', in Constance C. Relihan, ed., *Framing Elizabethan Fictions: Contemporary Approaches to Early Modern Narrative Prose*, Kent, OH, 1996, pp. 169–86.

'Masters and Servants in Moral and Religious Treatises, c. 1580–c. 1642', in Arthur Marwick, ed., *The Arts, Literature, and Society*, London and New York, 1990, pp. 48–75.

——'Ophelia's "false steward" Contextualized', *The Review of English Studies*, 46 (1995), pp. 48–56.

——'Popular Culture in the English Renaissance', in William Zunder and Suzanne Trill, eds, *Writing and the English Renaissance*, London and New York, 1996, pp. 106–22.

——'Tamburlaine: An Elizabethan Vagabond', *Studies in Philology*, 84 (1987), pp. 308–23.

——'*Tamburlaine* and the Body', *Criticism*, 33 (1991), pp. 31–47.

——'The "Trusty Servant": A Sixteenth-Century English Emblem', *Emblematica*, 6 (1992), pp. 237–53.

Butler, Martin, 'The Auspices of Thomas Randolph's *Hey for Honesty, Down with Knavery*', *Notes and Queries*, 35 (1988), pp. 491–2.

——'Massinger's *The City Madam* and the Caroline Audience', *Renaissance Drama*, 13 (1982), pp. 157–87.

——*Theatre and Crisis 1632–1642*, Cambridge, 1984.

Callaghan, Dympna, '"And all is semblative a woman's part": Body Politics and *Twelfth Night*', *Textual Practice*, 7 (1993), pp. 428–52.

Capp, Bernard, 'Popular Literature', in Barry Reay, ed., *Popular Culture in Seventeenth-Century England*, London and New York, 1988, pp. 198–243.

——'Separate Domains? Women and Authority in Early Modern England', in Paul Griffiths, Adam Fox and Steve Hindle, eds, *The Experience of Authority in Early Modern England*, Basingstoke and London, 1996, pp. 117–45.

Chaytor, Miranda, 'Household and Kinship: Ryton in the late 16th and early 17th centuries', *History Workshop*, 10, Autumn (1980), pp. 25–60.

——'Husband(ry): Narratives of Rape in the Seventeenth Century', *Gender and History*, 7 (1995), pp. 378–407.

Chitty, C. W., 'Aliens in England in the Sixteenth Century', *Race*, 8 (1966), pp. 129–45.

Clark, Peter, 'The Migrant in Kentish Towns 1580–1640', in Peter Clark and Paul Slack, eds, *Crisis and Order in English Towns 1500–1700*, London, 1972, pp. 117–63.

Colie, Rosalie L., 'Reason and Need: *King Lear* and the "Crisis" of the Aristocracy', in Rosalie L. Colie and F. T. Flahiff, eds, *Some Facets of 'King Lear'*, London, 1974, pp. 185–219.

Cooper, J. P., *Land, Men and Beliefs: Studies in Early-Modern History*, London, 1983.

Coward, Barry, *Social Change and Continuity in Early Modern England 1550–1750*, London and New York, 1988.

——*The Stanleys Lords Stanley and the Earls of Derby 1385–1672: The Origins, Wealth and Power of a Landowning Family*, Chetham Society, 3rd ser., 30 (1983).

Crawford, Patricia, 'Women's Published Writings 1600–1700', in Mary Prior, ed., *Women in English Society 1500–1800*, London and New York, 1985, pp. 211–82.

Cressy, David, *Literacy and the Social Order: Reading and Writing in Tudor and Stuart England*, Cambridge, 1980.

Croft, Pauline, 'Libels, Popular Literacy and Public Opinion in Early Modern England', *Historical Research*, 68 (1995), pp. 266–85.

Cross, Claire, 'Northern Women in the Early Modern Period: The Female Testators of Hull and Leeds 1520–1650', *Yorkshire Archaeological Journal*, 59 (1987), pp. 83–94.

Curtis, Mark H., 'The Alienated Intellectuals of Early Stuart England', *Past and Present*, 23, November (1962), pp. 25–43.

Davies, Natalie Zemon, *Society and Culture in Early Modern France*, Stanford, CA, 1975.

Delaney, Paul, '*King Lear* and the Decline of Feudalism', *Publications of the Modern Language Association of America*, 92 (1977), pp. 429–40.

Dickens, A. G., 'Estate and Household Management in Bedfordshire, c. 1540', *Bedfordshire Historical Record Society*, 36 (1956), pp. 38–47.

DiGangi, Mario, 'Asses and Wits: The Homoerotics of Mastery in Satiric Comedy', *English Literary Renaissance*, 25 (1995), pp. 179–208.

Dolan, Frances E., *Dangerous Familiars: Representations of Domestic Crime in England, 1550–1700*, Ithaca, NY and London, 1994.

Dollimore, Jonathan, 'Introduction: Shakespeare, Cultural Materialism and the New Historicism', in Jonathan Dollimore and Alan Sinfield, eds, *Political Shakespeare: New Essays in Cultural Materialism*, Manchester, 1985, pp. 2–17.

——review of *James I and the Politics of Literature: Jonson, Shakespeare, Donne and Their Contemporaries* by Jonathan Goldberg, Baltimore and London, 1983, *Criticism*, 26 (1984), pp. 83–6.

Duckworth, George E., *The Nature of Roman Comedy*, 5th edn, Princeton, NJ, 1971.

Dymond, David and Alec Betterton, *Lavenham: 700 Years of Textile Making*, Woodbridge, 1982.

Dynes, William R., 'The Trickster Figure in Jacobean City Comedy', *Studies in English Literature*, 33 (1993), pp. 365–84.

Elliott, Vivien Brodsky, 'Mobility and Marriage in Pre-Industrial England: A Demographic and Social Structural Analysis of Geographic and Social Mobility and Aspects of Marriage, 1570–1690, with Particular Reference to London and General Reference to Middlesex, Kent, Essex and Hertfordshire', unpublished PhD thesis, University of Cambridge, 1978.

Evett, David, '"Surprising Confrontations": Ideologies of Service in Shakespeare's England', *Renaissance Papers 1990*, pp. 67–78.

Fehrenbach, R. J., 'A Letter sent by the Maydens of London (1567)', *English Literary Renaissance*, 14 (1984), pp. 285–304.

Ferguson, Margaret W., 'Moderation and its Discontents: Recent Work on Renaissance Women (Review Essay)', *Feminist Studies*, 20 (1994), pp. 349–66.

Finch, Mary E., *The Wealth of Five Northamptonshire Families 1540–1640*, Northamptonshire Record Society, 19 (1956).

Fisher, F. J., 'The Development of London as a Centre of Conspicuous Consumption in the Sixteenth and Seventeenth Centuries', *Transactions of the Royal Historical Society*, 4th ser., 30 (1948), pp. 37–50.

——*The Fitzalan Chapel Guide*, Shoreham-by-Sea, n.d.

Fletcher, A. J. and J. Stevenson, 'Introduction', in Anthony Fletcher and John Stevenson, eds, *Order and Disorder in Early Modern England*, Cambridge, 1985, pp. 1–40.

Fletcher, Anthony, *A County Community in Peace and War: Sussex 1600–1660*, London and New York, 1975.

——*Tudor Rebellions*, London, 1968.

Foucault, Michel, *The History of Sexuality: An Introduction*, tr. Robert Hurley, Harmondsworth, 1990.

Freeburg, Victor Oscar, *Disguise Plots in Elizabethan Drama: A Study in Stage Tradition*, New York, 1965.

Freedman, Barbara, 'Elizabethan Protest, Plague, and Plays: Rereading the "Documents of Control"', *English Literary Renaissance*, 26 (1996), pp. 17–45.

Freeman, Arthur, 'Marlowe, Kyd, and the Dutch Church Libel', *English Literary Renaissance*, 3 (1973), pp. 44–52.

Friedman, Alice T., *House and Household in Elizabethan England: Wollaton Hall and the Willoughby Family*, Chicago and London, 1989.

Gasper, Julia, *The Dragon and the Dove: The Plays of Thomas Dekker*, Oxford, 1990.

Gay, Edwin F., 'The Temples of Stowe and Their Debts: Sir Thomas Temple and Sir Peter Temple, 1603–1653', *Huntington Library Quarterly*, 2 (1939), pp. 399–438.

Giddens, Anthony, *Central Problems in Social Theory: Action, Structure and Contradiction in Social Analysis*, London and Basingstoke, 1979.

Gossett, Suzanne, '"Best Men are Molded out of Faults": Marrying the Rapist in Jacobean Drama', *English Literary Renaissance*, 14 (1984), pp. 305–27.

Gowing, Laura, *Domestic Dangers: Women, Words, and Sex in Early Modern London*, Oxford, 1996.

Greenblatt, Stephen J., *Shakespearean Negotiations: The Circulation of Social Energy in Renaissance England*, Oxford, 1988.

Griffiths, Paul, 'Masterless Young People in Norwich, 1560–1645', in Paul Griffiths, Adam Fox and Steve Hindle, eds, *The Experience of Authority in Early Modern England*, Basingstoke and London, 1996, pp. 146–86.

——'The Structure of Prostitution in Elizabethan London', *Continuity and Change*, 8 (1993), pp. 39–63.

——*Youth and Authority: Formative Experiences in England 1560–1640*, Oxford, 1996.

Griffiths, R. G., 'Joyce Jeffreys of Ham Castle', *Transactions of the Worcestershire Archaeological Society*, 10 (1933), pp. 1–32.

Grimal, Pierre, *The Dictionary of Classical Mythology*, Oxford, 1986.

Gurr, Andrew, *Playgoing in Shakespeare's London*, Cambridge, 1987.

Hainsworth, D. R., *Stewards, Lords and People: The Estate Steward and his World in later Stuart England*, Cambridge, 1992.

Hall, Stuart, 'Metaphors of Transformation', in Allon White, *Carnival, Hysteria, and Writing: Collected Essays and Autobiography*, Oxford, 1993, pp. 1–25.

Hajnal, John, 'Two Kinds of Preindustrial Household Formation System', *Population and Development Review*, 8 (1982), pp. 449–94.

Hannay, Margaret Patterson, ed., *Silent But for the Word: Tudor Women as Patrons, Translators, and Writers of Religious Works*, Kent, OH, 1985.

Harte, N.B., 'State Control of Dress and Social Change in Pre-Industrial England', in D. C. Coleman and A.H. John, eds, *Trade, Government and Economy in Pre-Industrial England: Essays presented to F. J. Fisher*, London, 1976, pp. 132–65.

Haselkorn, Anne M. and Betty S. Travitsky, eds, *The Renaissance Englishwoman in Print: Counterbalancing the Canon*, Amherst, MA, 1991.

Heal, Felicity, 'The Crown, the Gentry and London: The Enforcement of Proclamation, 1596–1640', in Claire Cross, David Loades and J. J. Scarisbrick, eds, *Law and Government under the Tudors: Essays Presented to Sir Geoffrey Elton*, Cambridge, 1988, pp. 211–26.

——*Hospitality in Early Modern England*, Oxford, 1990.

——'Reciprocity and Exchange in the Late Medieval Household', in Barbara A. Hanawalt and David Wallace, eds, *Bodies and Disciplines: Intersections of Literature and History in Fifteenth-Century England*, Minneapolis and London, 1996, pp. 179–98.

Hegel, G. W. F., *Phenomenology of Spirit*, tr. A. V. Miller, Oxford, 1977.

Henry, G. Kenneth G., 'The Characters of Terence', *Studies in Philology*, 12 (1915), pp. 57–98.

Hobby, Elaine, *Virtue of Necessity: English Women's Writing, 1649–1688*, London, 1988.

Hoskins, W. G., 'The Elizabethan Merchants of Exeter', in S. T. Bindoff, J. Hurstfield and C. H. Williams, eds, *Elizabethan Government and Society: Essays Presented to Sir John Neale*, London, 1961, pp. 163–87.

——'Harvest Fluctuations and English Economic History, 1480–1619', *Agricultural History Review*, 12 (1964), pp. 28–46.

Hosley, Richard, 'The Formal Influence of Plautus and Terence', in John Russell Brown and Bernard Harris, eds, *Elizabethan Theatre*, Stratford-upon-Avon Studies 9, London, 1966, pp. 130–45.

Howard, Jean E., 'Scripts and/versus Playhouses: Ideological Production and the Renaissance Public Stage', in Valerie Wayne, ed., *The Matter of Difference: Materialist Feminist Criticism of Shakespeare*, Ithaca, NY, 1991, pp. 221–36.

Hull, Suzanne W., *Chaste, Silent and Obedient: English Books for Women 1475–1640*, San Marino, 1982.

Hutton, Ronald, *The Rise and Fall of Merry England*, Oxford and New York, 1996.

Hynes, William J., 'Mapping the Characteristics of Mythic Tricksters: A Heuristic Guide', in William J. Hynes and William G. Doty, eds, *Mythical Trickster Figures: Contours, Contexts, and Criticisms*, Tuscaloosa and London, 1993, pp. 33–45.

Ingram, Martin, 'Ridings, Rough Music and the "Reform of Popular Culture" in Early Modern England', *Past and Present*, 105, November (1984), pp. 79–113.

——'"Scolding women cucked or washed": A Crisis in Gender Relations in Early Modern England?', in Jenny Kermode and Garthine Walker, eds, *Women, Crime and the Courts in Early Modern England*, London, 1994, pp. 48–80.

Jack, Sybil M., *Trade and Industry in Tudor and Stuart England*, London, 1977.

James, M. E., 'The Concept of Order and the Northern Rising of 1569', *Past and Present*, 60, August (1973), pp. 49–83.

Jardine, Lisa, *Reading Shakespeare Historically*, London and New York, 1996.

Jones, Ann Rosalind, *The Currency of Eros: Women's Love Lyric in Europe, 1540–1620*, Bloomington and Indianapolis, 1990.

Jordan, W. K., *Philanthropy in England 1480–1660: A Study of the Changing Pattern of English Social Aspirations*, London, 1959.

Kerridge, Eric, *Textile Manufactures in Early Modern England*, Manchester, 1985.

Knowles, Ronald, 'The Farce of History: Miracle, Combat, and Rebellion in 2 *Henry VI*', in Cedric Brown, ed., *Patronage, Politics, and Literary Traditions in England, 1558–1658*, Detroit, 1993, pp. 192–210.

Kojève, Alexandre, *Introduction to the Reading of Hegel*, ed. Allan Bloom, trans. James H. Nichols, New York and London, 1969.

Krontiris, Tina, *Oppositional Voices: Women as Writers and Translators of Literature in the English Renaissance*, London and New York, 1992.

Kussmaul, Ann, *Servants in Husbandry in Early Modern England*, Cambridge, 1981.

Laroque, François, *Shakespeare's Festive World: Elizabethan Seasonal Entertainment and the Professional Stage*, tr. Janet Lloyd, Cambridge, 1991.

Laslett, Peter, 'Market Society and Political Theory', *Historical Journal*, 7 (1964), pp. 150–4.

Leinwand, Theodore B., 'Negotiation and New Historicism', *Publications of the Modern Language Association of America*, 105 (1990), pp. 477–90.

Lewalski, Barbara Kiefer, *Writing Women in Jacobean England*, Cambridge, MA, 1993.

Lindley, K. J., 'Riot Prevention and Control in Early Stuart London', *Transactions of the Royal Historical Society*, 5th ser., 33 (1983), pp. 109–26.

Linton, Joan Pong, '*Jack of Newbury* and Drake in California: Domestic and Colonial Narratives of English Cloth and Manhood', *English Literary History*, 59 (1992), pp. 23–51.

Liu, Alan, 'The Power of Formalism: The New Historicism', *English Literary History*, 56 (1989), pp. 721–71.

Lowe, Norman, *The Lancashire Textile Industry in the Sixteenth Century*, Chetham Society, 3rd ser., 20 (1972).

Macdonald, Michael, *Mystical Bedlam: Madness, Anxiety, and Healing in Seventeenth-Century England*, Cambridge, 1981.

McIntosh, Marjorie K., 'Servants and the Household Unit in an Elizabethan English Community', *Journal of Family History*, 9 (1984), pp. 3–23.

McLuskie, Kathleen E., *Dekker and Heywood*, Basingstoke and London, 1994.

Macpherson, C. B., *Democratic Theory: Essays in Retrieval*, Oxford, 1973.

——*The Political Theory of Possessive Individualism: Hobbes to Locke*, Oxford, 1962.

Manning, Roger B., *Village Revolts: Social Protest and Popular Disturbances in England, 1509–1640*, Oxford, 1988.

Marcus, Leah Sinanoglou, 'The Milieu of Milton's *Comus*: Judicial Reform at Ludlow and the Problem of Sexual Assault', *Criticism*, 25 (1983), pp. 293–327.

Mendenhall, T. C., *The Shrewsbury Drapers and the Welsh Wool Trade in the Sixteenth and Seventeenth Centuries*, London, 1953.

Mertes, Kate, *The English Noble Household 1250–1600: Good Governance and Politic Rule*, Oxford, 1988.

Moisan, Thomas, '"Knock me here soundly": Comic Misprision and Class Consciousness in Shakespeare', *Shakespeare Quarterly*, 42 (1991), pp. 276–90.

Montrose, Louis Adrian, '"The Place of a Brother" in *As You Like It*: Social Process and Comic Form', *Shakespeare Quarterly*, 32 (1981), pp. 28–54.

Moore, Peter R., 'Ophelia's False Steward', *Notes and Queries*, 41 (1994), pp. 488–9.

Morgan, Paul, 'Frances Wolfreston and "Hor Bouks": A Seventeenth-Century Woman Book-Collector', *The Library*, 11 (1989), pp. 197–219.

Neill, Michael, '"Hidden Malady": Death, Discovery, and Indistinction in *The Changeling*', *Renaissance Drama*, 22 (1991), pp. 95–121.

Newman, Karen, *Fashioning Femininity and English Renaissance Drama*, Chicago and London, 1991.

Nichols, John Gough, 'The Origin and Early History of the Family of Newdegate', *Surrey Archaeological Collections*, 6 (1874), pp. 227–67.

Orgel, Stephen, *Impersonations: The Performance of Gender in Shakespeare's England*, Cambridge, 1996.

Orlin, Lena Cowen, *Private Matters and Public Culture in Post-Reformation England*, Ithaca, NY and London, 1994.

Palliser, D. M., *The Age of Elizabeth: England under the Tudors 1547–1603*, London and New York, 1983.

Pelling, Margaret, 'Apprenticeship, Health and Social Cohesion in Early Modern London', *History Workshop*, 37, Spring (1994), pp. 33–56.

Pettegree, Andrew, *Foreign Protestant Communities in Sixteenth-Century London*, Oxford, 1986.

Plomer, Henry R., 'Some Elizabethan Book Sales', *The Library*, 7 (1916), pp. 318–29.

Plummer, Alfred, *The London Weavers' Company 1600–1970*, London and Boston, 1972.

Porter, Carolyn, 'Are We Being Historical Yet?', *South Atlantic Quarterly*, 87 (1988), pp. 743–86.

Prestwich, Menna, *Cranfield: Politics and Profits under the Early Stuarts*, Oxford, 1966.

Prior, Mary, 'Margerie Bonner: A Waiting Gentlewoman of Seventeenth Century Wroxton', *Oxfordshire Local History*, 2 (Autumn, 1984), pp. 4–10.

Ramsay, G. D., *The Wiltshire Woollen Industry in the Sixteenth and Seventeenth Centuries*, 2nd edn, London, 1965.

Rappaport, Steve, 'Social Structure and Mobility in Sixteenth-Century London: Part I', *London Journal*, 9 (1983), pp. 107–35.

——*Worlds within Worlds: Structures of Life in Sixteenth-century London*, Cambridge, 1989.

Rawcliffe, Carol and Susan Flower, 'English Noblemen and Their Advisers: Consultation and Collaboration in the Later Middle Ages', *Journal of British Studies*, 25 (1986), pp. 157–77.

Read, Evelyn, *Catherine, Duchess of Suffolk: A Portrait*, London, 1962.

Roberts, Michael Frederick, 'Wages and Wage-Earners in England: The Evidence of the Wage Assessments, 1563–1725', unpublished DPhil thesis, University of Oxford, 1981.

——'Women and Work in Sixteenth-century English Towns', in Penelope J. Corfield and Derek Keene, eds, *Work in Towns 850–1850*, Leicester, London and New York, 1990, pp. 86–102.

——'"Words they are Women, and Deeds they are Men": Images of Work and Gender in Early Modern England', in Lindsey Charles and Lorna Duffin, eds, *Women and Work in Pre-Industrial England*, London and Sydney, 1985, pp. 122–80.

Sackville-West, V., *Knole and the Sackvilles*, 4th edn, London, 1958.

Schleiner, Louise, 'Margaret Tyler, Translator and Waiting Woman', *English Language Notes*, 29, March (1992), pp. 1–8.

Scott, James C., *Domination and the Arts of Resistance: Hidden Transcripts*, New Haven, CT and London, 1990.

Scribner, R. W., *Popular Culture and Popular Movements in Reformation Germany*, London and Ronceverte, 1987.

Seaver, Paul, 'Declining Status in an Aspiring Age: The Problem of the Gentle Apprentice in Seventeenth-Century London', in Bonnelyn Kunze and Dwight D. Brautigam, eds, *Court, Country and Culture: Essays on Early Modern British History in Honour of Perez Zagorin*, Rochester, NY, 1992, pp. 129–47.

Segal, Erich, *Roman Laughter: The Comedy of Plautus*, Cambridge, MA, 1970.

Sharp, Buchanan, *In Contempt of All Authority: Rural Artisans and Riot in the West of England, 1586–1660*, Berkeley, Los Angeles and London, 1980.

Sharpe, J. A., *Crime in Early Modern England 1550–1750*, London and New York, 1984.

——*Early Modern England: A Social History 1550–1760*, London, 1987.

Sharpe, Pamela, 'Poor children as apprentices in Colyton, 1598–1830', *Continuity and Change*, 6 (1991), pp. 253–70.

Sil, Narasingha P., '"Jentell Mr. Heneage": A Forgotten Tudor Servant', *Notes and Queries*, 31 (1984), pp. 169–72.

Simpson, J. A. and E. S. C. Weiner, eds, *The Oxford English Dictionary*, 20 vols, Oxford, 1989.

Sinfield, Alan, *Faultlines: Cultural Materialism and the Politics of Dissident Reading*, Oxford, 1992.

Slack, Paul, *Poverty and Policy in Tudor and Stuart England*, London and New York, 1988.

Slater, Miriam, *Family Life in the Seventeenth Century: The Verneys of Claydon House*, London, 1984.

Smith, Stephen R., 'Almost Revolutionaries: The London Apprentices during the Civil Wars', *Huntington Library Quarterly*, 42 (1979), pp. 313–28.

——'The London Apprentices as Seventeenth-Century Adolescents', *Past and Present*, 61, November (1973), pp. 149–61.

——'The Social and Geographical Origins of London Apprentices, 1630–1660', *Guildhall Miscellany*, 4 (1973), pp. 195–206.

Spufford, Margaret, *Contrasting Communities: English Villagers in the Sixteenth and Seventeenth Centuries*, Cambridge, 1974.

Stallybrass, Peter and Allon White, *The Politics and Poetics of Transgression*, London, 1986.

Stevenson, Laura Caroline, *Praise and Paradox: Merchants and Craftsmen in Elizabethan Popular Literature*, Cambridge, 1984.

Stevenson, S. J., 'Social and Economic Contributions to the Pattern of "Suicide" in South-east England, 1530–1590', *Continuity and Change*, 2 (1987), pp. 225–62.

Stirm, Jan C., 'Representing Women's Relationships: Intersections of Class, Race and Generation in English Drama, 1580–1642', unpublished PhD thesis, University of California, Los Angeles, 1995.

Stone, Lawrence, *The Crisis of the Aristocracy 1558–1641*, Oxford, 1966.

——*Family and Fortune: Studies in Aristocratic Finance in the Sixteenth and Seventeenth Centuries*, Oxford, 1973.

Strier, Richard, *Resistant Structures: Particularity, Radicalism, and Renaissance Texts*, Berkeley, Los Angeles and London, 1995.

Suzuki, Mihoko, 'The London Apprentice Riots of the 1590s and the Fiction of Thomas Deloney', *Criticism*, 38 (1996), pp. 181–217.

Swain, John T., *Industry Before the Industrial Revolution: North-East Lancashire 1500–1640*, Chetham Society, 3rd ser., 32 (1986).

Thomas, Keith, 'The Levellers and the Franchise', in G. E. Aylmer, ed., *The Interregnum: The Quest for Settlement 1646–1660*, London and Basingstoke, 1972, pp. 57–78.

——'The Place of Laughter in Tudor and Stuart England', *The Times Literary Supplement*, 3906, 21 January (1977), pp. 77–81.

——'Women and the Civil War Sects', *Past and Present*, 13, April (1958), pp. 42–62.

Thomson, David, 'Welfare and the Historians', in Lloyd Bonfield, Richard M. Smith and Keith Wrightson, eds, *The World We Have Gained: Histories of Population and Social Structure*, Oxford, 1986, pp. 355–78.

Thomson, Gladys Scott, *Life in a Noble Household 1641–1700*, London, 1950.

Thrupp, Sylvia Lettice, *A Short History of the Worshipful Company of Bakers of London*, Croydon, 1933.

Traub, Valerie, *Desire and Anxiety: Circulations of Sexuality in Shakespearean Drama*, London and New York, 1992.

Underdown, David, *Revel, Riot, and Rebellion: Popular Politics and Culture in England 1603–1660*, Oxford and New York, 1987.

Walter, John, 'Grain Riots and Popular Attitudes to the Law: Maldon and the Crisis of 1629', in John Brewer and John Styles, eds, *An Ungovernable People: The English and their Law in the Seventeenth and Eighteenth Centuries*, London, 1980, pp. 47–84.

Walter, John, and Keith Wrightson, 'Dearth and the Social Order in Early Modern England', *Past and Present*, 71, May (1976), pp. 22–42.

Watt, Tessa, *Cheap Print and Popular Piety 1550–1640*, Cambridge, 1991.

Weil, Judith, '"Household stuff": Maestrie and Service in *The Taming of the Shrew*', in A. L. Magnusson and C. E. McGee, eds, *The Elizabethan Theatre, XIV*, Port Credit, 1994, pp. 71–82.

Weimann, Robert, *Shakespeare and the Popular Tradition in the Theater: Studies in the Social Dimension of Dramatic Form and Function*, tr. Robert Schwartz, Baltimore and London, 1987.

Whigham, Frank, *Seizures of the Will in Early Modern English Drama*, Cambridge, 1996.

White, Paul Whitfield, *Theatre and Reformation: Protestantism, Patronage, and Playing in Tudor England*, Cambridge, 1993.

Wilson, Richard and Richard Dutton, eds, *New Historicism and Renaissance Drama*, London and New York, 1992.

Wilson, Richard, *Will Power: Essays on Shakespearean Authority*, Hemel Hempstead, 1993.

Wilson, Scott, *Cultural Materialism: Theory and Practice*, Oxford, 1996.

Woodbridge, Linda, *Women and the English Renaissance: Literature and the Nature of Womankind, 1540–1620*, Brighton, 1984.

Wrightson, Keith, *English Society 1580–1680*, London, 1982.

——'Estates, Degrees, and Sorts: Changing Perceptions of Society in Tudor and Stuart England', in Penelope J. Corfield, ed., *Language, History and Class*, Oxford, 1991, pp. 30–52.

——'"Sorts of people" in Tudor and Stuart England', in Jonathan Barry and Christopher Brooks, eds, *The Middling Sort of People: Culture, Society and Politics in England, 1550–1800*, Basingstoke and London, 1994, pp. 28–51.

Wrigley, E. A. and R. S. Schofield, *The Population History of England 1541–1871*, London, 1981.

Würzbach, Natascha, *The Rise of the English Street Ballad, 1550–1650*, tr. Gayna Walls, Cambridge, 1990.

Yates, Frances A., *Astraea: The Imperial Theme in the Sixteenth Century*, London, Boston, Melbourne and Henley, 1985.

Young, Sidney, *The Annals of the Barber-Surgeons of London*, London, 1890.

Yungblut, Laura Hunt, *Strangers Settled Here Amongst Us: Politics, Perceptions and the Presence of Aliens in Elizabethan England*, London and New York, 1996.

Index